The Princeton Review®

Verbal Workout for the

GRE®

Sixth Edition

By the Staff of The Princeton Review

PrincetonReview.com

Penguin
Random
House

The Princeton Review

The Princeton Review
555 W. 18th Street
New York, NY 10011
E-mail: editorialsupport@review.com

Published in the United States by Penguin Random House LLC, New York, and in Canada by Random House of Canada, a division of Penguin Random House Ltd., Toronto.

Terms of Service: The Princeton Review Online Companion Tools ("Student Tools") for retail books are available for only the two most recent editions of that book. Student Tools may be activated only twice per eligible book purchased for two consecutive 12-month periods, for a total of 24 months of access. Activation of Student Tools more than twice per book is in direct violation of these Terms of Service and may result in discontinuation of access to Student Tools Services.

ISBN: 978-0-451-48785-8
eBook ISBN: 978-1-5247-1032-3
ISSN: 1559-8640

Permission has been granted to reprint portions of the following:

Death Comes to the Maiden: Sex and Execution 1431-1933, Camille Naish, © 2014, Routledge Library Editions, Women's History. Reproduced by permission of Taylor & Francis Books UK.

"The Evolution of Life on Earth" by Stephen Jay Gould. Reproduced with permission. Copyright © 1994 Scientific American, a division of Nature America, Inc. All rights reserved.

Gender Differences at Work: Women and Men in Non-traditional Occupations by Christine L. Williams. University of California Press, © 1989.

E.M. Forster: Perils of Humanism by Frederick Campbell Crews. Princeton University Press. © 1962.

California Indian Shamanism, edited by Lowell John Bean. Ballena Press, Menlo Park, CA.

Excerpt(s) from CITY OF WOMEN by Christine Stansell, copyright © 1982, 1986 by Christine Stansell. Used by permission of Alfred A. Knopf, an imprint of the Knopf Doubleday Publishing Group, a division of Penguin Random House LLC. All rights reserved.

"The Self-Reproducing Inflationary Universe" by Andrei Linde. Reproduced with permission. Copyright © 1994 Scientific American, a division of Nature America, Inc. All rights reserved.

Free Soil, Free Labor, Free Men: The Ideology for the Republican Party Before the Civil War by Eric Foner. Copyright © 1970. Reproduced with permission Oxford University Press, NY.

The Art of Enigma: The de Chirico Brothers and the Politics of Modernism by Keala Jewell. Copyright © 2004. Penn State University Press.

Editor: Selena Coppock
Production Artist: Craig Patches
Production Editors: Kathy G. Carter and Emily Epstein White

Printed in the United States of America on partially recycled paper.

10 9 8 7 6 5 4 3 2 1

Sixth Edition

Editorial
Rob Franek, Editor-in-Chief
Casey Cornelius, VP Content Development
Mary Beth Garrick, Director of Production
Selena Coppock, Managing Editor
Meave Shelton, Senior Editor
Colleen Day, Editor
Sarah Litt, Editor
Aaron Riccio, Editor
Orion McBean, Editorial Assistant

Penguin Random House Publishing Team
Tom Russell, VP, Publisher
Alison Stoltzfus, Publishing Director
Jake Eldred, Associate Managing Editor
Ellen Reed, Production Manager
Suzanne Lee, Designer

Acknowledgments

The editorial team would like to thank John Fulmer, our fearless GRE National Content Director and Jim Havens and Kyle Fox for their hard work on the sixth edition of this title.

Special thanks to Adam Robinson, who conceived of and perfected the Joe Bloggs approach to standardized tests and many of the other successful techniques used by The Princeton Review.

Register Your

1 Go to **PrincetonReview.com/cracking**

2 You'll see a welcome page where you can register your book using the following ISBN: 9780451487858.

3 After placing this free order, you'll either be asked to log in or to answer a few simple questions in order to set up a new Princeton Review account.

4 Finally, click on the "Student Tools" tab located at the top of the screen. It may take an hour or two for your registration to go through, but after that, you're good to go.

If you have noticed potential content errors, please email EditorialSupport@review.com with the full title of the book, its ISBN number (located above), and the page number of the error.

Experiencing technical issues?
Please e-mail TPRStudentTech@review.com with the following information:

- your full name
- e-mail address used to register the book
- full book title and ISBN
- your computer OS (Mac or PC) and Internet browser (Firefox, Safari, Chrome, etc.)
- description of technical issue

Book Online!

Once you've registered, you can...

- Read important advice about the GRE and graduate school
- Access crucial information about the graduate school application process, including a timeline and checklist
- Check to see if there have been any corrections or updates to this edition

Look For These Icons Throughout The Book

Proven Techniques

More Great Books

Applied Strategies

Study Break

The **Princeton** Review®

Contents

Chapter 1
Introduction

THE GRE AND YOU

So you've finally decided what to do with your post-college life. You're not going to pursue the vaunted M.D., nor are you going to chase the lucrative J.D. Rather, the initials you desire to follow your name are M.A., M.S., or Ph.D. In short, you want to go to graduate school. However, since you can't simply sign up for grad school, you're going to have to tackle the application process. That means writing essays, soliciting recommendations, gathering transcripts, and taking the Graduate Record Examination, otherwise known as the GRE. Nearly all graduate programs require the GRE, so no matter what field you intend to pursue, the GRE probably lies in your future. The GRE is written by the Educational Testing Service (ETS), the same folks who inflicted the SAT upon you during your high school days.

What Does the GRE Measure?

That's an excellent question. According to ETS, the GRE measures "analytical writing, verbal, and quantitative skills that have been acquired over a long period of time and that are not related to any specific field of study." Let's think about that for a moment. What seems to be missing from this statement? If you said, "Something directly related to how successful I will be as a grad student," you're on the right track. Notice that even ETS doesn't claim that the GRE measures how well you'll perform in a program of anthropology, or psychology, or religious studies, or art history, or physics. The GRE is not a test of intelligence or of your aptitude for graduate study. Despite this, graduate schools use it because it gives them an objective way to compare applicants whose other qualifications are often quite subjective.

So What Does the GRE *Really* Measure?

The GRE tests how well you solve GRE problems. It's true that in order to do that, you need some basic math skills, basic reading skills, basic writing skills, and a good vocabulary, but, perhaps most important, you need good test-taking skills. Many people (including those at ETS) view the GRE as some kind of general assessment of your ability. They believe that either you have what it takes, or you don't. But in reality the GRE tests very specific information and skills. You can learn that information and you can develop those skills. The key is to approach the GRE as a *specific* task, like learning to play the piano or hitting a golf ball. The same two things that will help you become a better piano player will help you become a better GRE test taker: 1) instruction and 2) practice. You will get both of these with this book.

Registering for the Test

The GRE is a computer-based test that you will take in a designated testing center. You can take the test year-round, on almost any day, morning or afternoon, weekday or weekend, subject to the availability of test appointments at the test center you want to use. The earlier you register, the more likely you are to get your preferred appointment. You can take the GRE only once every 21 days, and a maximum of five times in any 12-month period. In order to schedule a test, go to www.ets.org/gre or call 1-609-771-7670 or 1-866-473-4373 (toll free for test takers in the United States, American Samoa, Guam, Puerto Rico, U.S. Virgin Islands and Canada). Worldwide, the GRE currently (as of September 10, 2013) costs $205, payable by credit card, debit card, money order, certified check, voucher, or personal check. There's a $50 fee if you need to reschedule. These prices may change, so for up-to-date information, visit www.ets.org/gre.

How Important Is the GRE?

The definitive answer to this important question is this: It depends. How much weight the GRE is given varies from school to school, and from program to program. Some schools consider the GRE very important, while others tend to view it as a formality. Some don't use it at all for admissions, but only in awarding scholarships. Schools may also give different weight to the different sections of the GRE. If you're applying to a masters program in English Literature, for example, they might not care too much about your Math score, and focus instead on your Verbal and Analytical Writing scores. The best way to find out how important your GRE score will be is to contact the schools you're interested in and ask them. Most graduate programs are happy to talk about the application process and can let you know how they evaluate GRE scores.

In any case, there is always much more to a graduate school application than GRE scores. Your GPA, undergraduate institution, recommendations, personal statement, research or work experience, and interview are all part of the process. The GRE can be important, but it's never the whole story.

Dig Deeper!
For more GRE preparation, check out these other books from The Princeton Review:
Cracking the GRE
Math Workout for the GRE
Crash Course for the GRE

THE STRUCTURE OF THE GRE

Let's take a moment to review the basic structure of the GRE.

The Scored Sections

The GRE contains five scored sections:

- One 60-minute Analytical Writing section, which contains two essay questions
- Two 30-minute Verbal sections, which contain approximately 20 questions each

- Two 35-minute Math sections, which contain approximately 20 questions each

The first section will always be the Analytical Writing section, followed by the Math and Verbal sections, which can appear in any order. Almost all of the Verbal questions are multiple-choice; a few will ask you to highlight a sentence within a reading comprehension passage. The Math questions are also mostly multiple-choice, plus some Numeric Entry questions that require typing in an answer.

You will be able to see your Verbal and Math scores immediately upon completion of the test, but you will have to wait about two weeks before your Analytical Writing section is scored.

You will get a 1-minute break, enough time to close your eyes and catch a breath, between each section. You will also get a full 10-minute break after the third section. Be sure to use it to visit the bathroom, take a drink of water, refresh your mind, and get ready for the rest of the exam.

The Experimental Section

In addition to the five scored sections listed above, you will also have an unscored experimental section. This section is almost always a Math or Verbal section. It will look exactly like the other Math or Verbal sections, but it won't count at all toward your score. ETS administers the experimental section to gather data on questions before they appear on real GREs.

Thus, after your Analytical Writing section, you will actually see five multiple-choice sections: either three Verbal and two Math, or two Verbal and three Math, depending on whether you get a Verbal or Math experimental section. These sections can come in any order. You will have no way of knowing which section is experimental, so you need to do your best on all of them. Don't waste time worrying about which sections count and which section does not.

Here is how a typical GRE might look:

Analytical Writing – 60 minutes
Math – 35 minutes
10-minute break
Verbal – 30 minutes
Verbal – 30 minutes
Math – 35 minutes
Verbal – 30 minutes

Remember, the Analytical Writing section will always be first, and it will never be experimental. In the example above, the two Math sections were scored, but only two of the three Verbal sections were scored. One of the three was an experimental section, but we don't know which one. Of course, on your GRE you might see three Math sections instead of three Verbal sections, and they may come in any order. Be flexible, and you'll be ready for the test no matter what order the sections come in. In fact, they may not even include an experimental section! If so, count your lucky stars that you didn't have to waste your time on a meaningless section.

Research Section

The GRE will occasionally include an optional research section. This section will always be the final section of the test and will be clearly identified. ETS uses this section to test new oddball questions, or to collect demographic data. Nothing you do on the research section will change your score in any way.

HOW IS THE GRE SCORED?

You receive three separate scores for the GRE, corresponding to the three scored sections:

- A Verbal score from 130–170, in 1-point increments
- A Math score from 130–170, in 1-point increments
- An Analytical Writing score from 0 to 6, in half-point increments

THE GRE VERBAL SECTION UNMASKED

Let's look in more detail at the Verbal section. As we said before, the two scored Verbal sections contain 20 questions each. You are given 30 minutes for each Verbal section.

The GRE Verbal section contains three types of questions:

- Reading Comprehension (including Arguments)
- Text Completion
- Sentence Equivalence

The Text Completions are always first, followed by some Reading Comprehension, then the Sentence Equivalence questions, and finally some more Reading Comprehension. Roughly half of the questions are Reading Comprehension, and the other half fill-in-the-blanks style questions (Text Completions and Sentence Equivalence). Some questions will come in different varieties, such as Reading Comprehension questions that require choosing all the answers that apply, or that require selecting a sentence from the passage.

Within each section, you will be able to answer the questions in whatever order is easiest for you. You may skip any question you wish by clicking "Next," and you can return to that question anytime during the 30 minutes.

Once you have finished a section, however, you can't return to it. The GRE will use your results from the first scored Verbal section you complete to determine which questions to give you on your second scored Verbal section. If you do well on the first section, you'll get harder questions. If you don't do as well, you'll get easier questions. This is what makes the Revised GRE "adaptive by section."

How does this affect your test-taking strategy? It doesn't. You should still try your best on every single section, whether it's the first or second section of that type. In fact, when you get to the second Verbal section, don't try to guess whether or not it's easier than the first one. People are incredibly bad at guessing how hard questions are for other people, and if you're focusing on anything but how to answer the question in front of you, you're wasting your time. Don't forget that either the first or second Verbal section might have been the experimental section! Ignore the fact that the GRE is adaptive, and instead focus on the section you're currently working on, not the section you already finished. Every question in a section has an equal impact on your score, so focus only on answering questions correctly.

Applied Strategies
We'll dig deeper into our Princeton Review strategies later in the book.

THE ANALYTICAL WRITING SECTION DEMYSTIFIED

In the Analytical Writing chapter, you'll learn all you need to know about writing high-scoring essays. But in the meantime, we'll examine a few of the basics of this section.

The Analytical Writing section requires you to write two essays:

- One Issue essay in 30 minutes
- One Argument essay in 30 minutes

How the Essays Are Scored

Each essay will receive a score from a human grader from 0 to 6. That score will be checked against proprietary software that rates the original grader. If the human- and computer-generated scores differ by a certain amount, another human grader will provide a second evaluation. In that case, the two human-based scores are averaged for each essay, and then the scores for the two essays are averaged and rounded to the nearest half-point.

The only number that schools ever see is the final score. They don't see how you scored on the individual essays. However, ETS plans to eventually make the individual essays themselves available to schools, so that they could read them if they choose.

Analytical Writing Percentiles

Essay Score	Percentile
6	99
5.5	98
5	93
4.5	82
4	59
3.5	42
3	17
2.5	7
2	2
1.5	1
1	0
0.5	0
0	0

These are the most recent percentiles ETS has published; however, the current percentiles may be slightly higher or lower.

HOW TO USE THIS BOOK

There are probably two categories of people who have purchased this book. See if you belong in one of these.

1. People who have also bought a book that covers the whole GRE (such as, perhaps, the excellent *Cracking the GRE*) and are simply looking for some more verbal practice
2. People who are very comfortable with the math on the GRE and want to focus their preparation mostly or exclusively on the Verbal section

If you fit into the first category, then you will already know much of the information in this book. However, it's still worth reading all of it. First, doing so will reinforce the points and techniques that you've already studied. Also, the material is presented in a slightly different way in this book, and you will benefit from seeing the same techniques described in different words.

If you fit into the second category, then you obviously will want to study all the material carefully to learn how to approach each type of question. Make sure to practice the techniques when you do the practice sets, and read the explanations carefully to ensure that you pick up both the big picture and the details of our methods.

If you fit into a third category, well, we're sure you'll be able to figure out how to use the book to your advantage.

Create a study schedule for yourself that includes study time and break time. It's important not to burn yourself out!

Whatever your situation, one thing you definitely must do is obtain as much real GRE material as you can to practice on. The most important book to get ahold of is *The Official Guide to the GRE® revised General Test, Second Edition*. This book is published by ETS, and contains questions for every single Math and Verbal question type, as well as practice essay prompts, and a CD-ROM with two practice exams. You can buy it (or order it online) at any large bookstore or directly from ETS at www.ets.org.

Included on a CD-ROM inside every copy of *The Official Guide to the GRE® revised General Test* is a copy of the GRE *POWERPREP II* software. *POWERPREP II* contains a computer-based GRE, sample writing topics, sample essays with commentary, a math review, and some tutorials. The most important part is the practice tests. The GRE is a computer-based test, so part of your preparation must include practice on a computer. By taking the *POWERPREP II* computer test, you'll become familiar with the layout of the buttons and the feel of the computer format, and have the opportunity to practice our techniques in a realistic setting. We recommend taking the computer test only after you've completed all the material in this book. You can also download *POWERPREP II* for free from the GRE website at www.ets.org/gre.

The most important thing you need to do is work hard. No GRE book can help you if you don't put in the time to learn the techniques, practice the techniques, and then use the techniques on the actual exam. As in many other situations, the results you get out of your GRE preparation will be largely determined by the amount of effort you put into it.

So, let's get to work!

Chapter 2
Strategies

STRATEGIZE

Before we get into the specific techniques for tackling the verbal questions, we need to discuss some of the overall strategies that are important on the GRE. Some of these will make perfect sense, but others may seem counterintuitive. Trust us that everything we recommend here has been tested, refined, and proven through a great deal of experience. Stick with it, and practice until it all becomes automatic and second-nature.

We'll have a lot to say about the computer shortly, but before looking at that, we're going to discuss a few things that are crucial to scoring your best on the Verbal section.

Proven Techniques

Be Methodical

One reason many people particularly despise the Verbal section of the GRE is that there is a specific disadvantage to verbal questions that doesn't exist on math questions. Math questions always have answers that are exact and provable, whereas the answers to verbal questions may often seem debatable. They involve shades of meaning and nuance that you simply don't have to deal with in math questions. When $x = 7$, you just look for the 7 in the answer choices, but you often do not have that same certainty that the answer you choose for a verbal question is correct.

Unfortunately, what many people take from this is the idea that answering verbal questions is a matter of groping your way toward the right answer and picking the one that smells/tastes/feels right. If that's the way you approach verbal questions, it's going to be hard for you to improve. The key to becoming better at solving verbal questions is to adopt a systematic approach. You need a step-by-step method for attacking each part of the Verbal section, and you need to apply that method consistently. Not surprisingly, we will be showing you these techniques in the subsequent chapters.

Meet Your New Best Friend: POE

This POE is not related to Edgar Allan, but is rather the Process of Elimination. You should use the Process of Elimination on every question in the Verbal section. To understand why POE is so important, you need to look at several elements of the GRE. The first is that most of the questions on the GRE are multiple-choice. The multiple-choice questions will have anywhere between 3 and 6 answer choices that you must choose between. However, there are more wrong answers on the Verbal section than right ones. In this book, we will teach you strategies to spot the wrong answers. And when you spot them and eliminate them, you narrow the range of options you have to choose from, thus increasing your chances of picking the correct answer, even if you end up guessing.

Another important reason is based on the nature of verbal questions themselves. When answering verbal questions under test conditions, you may often feel as though two or more answers could be correct. Of course, only one answer can be defended as correct by reference to the sentence or passage. For ETS, there must be only one answer that can be defended as correct. However, they are very good at making two or more answers sound correct, so you may often feel as though you must pick the best of the answers that you have left. That's why process of elimination is important. If you can find good reasons to eliminate an answer, choose what's left—even if you aren't in love with the remaining answer.

It's important to understand that POE is not just a matter of crossing off answer choices as you go. It's not simply a physical process. Rather, it's an active mental process that evaluates answer choices by looking for flaws, looking for reasons to get rid of them. Don't look for answer choices that you like, because most of the time, either you won't like any of them, or you will like more than one and won't be able to decide among them. Instead, get into the habit of making the best case you can *against* each answer choice, and you'll be much more successful.

Watch Out for Traps

ETS has given the GRE to hundreds of thousands of students, and because of all this data and experience you can believe one thing: They know how you think. Don't feel bad about this. They know how you think because most of us think in very similar ways. We all share many of the same associations and tendencies. It's simply part of our nature. ETS has learned how to take advantage of this by writing trap answers, sometimes called "distractors," because they distract you from the right answer. For example, on a tough Text Completion or Sentence Equivalence question, ETS loves to include an answer choice that contains words that remind you of the original sentence, but don't actually fit. Say you get a sentence like "Vincent approached each canvas _____ , carefully considering the perfect location for his next brush stroke." ETS knows that if they put an answer choice such as *artistically*, many people will choose it because Vincent is an artist, and it seems like the best thing they can find. Don't fall for it. If the answer could be found that easily, it wouldn't be a GRE question.

Applied Strategies

Scratch Paper

The GRE is a computer-based test, so you can't write on the problems themselves. (The test center employees get very unhappy if you write on their computer screens.) All your work must be done on scratch paper. For Verbal questions, there are between 3 and 6 answer choices. If you have a Sentence Equivalence question, which requires choosing two out of the six answer choices that could fit into a sentence, then you don't want to waste time trying to remember which answers worked and which didn't. This is exactly what the scratch paper is for. As soon as you see the question, start writing.

Later on in the book, we'll discuss exactly what to write for each particular question type, but for every single question type you'll write down a letter for each answer choice. For a Sentence Equivalence question, since there are six answer choices, you'll write A B C D E F vertically on your scratch paper. As you work on the problem, you'll cross off answers that you know are wrong. After that, you can focus on figuring out which two of the answers you have left are correct.

Get used to using a simple notation on your scratch paper to tell you which answers are still possible. If an answer is clearly wrong, cross it off. If an answer seems like it could work, put a check mark next to it. If an answer contains a word you don't know, put a question mark next to it. You may need to look at the answer choices you haven't crossed off or question marked a couple of times until you've crossed off all the wrong answers.

Your scratch paper for a Text Completion question could look something like this:

2. A̶
    B ✓
    C̶
    D̶
    E ?

There's a bit more you'd write for this type of question, but for now let's focus on the answers. Even without the question or answer choices, which answer should you pick here? Pick (B). Although you put a question mark next to (E) because you didn't know the word, it doesn't matter what that word means if you knew what (B) was, and that word works with the sentence.

Notice that we wrote down the question number? Since you can skip questions and return to them later, you may end up selecting one answer for now and returning to this question later if you have time. If you do return to this question, you don't want to have to redo all that nice writing you did on your scratch paper. If you've numbered each question's answer choices on your scratch paper, then returning to half-completed problems is much easier.

What if your scratch paper looks like this? Which answer choice would you pick?

4. A̶
    B̶
    C
    D̶
    E̶

That may seem like an obvious question, and it is. Pick (C), because it's the only answer left. Clearly (C) wasn't a very good answer; otherwise it would have gotten a checkmark. But it wasn't obviously wrong, so you moved on and looked at the other answer choices. Remember this: Sometimes the correct answer is not very good, but it's the only one answer that can be defended as correct and that's good enough.

There are three major advantages to using your scratch paper on every single problem. The first is that, as already mentioned, you don't want to have to waste time and brainpower remembering which answers worked and which didn't. If you have all that information written down, you can let your weary brain focus on moving forward, rather than remembering what you already did.

The second is that you are more likely to know when it's time to guess on a problem. Say you've got this on your scratch paper:

5.   A ?
       ~~B~~
       C ?
       D ?
       ~~E~~

You've crossed off two answers, but have question marks next to the other three answer choices. That means there are three words on the screen that you don't know. At that point, it's a better use of your time to guess one of those three mystery words and go work on other questions than it is to sit and stare at those words, hoping that you magically remember one of the definitions.

The last reason to use your scratch paper is so that you don't have to redo your work when you return to problems. If you've already crossed off three answers on a Reading Comprehension question and decided to move on, then when you come back to that question you don't want to waste time rereading the answer choices you already know are wrong.

This book, of course, is not a computer screen, and you may be tempted to just cross off answers in the book, rather than write the letters for the answer choices on your scratch paper. Resist that temptation. As much as possible, set up your scratch paper while doing practice problems in this book in the exact same way you will eventually set it up while doing the actual test. Using your scratch paper should become an automatic response to seeing a GRE question, and if you don't start right now, then you'll be in for a shock when you get to the testing center and you're not used to looking down at your scratch paper to know which answers you have left.

At the test center, you'll be given six sheets of scratch paper. If necessary, you can ask for more, but the proctor will take away all your old paper at the same time. Also, if you run out of paper in the middle of a section, you'll need to raise your hand and wait for a proctor to notice, collect new scratch paper, and bring it in to you. You don't want to waste your precious time waiting for the proctor to attend to you. Time is ticking away! So even though your scratch paper is technically unlimited, don't be extravagant. Try to make it last. Use your 10-minute break to get more paper.

Vocabulary

It might seem odd to think of vocabulary as a strategy, but learning vocabulary is one of the most important things you must do to maximize your score on the GRE Verbal section. The Text Completion and Sentence Equivalence sections are hugely vocabulary-dependent. Only the reading comprehension questions give you a partial respite from this vocabulary obsession.

This means that you have to tackle the vocabulary issue directly. The techniques we'll be showing you are strong, but at some point vocabulary will put a ceiling on your score. The more words you know, the higher that ceiling is. Studying words may be dull, but you'll know how serious you really are about raising your GRE Verbal score by how diligently you work to expand your vocabulary.

To assist you with this, we have included Chapter 7, which contains lists of words that commonly appear on the GRE (which also appear in *Cracking the GRE*) and additional word lists (which do not). Furthermore, there are drills, quizzes, sample questions, and advice for building your vocabulary. Study these words assiduously, and you'll give yourself a big advantage on test day. But don't wait until you've worked through the rest of the book to turn to the vocabulary chapter. Start working on vocabulary from the very beginning. You need to spread it out over the whole period of your GRE preparation for it to be effective.

Ultimately, the most successful path to a higher GRE Verbal score is the combination of better technique and better vocabulary. Either one alone will help raise your score, but truly high scores and stellar improvements require both.

More Great Books
For even more GRE prep, check out other books from your pals at The Princeton Review: *Cracking the GRE, Crash Course for the GRE,* and *Math Workout for the GRE.*

COMPUTER STRATEGIES

Now we're ready to tackle the computer. Taking a test on a computer is strange. If you haven't taken one before, you'll probably discover that it's stranger than you anticipated. This is one reason why it's so important to take the *POWERPREP II* tests mentioned in the previous chapter. You will not be comfortable taking the real GRE unless you have some experience with the computer format.

In addition to experience, however, you need to have knowledge about how the computer test works and strategies that take advantage of it. Here we'll be looking at the details of the computer format. Let's start with a look at the computer screen itself and a quick explanation of what the various buttons do.

Basic Format

For each blank select one entry from the corresponding column of choices. Fill all blanks in the way that best completes the text.

Though Adam was incredulous upon hearing Madam Sofia's psychic reading, after a few weeks had passed, he was (i) _____ by how remarkably (ii) _____ she had turned out to be.

Blank (i)
dubious
stupefied
blase

Blank (ii)
prescient
exhaustive
mundane

Click on your choices.

As you can see, the question will be in the middle of the screen, and the answers will be below the question. There are several ways that the GRE can present answer choices, each of which affects how you will select answers and how you will use your scratch paper.

The answers to Text Completion questions will have words inside a table, like this:

exacerbate
plummet
mitigate
rescind
allege

If the question is a sentence with one blank, then there will be five words. You will have to choose one of the words.

For some Text Completion questions, you will be presented with a sentence that contains two or three blanks. The answer choices of a two-blank Text Completion will look like this:

Blank (i)
querulous
abysmal
diffident

Blank (ii)
preoccupation with
affection for
predilection for

For each blank, you must choose the correct word for the blank from three potential answer choices. If you don't choose the correct answer for every blank, the question is marked wrong and you will receive no credit for that question.

For some Reading Comprehension questions, you will be asked a question followed by 5 answer choices, which looks like this:

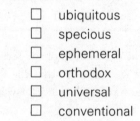

- refute an erroneous theory
- assert a controversial claim
- describe a possible flaw
- contradict an earlier statement
- highlight a relevant notion

In this case, there is only one correct answer. However, in some other Reading Comprehension questions, you will be presented with only three answer choices. In this case, there may be more than one correct answer choice, and you must select them all to get credit for the question. Other Reading Comprehension questions will ask you to select the correct sentence from the passage. In this case, you will need to select the single correct sentence on the text of the passage to receive credit.

For Sentence Equivalence questions, there will be six answer choices, presented like this:

- ☐ ubiquitous
- ☐ specious
- ☐ ephemeral
- ☐ orthodox
- ☐ universal
- ☐ conventional

For Sentence Equivalence questions, there will always be two answers that work, and you must choose both correct answers to get credit for that question.

Once you've selected an answer or answers, you must click the Next button to go the next question. Now that we know how the answer choices work, let's turn our attention to the screen itself.

The top of the screen contains the following buttons, from left to right:

- **Quit Test:** This button will end your test. Don't use it unless you're so ill you have to leave the test center. Otherwise, even if you decide that you're going to cancel your score at the end of the test, continue taking the test if you can. You may change your mind at the end, and even if you don't, the extra practice and experience will be helpful.
- **Exit Section:** Clicking this button will allow you to exit the section you're working on and move on to the next one. Don't use it unless you've answered every single question in the section and reviewed the questions you weren't sure about.
- **Review:** This button will show you a list of all the questions in the section, by question number. Whether or not you've answered each question is listed next to each question number. Use this button to return to questions you skipped; also, click this button when the timer starts blinking at the two-minute warning, and fill in your Letter of the Day (LOTD) for any unanswered questions (see page 19).

- **Mark:** Clicking this button will mark the current question. This mark will appear on the Review screen, allowing you to easily see which questions you wanted to return to.
- **Help:** Clicking this button will bring up a screen with directions for the current question type. Don't waste your time with this on the actual test. It won't help you solve problems, and you should already know how the buttons and questions work by the time you take the real test.
- **Back:** This button will return you to the previous question. Any answer you selected for the current question will be saved.
- **Next:** This button will take you to the next question. You must click this button to move to the next question after selecting an answer. You do not need to pick an answer to move on to the next question.
- **Hide Time:** This button hides the onscreen timer. Ignore this button. Seeing how much time you have left in the section will help with your pacing (more on that in a bit), and without the timer you may answer questions too quickly or too slowly. However, some people find that they just can't concentrate with the timer counting down in front of them, and they need to hide the timer in order to focus on the questions. In any case, when the section is almost over, the timer reappears (if it was hidden) and you can't hide it any longer.

Keep Moving

You've got 20 questions to answer in 30 minutes. If a tough question comes up, and you're not sure how to solve it, what should you do? Sit and stare at it until time runs out? Of course not. Remember that Mark button we mentioned earlier? Use it. Click the Mark button so that you know to return to that question when you've completed everything else in the section.

Get used to completing each section in two passes. On the first pass, do all the Text Completion and Sentence Equivalence questions, because they take less time than Reading Comprehension questions. With the fill-in-the-blanks questions, either you know the vocabulary and you get the correct answer(s) quickly, or you don't know the vocabulary and you guess quickly. This way, you have the bulk of your time left to work on Reading Comprehension. As soon as a question gives you trouble, run away. Click Mark, then click Next, and forget about that tough question for now (unless it's the final question on a Reading Comprehension passage, in which case just pick your Letter of the Day and move on). Focus on the question that's currently in front of you. Once you have done all the other questions from the same Reading Comprehension passage, you can return to the question you marked and—hopefully—see it with "fresh eyes." If not, choose your Letter of the Day (LOTD) and move on to the next passage.

Your first pass should be a confidence builder. As you begin to study for the GRE, the first pass may not inspire much confidence, but as you get to know the different question types better and build your vocabulary, you'll find that there are a certain number of questions in any given section that you can answer without too much trouble. Your goal on your first pass is to answer those questions.

Once you click Next on question 20 (the last question), the GRE will remind you that you can return to any previous questions. Click on Review and look at which questions you left unanswered. Take a look at the timer. How much time do you have left? How many questions? Out of the passages you have left, choose the easiest. Work on that one. If you can't answer any of the questions for that passage, guess and move on.

Pacing

Two of the most important skills for the GRE are how to use your scratch paper, which we've discussed, and pacing. Pacing does not mean rushing; it means knowing how much time to spend on each question. How each person paces himself or herself will change depending on that person's skills, so this is when practice, such as with GRE's *POWERPREP II* software, is key.

However, everyone will follow the same basic timeframe. On your first pass, you shouldn't spend too much time on any one question. Reading Comprehension questions may take some time here, because you'll need to parse the passage, but don't spend more than three minutes on any single question. You're not rushing here; you're choosing the easy battles.

On your second pass, take into account how much time and how many questions you have left. You're not going to rush through all these questions. Instead you're going to choose what look like the easiest passages of what's left, answer those questions to the best of your ability, and if you don't have time for some other questions, fill in your Letter of the Day (see page 19). If you have three minutes and five questions, you may have time to work on only two or three of those remaining questions. That's fine. It's better to take your time on a few questions, and get some of them correct (then, quickly guess on the others), than it is to rush through all five questions and get almost all of them incorrect.

Guessing

Don't be afraid to guess. In fact, get used to it. The GRE uses tough vocabulary and dense passages. Let's say you've eliminated three incorrect answers, and you have two answer choices left: perorate and adumbrate. You know you're looking for a word that means to deliver a big fancy speech, but now you're down to these two words you've never seen before. In that case, guess and move on. Remember that you've got other questions you can spend that time on, and you have to answer every single question. So congratulate yourself on crossing off so many incorrect answers, pick one of the answers left, and worry about some other questions. (By the way, perorate means to deliver a speech either formally or for a long time.)

Proven Techniques

Guessing is not great, but it's a basic part of taking the GRE. Once your only options on a question are "Guess and move on," or "Stare at the question and the timer until you have a nervous breakdown," then guess. Remind yourself that you're doing what a smart test taker should do by not letting one question ruin both your score and your confidence.

The last important thing to know is that you must answer every single question on the test. There is no penalty for incorrect answers, so do not leave any questions blank. Depending on your particular pacing, you may not have time to work on every question, which means there may be some questions at the end that you have to guess on. That's fine. If you did the questions that you spent time on correctly, then guessing on a couple of questions at the end is not going to affect your score in any major way. However, you should pick one letter (your Letter of the Day, or LOTD) to guess on every question you don't have time to work on; choosing the same answer every time will increase your chances of guessing correctly.

A Final Note About the Computer

One final feature of the computer-based GRE is that you'll get your Math and Verbal scores immediately at the end of the test (the essays still need to be read, so you'll receive your Analytical Writing score in about two weeks along with your official score report). Once you've completed the multiple-choice sections, the computer will give you the option to accept or cancel your scores. Of course you have to make that decision before learning what they are. If you choose to cancel, you will never find out how you did. If you accept, you can't cancel them later. However, thanks to the "Score Choice" option, which allows you to pick which scores are sent to which graduate programs, no one but you ever has to know your scores for this administration of the test. So, unless you were ill or there was a major distraction during the test (e.g., the person seated next to you had a seizure and was hauled away by paramedics), you should accept your scores. There's no reliable way to know how you did except by seeing the scores. Remember, the test is supposed to be hard for everyone.

Chapter 3
Text Completions

THE GOAL: FILL IN THE BLANK

Your job on any given Text Completion question is to pick the answer choice that best completes the sentence by filling in the blank or blanks. Not too hard, right? Well, not too hard if you know what *not* to do.

Here's an example question and an outline of what not to do to answer it:

> Most of Newton's biographers refer to the _____ story of the apple tree and the discovery of gravity, despite the story's lack of verifiable sources.

humorous
empirical
baffling
apocryphal
comprehensible

And here's what most people do:

(A)   Most of Newton's biographers refer to the *humorous* story of the apple tree and the discovery of gravity, despite the story's lack of verifiable sources. *(Was the story humorous? What happened in that story again? Something about being hit in the head by a snake with an apple, right? I'm not sure about this answer.)*

(B)   Most of Newton's biographers refer to the *empirical* story of the apple tree and the discovery of gravity, despite the story's lack of verifiable sources. *(Empirical? What's that mean? Something about an empire? Maybe the Roman empire? Does it mean that he wore a toga? Did Newton wear a toga? I don't think so, so this answer is probably wrong.)*

(C)   Most of Newton's biographers refer to the *baffling* story of the apple tree and the discovery of gravity, despite the story's lack of verifiable sources. *(I'm baffled about the story, so this makes sense to me.)*

(D)   Most of Newton's biographers refer to the *apocryphal* story of the apple tree and the discovery of gravity, despite the story's lack of verifiable sources. *(Is apocryphal related to apocalypse? Did Newton's discovery of gravity almost cause the world to end? Not sure . . . better ignore this answer choice.)*

(E)   Most of Newton's biographers refer to the *comprehensible* story of the apple tree and the discovery of gravity, despite the story's lack of verifiable sources. *(Stories can be comprehensible. Sure. That makes sense.)*

In other words, when you just use the answer choices to fill in the blank or blanks, it is not very effective. People tend to do this because they think it's the fastest way to answer a Text Completion question, but guess what? It's not. In fact, it's the slowest way, because more than one answer choice may seem as if it could work.

A Better Approach

Rather than rereading the same sentence or paragraph over and over again, here's a better way. The first thing you should do, as with all GRE questions, is start writing stuff down. For Text Completion questions, write A B C D E vertically on your paper. (We're just going to talk about one-blank Text Completion questions, with five answer choices, for now. Later in the chapter, we'll explain what to do with Text Completion questions with two or three blanks, for which there are three possible answers per blank. Of course, your first job will be to write A B C and D E F for two-blank Text Completions, and A B C, D E F, and G H I for three-blank completions.) Once you've got your letters on the paper, you're all set up to do some Process of Elimination, so let's figure out what we need to eliminate.

Read the sentence. Do not read the answer choices. The answer choices are there to sound nice, and to sound as if they fit nicely in the sentence, which is exactly why ETS put them there. We don't care how good a word sounds in a sentence: We only care whether a word means exactly what we know the blank has to mean.

First, look for whom or what the blank is describing. For adjectives, this is an easy task—it will be describing the word that follows. For nouns and verbs, however, this isn't quite so easy, and you'll have to stitch together a few phrases from the text. Second, look for other terms in the sentence that provide insight into the blank. Sometimes these are easy to find, but at other times will be hiding in plain sight. Third, try to think of a word or phrase that makes sense for the blank. This word or phrase doesn't have to be a fancy-pants GRE word; it just has to mean what you know the blank has to mean. Simple words are fine. In fact, simple words are usually better. The fancy word is ETS's job. Your job is to know the definition of the word that fits in the blank.

Once you have your own word or phrase for the blank, write that word or phrase down on your scratch paper, right next to your A B C D E. Now it's time to do some Process of Elimination. We'll use the same POE marks we talked about in Chapter 1: If an answer choice kind of matches the word or phrase you wrote down, put a check mark. If an answer choice does not match the word or phrase you wrote down, cross off that answer choice. And, last but not least, if an answer choice contains a word you don't know, put a question mark next to it, and do not cross it off.

That's it. After you've gone through the five answers, hopefully you have at least one check mark. If not, guess one of the answers you put a question mark next to, and move on. Notice that although you'll spend more time than you're used to at the beginning of the question, trying to think of and write down your own word or phrase, you will more than make up for that time when you do POE. Think of all the time you'll save over the "(A) Most of Newton's . . . (B) Most of Newton's . . . (C) Most of Newton's" method of rereading the same question over and over again to find which word sounds right.

To summarize:

- Write down letters for each answer choice: A B C D E
- Read the sentence, but not the answers.
- Come up with your own word or phrase for the blank.
- Cross off answer choices that don't match your word or phrase, and mark those that do match with a check.
- *Never* eliminate an answer choice if you don't know what the word means.

It's Your Word

Let's take a look at an example. Remember, the first thing to do is to ignore the answer choices.

The actress, though portrayed by the media as an arrogant prima donna, was, in fact, both charming and _____.

improvident
gracious
enthusiastic
exceptional
lithesome

What word might fit into the blank? *Nice, modest, delightful*. Anything in that vein. Now that you have your own word, go to the answer choices and pick the one that most closely matches your word. The best match doesn't have to be your word exactly—it doesn't even have to be a synonym of your word. It just needs to get across the same idea or feeling.

To go back to the above example: You want to find a word that matches *nice*. Don't cross out (A) if you don't know what *improvident* means. Put a ? next to (A) on your scratch paper, and move on. Don't start playing the word association "what does this word sound like?" game. What about (B)? Does it work? Sure, *gracious* is a good match for *nice*. Put a check mark next to (B) on your scratch paper, and read the next answer. For (C), *enthusiastic* doesn't mean nice. Although someone who is *enthusiastic* COULD be nice, they could also be mean. Cross off (C) on your scratch paper. Same goes for (D), because *exceptional* doesn't match *nice*. If you don't know what *lithesome* means, then put a ? next to (E). Your scratch paper should look something like this:

A ?
B ✓
Є
Đ
E ?

Even though you didn't know what *improvident* or *lithesome* meant, you should know which answer to choose just by looking at your scratch paper. Since (B) got a check mark, then (B) is the answer.

Note that in working through this example, we went through each and every answer choice. On any Text Completion—on any Verbal question—you *have* to do this. You must. Why? Because you may come across an answer choice that seems to work, but another answer choice further down the road works even better. The lesson: Always, always look at every single answer choice. Remember that your job is to find and eliminate answers that don't work. Let's try another Text Completion.

> Although perfumes were first created from the natural oils of plants, chemists have, since the early nineteenth century, produced thousands that contain _____ ingredients.

uncultivated
piquant
synthetic
aromatic
variable

Did you remember to ignore the answer choices? What word did you fill in for the blank? Probably something along the lines of *man-made*. (A) doesn't match your word, so eliminate it. (B) is a harder word. If you don't know what *piquant* means, then you have to keep it. (C) looks good—*synthetic* is a good match for *man-made*—but don't forget to check out (D) and (E). *Aromatic* (a trap answer that sounds good in a sentence about perfumes) and *variable* aren't close to *man-made* at all. So you're left with (B) and (C). Since (B) has a ? and (C) has a ✓, pick (C).

Quick Quiz #1

In the following questions, come up with your own word for the blank. Suggested answers are on page 46.

1. The kidnapping of the son of Charles A. Lindbergh in 1932 so _____ the public that laws were soon adopted with severe penalties for the offense.

2. Though, in his lifetime, Mark Twain received much (i) _____, today's critics esteem him to such a degree that they (ii) _____ him.

3. By (i) _____ all of the genes on the human chromosomes, the Human Genome Project, established in 1990, hopes to gain (ii) _____ into human evolution and study the genetic similarities (iii) _____ by all species.

4. Even with the (i) _____ of the battering ram and catapult, which reduced the effectiveness of large-scale fortifications, castles during the Middle Ages still remained (ii) _____.

5. Mosses, though limited to (i) _____ habitats because they require water for fertilization and lack a vascular system for absorbing water, are considered (ii) _____ plants due to their resilience.

6. The _____ sources that Fahey drew upon extensively in the mid-1960s can be clearly heard in compositions such as the motley "Stomping Tonight," which incorporates elements from the classical music of Vaughan Williams, a Gregorian chant, and the blues of Skip James.

7. The judge did not wish to _____ the tensions between the feuding parties by seeming to favor one side over the other.

A CLUE, A CLUE, A CLUE

Let's take a look at a Text Completion that you'll never see on the real GRE.

ETS is _____ company.

a nonprofit
a wealthy
a devious
a cautious
an enormous

How should you always approach a Text Completion? By ignoring the answer choices and coming up with your own word for the blank. But if you do that for this particular question, guess what? Anything could go in the blank, and (A) through (E) could all be right.

This particular question would never show up on the real GRE because there is no right answer—any of the five answer choices could work. But what if we changed the question a little so that it looked like the following:

ETS, which earns over four million dollars each year, is _____ company.

a nonprofit
a wealthy
a devious
a cautious
an enormous

What's the answer now? (B), right? How do you know (B) is correct? You know the answer is (B) because of the clause "which earns over four million dollars each year." That clause gave you a clue as to what belonged in the blank. Let's change the question again.

ETS, which likes to trick test takers on hard questions, is _____ company.

a nonprofit
a wealthy
a devious
a cautious
an enormous

The answer now is (C). What tells you the answer is (C)? The clue "likes to trick test takers."

On every single Text Completion, there must be a clue that tells you what belongs in the blank. Without a clue, there would be no right answer. So, anytime you're coming up with your own word for the blank, look for the clue to help you out. In fact, often you can repeat the clue itself in the blank. For example, in the last question, you might have said, "ETS . . . is a *tricky* company." *Tricky* is the word you came up with based on the clue.

To make identifying the clue easier, ask, "Whom or What is the blank describing?" and "What else in the sentence gives me insight into that person or thing?" The part of the sentence that provides insight into the blank is the clue. For example, in the last question, the blank describes ETS, and "likes to trick test takers" is the part of the sentence that provides insight into ETS. When identifying the clue is difficult, use the *Who* or *What* and *Insight* questions to narrow in on the clue.

Keep in mind that clues can show up anywhere in the sentence: at the beginning, in the middle, or at the end. If you're having trouble finding the clue, look for the most descriptive part of the sentence. That's usually where the clue is. Try to identify the clue in the following example:

> Hadrian, one of Rome's second-century emperors, focused his efforts primarily on _____ matters, traveling throughout Rome's territory and personally ensuring that the government of each province was operating efficiently.

| foreign |
| dubious |
| municipal |
| inconsequential |
| martial |

Proven Techniques

Don't worry if you don't know anything about Roman emperors; the sentence gives us all the information we need. What does it tell us about this Hadrian guy? Well, we know that he spent time *traveling throughout Rome's territory and personally ensuring that the government of each province was operating efficiently.* Let's use that clue to come up with a word for the blank. Since he cared about the government of each province, our word can be something like "provincial."

Now let's do some POE. Does (A), *foreign*, mean "provincial?" Nope; in fact, *foreign* is the opposite of *Rome's territory*, where Hadrian was traveling. Cross it off. Same with (B), *dubious*. Since *municipal* sort of matches "provincial," put a check mark next to (C). (D), *inconsequential*, doesn't match with our word, nor does (E). Cross both of them off. The answer is (C).

Notice that everything we need to know about the blank is inside the sentence itself. There will always be a clue in every sentence to tell you what the meaning of the word in the blank must be.

TRANSITIONS

Besides the clue, there are other parts of the sentence that tell you what should go in the blank. These other parts of the sentence are transitions.

Transitions are, for the most part, small words. They're important, though, because they usually give structure to the sentence: Either they keep the sentence going in the same direction, or they change the direction of the sentence.

Let's take a look at two classic transitions: *and* and *but*. Fill in the blank for each of the sentences below.

- I don't want to go to the party, and _____ .
- I don't want to go to the party, but _____ .

For the first sentence, you might have come up with something like "I don't want to go to the party, and you can't make me go." For the second sentence, you might have had something along the lines of "I don't want to go to the party, but I'll go anyway."

Notice the function of *and* in the first sentence. It continues the flow of the sentence. In contrast, *but* in the second sentence changes the flow—it takes the sentence in the opposite direction.

Let's take a look at a question you've already seen to get an idea of how transitions work.

The actress, though portrayed by the media as an arrogant prima donna, was, in fact, both charming and _____ .

improvident
gracious
enthusiastic
exceptional
lithesome

First, let's stop and look for the clue. The blank is describing the actress, and the part of the sentence which provides insight into the actress is "portrayed by the media as an arrogant prima donna." Now, let's look for transitions. Do you see any?

There are not one, but two, transitions in this sentence. The first is the word "though" and the second is the word "and." The "though" tells you the sentence is going to change in direction. Therefore, what goes in the blank should be the opposite of "an arrogant prima donna." What about the second transition? The "and" tells you the sentence is going to continue in the same direction. So what goes in the blank should be similar to "charming."

More Transitions

Not all sentences have transitions, but many do. The chart below shows some of the most common transitions.

Same-Direction Transitions	Changing-Direction Transitions
and	but, yet
since	though, although, even though
because	however
so	despite, in spite of
not only . . . but also	rather, instead
thus	whereas
therefore	while
consequently	notwithstanding
hence	ironically
:	however
;	

Transitions aren't always words. Note that the last two transitions in the same-direction column are punctuation marks. ETS loves to use the colon (:) and semicolon (;), so always be on the watch for them. Take a look at an example:

> Born of the blood of Uranus, the mythic Furies are _____ creatures: they punish those who have wronged blood relatives, regardless of the perpetrators' motivations.

vehement
unforgiving
gloomy
quarrelsome
caustic

The clue is everything that comes after the colon; the transition is the colon itself. Therefore, you know that whatever goes in the blank should continue the direction of "they punish those who have wronged blood relatives, regardless of the perpetrators' motivations."

Given the clue and the transition, a good word for the blank is "punishing." You can eliminate (A) since *vehement* isn't a good match. (B) looks okay, so mark it with a check. (C) definitely isn't right, and neither is (D). (E) doesn't fit either since *caustic* means sarcastic, so you're left with (B) as the correct answer. Notice that *unforgiving* doesn't exactly match our predicted answer, but all the other choices are much worse!

Quick Quiz #2

In the following questions, underline the clue and circle any transitions. Then, use the clue and transitions to help you determine what word should go in the blank. Remember, the clue is the part of the sentence which provides insight into the blank. Also, don't forget you can often repeat a part of the clue as the word that goes in the blank. The answers are on page 46.

1. In the Bible, handwriting appeared on the wall at the feast of Belshazzar, a _____ of doom according to Daniel; that night, Babylon fell to Cypress.

2. By the late nineteenth century, many of the congressmen had become staunch _____ : they firmly believed that the United States should avoid all foreign wars and entanglements.

3. Jane's naiveté was often charming, but her (i) _____ all too easily led her to be deceived and therefore (ii) _____.

4. The jealousy of the goddess Hera has been (i) _____ in Greek mythology: numerous stories tell of her (ii) _____ Zeus and his philandering.

5. Many park designers are moving away from the concept of (i) _____ play for children, instead opting for the freedom offered by open space and other (ii) _____ activities. However, this has come at a cost in our (iii) _____ society, in which protective parents are willing to sue anyone felt to be responsible for their child's skinned knee or stubbed toe.

6. It remains a mystery as to how the _____ of the early universe evolved into its present-day diversity.

NO WORD OF YOUR OWN?

Together the clue and the transitions help you come up with your own word for the blank. There are times, however, when you won't be able to come up with your own word—even though you've found the clue and the transitions. What do you do then?

You can still use the clue and the transitions to help you. Even though you may not be able to come up with your own word, you can often tell whether what goes in that blank is positive or negative. If you know the word is positive, then you can eliminate any answer choice that contains a negative word. If you know the word is negative, then you can eliminate any answer choice that contains a positive word.

A word of caution: Don't use this approach as a crutch. It's going to be very tempting to use this technique instead of coming up with your own word, but you shouldn't. Your first goal is always to come up with your own word. Only if you can't do that should you move on to Positive/Negative. For those times when you do use Positive/Negative, remember that you still need to find the clue and transitions. Otherwise you won't know what should go in the blank. Let's try applying Positive/Negative to a question.

> Because he did not want
> to appear _____, the junior
> executive refused to dispute the
> board's decision, in spite of his
> belief that the decision would
> impair employee morale.
>
> A   –
> B   –
> C   +
> D   –
> E   +

Let's say that you can't come up with your own word, which means you need to rely on Positive/Negative. What's the clue in the sentence? The insight is *refused to dispute the board's decision*. There's also the same-direction transition *Because* and the opposite-direction transition *in spite of*. Together, the clue and transitions tell you that a negative word belongs in the blank. (Who would not want to appear positive?) So what can you eliminate? (C) and (E).

This is a good example of how Positive/Negative can be a helpful technique. You can't figure out exactly what should go in the blank, but you can still manage to eliminate two answer choices. If you get stuck after that, you now have a one-in-three chance of getting the question right.

Here's what the complete question looks like:

> Because he did not want
> to appear ____, the junior
> executive refused to dispute the
> board's decision, in spite of his
> belief that the decision would
> impair employee morale.

contentious
indecisive
solicitous
overzealous
steadfast

(C) and (E) are gone because they're positive words. You can't eliminate (A) if you don't know what *contentious* means. (B) doesn't work because the clue is *refused* to *dispute*. That doesn't work with *indecisive*. For the same reason, (D) doesn't work either. So the correct answer is (A). Even though you might not know *contentious*, you can still get to the credited response.

Quick Quiz #3

Find the clue and transitions in the following questions and determine whether the word in the blank should be positive or negative. The answers are on page 47.

1. It was only after the end of the grueling and seemingly ceaseless campaign that the soldiers were allowed any measure of _____.

2. Even when injured, Jane has always been a (i) _____ opponent; indeed, a problematic back and foot did not (ii) _____ her from winning several championships during the 2002 season.

3. The nouveau riche often strive for the same social standing as the established wealthy, but they usually find themselves left with only the _____ of affluence.

4. Of particular note is her assertion that verbal transmissions of (i) _____ were not necessary to result in (ii) _____ effects in neighboring social groups; the more violent one group was, the likely nearby social groups were similarly bellicose. A similar effect was not viewed with group feelings of (iii) _____, indicating that conflict spreads far more easily than does amicability.

5. Though it is important to stand by one's beliefs, it is also important not to cling _____ to them.

6. Barbados's approach to debt, however, was radically different from those of similar countries in (i) _____ economic times: By forcing management and workers to discuss outcomes beneficial to both parties, Barbados disproved the most dire forecasts and (ii) _____ in a striking fashion.

7. The novelist's primary skill is his (i) _____ prose, which elevates even his most (ii) _____ scene.

Study Break

Don't burn yourself out while preparing for the GRE. Be sure to give yourself occasional breaks from studying. You may wish to schedule these at set times ("after 2 hours of studying I'll reward myself with a trip to the kitchen for some ice cream") or as a reward for a productive day ("once I'm done studying for the day, I'll reward myself with a walk around the park")—find the system that works for you. But remember: your brain needs time off to process everything you are learning, so be sure to give yourself study breaks.

TWO OR THREE BLANKS

So far we've talked mostly about Text Completion questions with only one blank. However, some of the Text Completion questions will have two or three blanks. These Text Completion questions will often be a full paragraph. For each blank, you'll have to choose one out of three possible words.

When you're presented with a two-blank or three-blank Text Completion, treat that question as if it were a series of one-blank questions. Write down letters on your scratch paper (A B C, D E F, and possibly G H I). Read the full sentence or paragraph. If you notice that one of the blanks has an obvious clue, start with that blank. If none are obvious, select the first blank and try to identify the clue by asking, "Whom or What is the blank describing?" and "What else in the sentence gives me insight into that person or thing?" Ignoring the answers, write down a prediction word for that blank. Now look at the set of answers for that blank. Cross off the words that don't match your predicted answer, and put a check beside the word that matches your word or phrase. Put a question mark next to any word you don't know. Then, move on to the next blank, and then the next.

Sometimes with two- or three-blank Text Completion questions, you may not know the answer to every single blank. In that case, click on the answers you know, guess an answer from what you have remaining in the other blank(s), click the Mark button, make sure that you wrote down the question number next to your work on your scratch paper, and then click Next. Work another question or two; then return to this question (and your scratch paper for the question). You may notice something about the question or answers that you missed the first time. If not, then just guess and move on. Remember, you're going to hit some tough questions, and you may not be able to answer them all on the first pass. That's why there's a Mark button. Use it!

Let's try a really long three-blank question. Remember, read the question but ignore the answers.

Economic policy is primarily reactionary, designed solely to avoid downturns rather than foster upturns. As a result, economic policies tend to be (i) _____ the previous crisis, rather than focusing on (ii) _____ management of the current boom. As a result, unrestrained financial growth leads to rampant speculation, and soon even seemingly (iii) _____ investments collapse as another recession begins.

Blank (i)	Blank (ii)	Blank (iii)
ignorant of	prudent	solid
responses to	sparing	tenuous
peripheral to	irrational	unstable

That was practically an entire economics textbook, wasn't it? Let's take it apart piece by piece. We'll start with the third blank, because there's a nice clue and transition close by. We know that the *investments collapse*, which means that there was something wrong with the investments. However, before that clue we have the transition *even seemingly*, which tells us that although the investments were bad, they didn't seem so bad. We could describe our investments-that-seemed-like-they-weren't-bad with the word "safe."

Now look at the answers for Blank (iii). *Solid* matches "safe," because a solid investment is definitely a safe investment, so put a check mark next to (G). For (H), *tenuous* doesn't match "safe," so cross it off (or put a question mark next to it if you don't know what *tenuous* means). For (I), *unstable* definitely doesn't match "safe," so cross it off. You have only (G) left, so click on the first word for Blank (iii), *solid*.

Let's try Blank (i) next, because it also has a nice clue for the blank. What's the sentence tell us about *economic policies*? That they are *purely reactionary*. Let's "recycle" the clue for the first blank, and write down "reactions." Cross off (A) and (C), leaving (B), *responses to*.

Now it's time for the middle blank. Most of the work is done at this point, and we now have a much better idea of what this paragraph is about. Blank (ii) is a bit tougher, but there is a clue hiding in the paragraph. What does the paragraph tell us about *management of the current boom*? Well, we know the author thinks that financial policy should *foster upturns*, so we want "helpful" management. (D), *prudent*, means careful, which basically matches our word. (E) and (F) don't, so cross them both off. Our answers are *responses to*, *prudent*, and *solid*.

Don't bite off more than you can chew. If you get a two- or three-blank Text Completion, just work on one blank at a time. Once you figure out what should go in one blank, use POE *right away*. As you solve each blank, you'll notice that a formerly insurmountable wall of text has become a couple of simple sentences.

Relationship Between the Blanks

There are a few two- and three-blank questions for which you can't know *exactly* what should go in the blanks. These are rare; most of the time, there'll be a clear clue for each blank. Sometimes, however, there will be questions without a nice clue for one or more of the blanks. In that case, you have to see how the blanks relate to one another.

For instance, let's look at this Text Completion question:

Dorsey's film criticisms are (i)
_____ in that his critiques (ii)
_____ the accepted views of
most commentators of film.

Blank (i)	Blank (ii)
impartial	distill
unconventional	conform to
celebrated	defy

The problem with this sentence is there is no clue as to what Dorsey's film criticisms are like. Do they agree with the accepted views? Do they go against them? There's no way to know for sure. Therefore, let's see how the blanks relate. Make up your own word for one of the blanks, and see how it affects the other blank. Then make up another word for the same blank, and see how it affects the other.

Starting with Blank (ii), let's say that his critiques "match" the accepted views. In that case, his film criticisms are "typical" reviews, because he goes along with whatever everyone else says. But what if for Blank (ii) we say his critiques "go against" the accepted views? In that case, his reviews are "unusual." Write down both pairs: "typical . . . match" and "unusual . . . go against."

Now look at the answer choices for the first blank. *Impartial* doesn't match either "typical" or "unusual," so cross off (A). *Unconventional* matches "unusual"; put a check next to (B) and the small letters (d), (e) and (f) to go with (B). Now compare the words for the second blank with the other half of this pair, "go against."

Distill and *conform* to can be eliminated, but *defy* matches the second word in the correct pair of predicted answers. For this kind of Text Completion only, once you see two check marks, you can safely choose them both. The correct answers are (B) and (F).

Remember, these types of Text Completions don't show up that often, so you should mostly focus on trying to find clues and transitions.

IN SUMMARY...

A text completion is hard only when you get distracted by the answer choices and forget about the sentence itself. Focus on the sentence—that's where the clue and transitions are.

1. Ignore the answer choices. Remember, it's the sentence that's important.
2. Come up with your own word for the blank. Ask, "*Whom* or *What* is the blank describing?" and "What else in the sentence provides *insight* into that person or thing?" Use the clue and transitions to come up with your word. Recycle part of the clue whenever possible.
3. If you can't come up with your own word, use the clue and transitions to determine whether what goes in the blank is a positive or negative word.
4. If it's a two- or three-blank Text Completion, focus on one blank at a time.
5. If the clue for one blank is actually the other blank, write down both possible pairs of words and look for two check marks.

Practice Drill #1

<u>Directions:</u> Each sentence below has one, two, or three blanks, each blank indicating that something has been omitted. Beneath the sentence are five lettered words or sets of words. Choose the word or set of words for each blank that <u>best</u> fits the meaning of the sentence as a whole. The answers are on page 48.

1. The couple thought that the values represented in traditional services were _____, so they decided to write their own, more modern, wedding vows.

bigoted
archaic
dogmatic
ineloquent
somber

2. An experienced film critic is one who not only calls attention to the (i) _____ of a particular feature, but also puts forth legitimate (ii) _____ that, if employed, would create a more satisfying product.

Blank (i)	Blank (ii)
fascinations	recommendations
origins	statistics
shortcomings	controversies

3. Louis was so painfully shy that his friends had to cajole him not to _____ even the smallest social gathering.

confront
subdue
flout
shun
attend

4. The salmon was prepared with such care that even those who did not have _____ seafood found the meal to be delicious.

a contention with
an assurance of
a penchant for
a preconception of
an endorsement of

5. The movement in literature known as realism was so named because of its attempt to describe life without idealization or romantic subjectivity; similarly, the realist movement in art had as its intent the (i) _____ of natural forms without (ii) _____.

Blank (i)	Blank (ii)
obfuscation	vulgarity
rendering	embellishment
adulteration	intrusion

6. Before she applied for the position, Laura thought her qualifications might be considered (i) _____. However, when she learned of the financial (ii) _____ the company was facing, she hoped that her lack of experience might be made up for by her willingness to accept (iii) _____ salary.

Blank (i)	Blank (ii)	Blank (iii)
exemplary	distress	a peremptory
inadequate	approbation	a commensurate
esoteric	abundance	an opulent

7. Known as "The City of Trees," Sacramento has more trees per capita than does Paris, is filled with tree-lined streets and thoroughfares, and even has (i) _____ art installation in City Hall. However, recent budget cuts have (ii) _____ the Urban Forestry workforce, causing some concern about the future of Sacramento's green canopy.

Blank (i)	Blank (ii)
an arboreal	amalgamated
an impressionist	ameliorated
a terrestrial	abridged

Practice Drill #2

<u>Directions:</u> Each sentence below has one, two, or three blanks, each blank indicating that something has been omitted. Beneath the sentence are five lettered words or sets of words. Choose the word or set of words for each blank that <u>best</u> fits the meaning of the sentence as a whole. The answers are on page 50.

1. In conducting field research, one must observe every detail, no matter how small, for it is often the seemingly unimportant that actually leads to scientific ____.

recessions
obstructions
incapacities
breakthroughs
dissolutions

2. The young researcher's conclusions flew in the face of established scientific knowledge; she therefore stated her findings (i) ____ in her paper. Despite her confidence in her theories, she wanted to avoid accusations of (ii) ____ that might come from more seasoned academics, and determined that she could forgo recognition for the time being. Once her ideas were corroborated by additional experimentation, she would receive her due (iii) ____.

Blank (i)	Blank (ii)	Blank (iii)
eruditely	brazenness	compensation
facetiously	avarice	kudos
diffidently	deference	diligence

3. Whereas the flexing of a muscle is viewed as a motion that requires ____ effort, breathing is considered an involuntary act.

careful
conscious
minimal
thoughtful
intensive

4. Initially (i) ____ the homeowner's claims of supernatural activity, the Ghost Hunters soon discovered that the house was indeed haunted, but that the ghost was more playful and curious than the traditionally (ii) ____ and solitary spirits they had encountered other places.

Blank (i)	Blank (ii)
credulous of	lugubrious
dubious of	jocund
receptive to	inquisitive

5. The judge was known for his (i) ____ treatment of controversial cases. Hence, it was rare for anyone in the courtroom to request a (ii) ____ for his cases, though he presided over some in which jurists with strong opinions about the subject matter of the case would feel compelled to (iii) ____ themselves.

Blank (i)	Blank (ii)	Blank (iii)
iniquitous	modification	regale
biased	remonstration	recuse
disinterested	proxy	foment

6. It is easy to assume that the more slow and (i) ____ the study of a disease, the more likely a cure will be found. Historically, however, cures for major diseases have often been found through (ii) ____ breakthroughs and accidental discoveries.

Blank (i)	Blank (ii)
subtle	precipitous
exhaustive	lucid
fortuitous	deliberate

Practice Drill #3

<u>Directions:</u> Each sentence below has one, two, or three blanks, each blank indicating that something has been omitted. Beneath the sentence are five lettered words or sets of words. Choose the word or set of words for each blank that <u>best</u> fits the meaning of the sentence as a whole. The answers are on page 52.

1. Scientists cannot (i) _____ date when whales evolved to feed using baleen, a filtering structure used to (ii) _____ prey from seawater. Because it is made of keratin, a protein, baleen rarely fossilizes, and the carbon-dating of any fossils found does not conclusively prove age. However, some researchers have attempted to date the modification by (iii) _____ baleen-related skull modifications and formations of the jaw.

Blank (i)	Blank (ii)	Blank (iii)
germanely	sieve	hypothesizing
definitively	consume	assaying
cogently	locate	validating

2. Cleopatra of Egypt and Antony of Rome were allies both militarily and amorously and, together, their armies were (i) _____ at the Battle of Actium. In the chaotic aftermath of the defeat, the two fled and were separated and, tragically, upon hearing a false rumor that his (ii) _____ in battle and (iii) _____ had committed suicide, Antony fell on his sword and killed himself.

Blank (i)	Blank (ii)	Blank (iii)
routed	collaborator	hostility
consoled	antagonist	romance
invigorated	liaison	invasion

3. While there isn't yet enough evidence to prove that any one food can (i) _____ the risk of lung cancer, a "heart-healthy" diet can (ii) _____ other risk factors, such as obesity, that can lead to various forms of cancer.

Blank (i)	Blank (ii)
increase	attack
reduce	detach
assert	diminish

4. Despite his _____ job performance, the administrator did not receive credit for his accomplishments.

incompetent
noticeable
effective
lugubrious
aggressive

5. Although she conveyed the message calmly and without distress, Lin's expression betrayed the message's _____ nature.

facetious
impartial
puerile
uncommunicative
dire

6. Shi-yu's art is to be admired not for its realism, but rather for its distortion of reality: he creates _____ of the world, exaggerating not only its beauty but also its meanness and pettiness.

a mockery
a personification
a caricature
a sublimation
an allegory

7. Though Bernie is warm and magnanimous, she is just as (i) _____, combining her generous nature with an admirable (ii) _____.

Blank (i)	Blank (ii)
affable	recalcitrance
unyielding	benevolence
cantankerous	tenacity

Practice Drill #4

<u>Directions:</u> Each sentence below has one, two, or three blanks, each blank indicating that something has been omitted. Beneath the sentence are five lettered words or sets of words. Choose the word or set of words for each blank that <u>best</u> fits the meaning of the sentence as a whole. The answers are on page 54.

1. The new film was practically a (i) _____ to Canada, with its shots of Toronto landmarks such as Honest Ed's, Sonic Boom record store, and Parliament Street. Even the actors' T-shirts, such as a Canadian coffee shop T-shirt and a Canadian indie-rock band shirt, stress to viewers that the film is (ii) _____ Canadian.

Blank (i)	Blank (ii)
breach	unreservedly
dearth	obscurely
paean	cinematically

2. Some scientists believe that certain human beings may be more _____ than others because the former possess a gene that predisposes them toward aggressive behavior.

reserved
timorous
self-possessed
uncouth
quarrelsome

3. The formerly esoteric debate over teacher tenure has recently gained enormous (i) _____; while some believe that tenure is necessary to prohibit arbitrary exercise of (ii) _____ power and to preserve academic freedom, others see tenure as a profligate waste of resources and an obstacle to school improvement. Only through comprehensive comparative studies will we be able to enact a model of teacher recruitment and hiring that will best serve the needs of students, but such studies are difficult to conduct, as districts are often (iii) _____ to experiment with new hiring methods before they have been tested elsewhere.

Blank (i)	Blank (ii)	Blank (iii)
accord	autocratic	eager
ire	whimsical	wanton
prominence	titanic	loath

4. While some (i) _____, such as Lewis Carroll's lasting creation "chortle"—derived from the words "snort" and "chuckle"—add meaning and richness to our language, others, such as the recent "reintarnation," can make the speaker simply seem (ii) _____.

Blank (i)	Blank (ii)
chorals	antipodal
neologisms	erudite
canons	benighted

5. While the modern concept of the robot is often (i) _____ to the American science fiction writer Isaac Asimov, the word was actually brought into usage by Karel Čapek, a Czech writer. Čapek wrote about a servant class of creatures who looked almost (ii) _____ to humans, but were actually artificial clones. Čapek noted in his late papers that his brother had contributed the word "robot," deriving it from a Czech word for "slave." Robots, to Čapek, did not symbolize the dream of a future technologically advanced era, but rather the horror of his current world, filled with the (iii) _____ of fascist dictatorships and mass production.

Blank (i)	Blank (ii)	Blank (iii)
proposed	identical	nuisances
attributed	amenable	actualities
queried	comely	scourges

6. The class was purportedly an exhaustive study of Jane Austen's works, yet since it failed to include either *Emma* or *Pride and Prejudice* in its analysis, it was, by no means, _____.

prudent
acceptable
comprehensive
adequate
authoritative

7. The well-behaved children were (i) _____ and required no (ii) _____ so their parents were always happy to take them on trips.

Blank (i)	Blank (ii)
decorous	supervision
finicky	affluence
exquisite	encumbrance

Practice Drill #5

<u>Directions:</u> Each sentence below has one, two, or three blanks, each blank indicating that something has been omitted. Beneath the sentence are five lettered words or sets of words. Choose the word or set of words for each blank that <u>best</u> fits the meaning of the sentence as a whole. The answers are on page 56.

1. The two friends, both English teachers, had a tendency to endlessly (i) _____ over small grammatical points; no one else cared whether the word in question was the predicate nominative or predicate adjective of the sentence, but determining who was right was, for them, (ii) _____.

Blank (i)	Blank (ii)
prevail	irrelevant
quibble	paramount
exult	didactic

2. Although honesty is a trait to be valued, it is not always appropriate; when one is too forthright, one can often be _____.

objective
equitable
deluded
tactless
corrupt

3. Reading D.H. Lawrence's novel *Sons and Lovers* today, it can be easy to forget that the book's depictions of amorous relationships between men and women were considered (i) _____ for many years after its publication. The types of relationships Lawrence describes, once thought worthy of censure, now seem to appear on film and television on a daily basis and might be considered (ii) _____. Whether one considers it beneficial or harmful, this cultural (iii) _____ marks a profound shift in attitudes toward male/female relationships.

Blank (i)	Blank (ii)	Blank (iii)
prurient	descriptive	transformation
patronizing	pedestrian	assimilation
sacrosanct	vulgar	bias

4. Interpreting data on controversial issues generated from live, as opposed to automated, telephone polls can be complicated by the fact that responders sometimes (i) _____ their views to live pollsters if they believe those views may be considered socially unacceptable. In contrast, automated polling may minimize the (ii) _____ these responders feel, and generate more accurate data.

Blank (i)	Blank (ii)
demonstrate	stagnation
expound	relief
misrepresent	stigma

5. Despite the fact that the (i) _____ writer had no previous publishing experience, she was still able to get a contract for her (ii) _____ novel through hard work and (iii) _____.

Blank (i)	Blank (ii)	Blank (iii)
seasoned	debut	indolence
neophyte	fictional	tenacity
successful	subsequent	savvy

6. Unfortunately, Jeannie's shy demeanor was often misinterpreted by those who did not know her: indeed, strangers typically construed her _____ behavior as coyness.

unresponsive
supercilious
amenable
acquiescent
demure

7. At first, the collector was (i) _____ of the woman's claims that the gold bar was sunken treasure. After he (ii) _____ the bar, though, he found that coral had grown on the back of it, indicating that the bar had been underwater for years. This discovery (iii) _____ the woman's claim.

Blank (i)	Blank (ii)	Blank (iii)
dubious	briefed	nullified
convinced	assayed	substantiated
enamored	scrutinized	belied

ANSWERS AND EXPLANATIONS

Quick Quiz #1

1. outraged

2. acclaim . . . deify

3. mapping . . . insight . . . shared

4. advent . . . defensible

5. moist . . . hardy

6. diverse

7. exacerbate

Quick Quiz #2

1. In the Bible, handwriting appeared on the wall at the feast of Belshazzar, a _____ of doom according to Daniel; that night, Babylon fell to Cypress.

   portent

2. By the late nineteenth century, many of the congressmen had become staunch _____: they firmly believed that the United States should avoid all foreign wars and entanglements.

   isolationists

3. Jane's naiveté was often charming, but her (i) _____ all too easily led her to be deceived and therefore (ii) _____.

   credulousness . . . duped

4. The jealousy of the goddess Hera has been (i) _____ in Greek mythology: numerous stories tell of her (ii) _____ Zeus and his philandering.

   well documented . . . resentment toward

5. Many park designers are moving away from the concept of (i) _____ play for children, instead opting for the freedom offered by open space and other (ii) _____ activities. However, this has come at a cost in our (iii) _____ society, in which protective parents are willing to sue anyone felt to be responsible for their child's skinned knee or stubbed toe.

   constrained . . . unrestricted . . . litigious

6. It remains a mystery as to how the _____ of the early universe evolved into its present-day diversity.

   homogeneity

Quick Quiz #3

1. It was (only after the end) of the grueling and seemingly ceaseless campaign that the soldiers were allowed any measure of _____.

   +

   respite

2. Even when injured, Jane has always been a (i) _____ opponent; indeed, a problematic back and foot did not (ii) _____ her from winning several championships during the 2002 season.

   + . . . −

   formidable . . . keep

3. The nouveau riche often strive for the same social standing as the established wealthy, (but) they usually find themselves left with only the _____ of affluence.

   −

   trappings

4. Of particular note is her assertion that verbal transmissions of (i) _____ were not necessary to result in (ii) _____ effects in neighboring social groups; the more violent one group was, the likely nearby social groups were similarly bellicose. A similar effect was (not viewed) with group feelings of (iii) _____ , indicating that conflict spreads far more easily than does amicability.

   − . . . − . . . +

   hostility . . . tumultuous . . . sociability

5. (Though) it is important to stand by one's beliefs, it is also important not to cling _____ to them.

   −

   dogmatically

6. Barbados's approach to debt, however, was radically different from those of (similar) countries in (i) _____ economic times: By forcing management and workers to discuss outcomes beneficial to both parties, Barbados (disproved) the most dire forecasts and (ii) _____ in a striking fashion.

   − . . . +

   dreadful . . rebounded

7. The novelist's primary skill is his (i) _____ prose, which elevates (even) his most (ii) _____ scene.

   + . . . −

   rousing . . . banal

Practice Drill #1

1. **B** The blank describes what *the couple thought* about *the values represented in traditional services*. The clue is *modern*. The transition word *more* indicates that the word for the blank is an opposite of the clue, so use "old-fashioned" as a word for the blank. Choices (A), (D), and (E)—*bigoted, ineloquent, somber*—can be eliminated because they don't match "old-fashioned." For (C), while something that is *dogmatic* may be old-fashioned, the word means a belief that is established, which may not be old-fashioned, so eliminate (C). The correct answer is (B), *archaic*.

2. **shortcomings** and **recommendations**

   The first blank is an easy place to start, and describes a quality *of a particular feature* which *an experienced film critic . . . calls attention to.* The clue for the first blank is *satisfying*. The transition word *more* indicates that the word for the first blank is an opposite of the clue. If a feature is unsatisfying, there is something wrong with it, so use "flaws" as a word for the first blank. Choices (A) and (B) can be eliminated because they don't match "flaws," so (C), *shortcomings*, is the answer for the first blank. Now look at the second blank, which refers to what the *critic . . . puts forth*. The clue is *if employed, would create a more satisfying product.* Something that could be employed to make a product with flaws more satisfying would be a "suggestion," so use that for the second blank. Choices (E) and (F) can be eliminated because they don't match "suggestion," so the correct answer for the second blank is (D), *recommendations.* The correct answer is (C) and (D).

3. **D** The blank refers to what Louis's *friends had to cajole him not to* do. The clue is *painfully shy* and *smallest social gathering*. The transition words *so . . . even* indicate that Louis's shyness was so extreme that it would impact *the smallest social gathering*. Thus, an extremely shy reaction to the smallest social gathering is to "avoid" it, so use that as a word for the blank. Choices (A), (B), (C), and (E)—*confront, subdue, flout, attend*—can be eliminated because they don't match "avoid." The correct answer is (D), *shun*.

4. **C** The blank refers to a perception that some people, *those, did not have* toward *seafood*. The clue is *prepared with . . . care* and *found the meal to be delicious*. The transition words *such . . . even* indicate that finding *the meal to be delicious* is somehow extreme. Since the meal was *prepared with . . . care*, it would be normal to find it delicious, so the blank refers to the perception of people who do not like seafood. Since the blank refers to a perception these people did not have, use "a fondness for" as a phrase for the blank. Choices (A), (B), and (D)—*a contention with, an assurance of, a preconception of*—can be eliminated because they don't match "a fondness for." Choice (E), *an endorsement of*, means a support or recommendation of seafood, which doesn't match "a fondness for," because it refers to how those people might describe seafood to a third party, so eliminate (E). The correct answer is (C), *a penchant for.*

5. **rendering** and **embellishment**

   The second blank is an easy place to start, and refers to a quality that *the realist movement in art* did not have. The clue for the second blank is *idealization or romantic subjectivity*. The transition word *similarly* indicates that *realism . . . in literature* can be compared to *the realist movement in art*, so recycle "idealization" as a word for the second blank. Choices (D) and (F)—*vulgarity, intrusion—*

be eliminated because they don't match "idealization," so the correct answer for the second blank is (E), *embellishment*. Now look at the first blank, which refers to what *the realist movement in art* intended to do to *natural forms*. The clue for the first blank is *describe... without idealization or romantic subjectivity*. Again, the transition word *similarly* indicates that *realism... in literature* can be compared to *the realist movement in art*, so recycle "describe" as a word for the first blank. Choices (A) and (C)—*obfuscation, adulteration*—can be eliminated because they refer to some kind of distortion of a reality, so the correct answer for the first blank is (B), *rendering*. The correct answer is (B) and (E).

6. **inadequate**, **distress**, and **a commensurate**

    The first blank is an easy place to start, and refers to what *Laura thought her qualifications might be considered*. The clue for the first blank is *lack of experience,* so recycle "lacking" as a word for the first blank. Choices (A) and (C) can be eliminated, because they don't match "lacking," so the correct answer for the first blank is *inadequate*. Now look at the third blank, which refers to the type of *salary* that *Laura* is willing *to accept*. The clue for the third blank is *lack of experience.* The words *made up for* indicate a transition. Since the question centers on how *Laura... might be considered, the contrast applies to how the company would feel about hiring Laura,* and a *lack of experience* is negative, so the type of *Salary* that would be considered positive is a "low" one, so use that as a word for the third blank. While none of the choices for the third blank match "low," (I), *an opulent,* can be eliminated as the opposite of "low." Choice (G), *a peremptory,* indicates an urgent or arrogant salary, which cannot be a match for "low," so eliminate (G). Choice (H), *a commensurate,* indicates a matching salary, which can agree with *lack of experience* to mean a low salary, so the correct answer for the third blank is (H), *a commensurate.* Now look at the second blank, which refers to something *financial... the company was facing.* The clue for the second blank is *considered inadequate.* The transition words *before... however* indicate that Laura's *lack of experience* might not *be considered inadequate.* A *financial* situation a *company* is *facing* which might make a *lack of experience* less of a problem is "trouble," so use that as a word for the second blank. Choices (E) and (F) can be eliminated because they don't match "trouble," so the correct answer for the second blank is (D), *distress.* The correct answer is (B), (D), and (H).

7. **an arboreal** and **abridged**

    The first blank is an easy place to start, and refers to the type of *art installation in* Sacramento's *City Hall.* The clue for the first blank is *the city of trees.* The transition word *even* indicates that the focus on *trees* is so extreme that it extends to the *art installation,* so use "a tree focused" as a phrase for the first blank. Choice (B) can be eliminated because it does not match "a tree focused." Choice (C) may seem appealing, but *terrestrial* means land-based, which does not specifically refer to trees, so eliminate (C). The correct answer for the first blank is (A), *an arboreal.* Now look at the second blank, which refers what *recent budget cuts* have done to *the Urban Forestry workforce.* The clue for the second blank is *concern about the future of Sacramento's green canopy.* The transition word *causing* indicates that the *budget cuts* are cause for *concern,* so the *workforce* is "hurt," and use that as a word for the second blank. Choices (D) and (E) can be eliminated because they do not match "hurt," so the correct answer for the second blank is (F), *abridged.* The correct answer is (A) and (F).

Practice Drill #2

1. **D** The blank refers to something described as *scientific*. The clue is *must observe every detail, no matter how small and seemingly unimportant*. The transition word *actually* indicates that the blank refers to something that is "important," so use that as a word for the blank. Choices (A), (B), (C), and (E)—*recessions, obstructions, incapacities, dissolutions*—can be eliminated because they do not match "important," so the correct answer is (D), *breakthroughs*.

2. **diffidently, brazenness**, and **kudos**

    The second blank is an easy place to start, and refers to the kind of *accusations* the *young researcher . . . wanted to avoid*. The clue for the second blank is *confidence in her theories*. The transition word *despite* indicates that the researcher *wanted to avoid accusations of* "unsupported conclusions," so use that as a phrase for that second blank. None of the choices match "unsupported conclusions," but (E) and (F) can be eliminated because they indicate ill-intent and submission, neither of which can be used to match "unsupported conclusions." Choice (D), *brazenness*, can match "unsupported conclusions," since the *researcher's conclusions* contradicted *established knowledge*, so the correct answer for the second blank is (D), *brazenness*. Now look at the third blank, which refers to something the *researcher* would be *due*. The clue for the third blank is *forgo recognition*. The transition words *for the time being* and *once* indicate the word for the blank will match the clue, so recycle "recognition" as a word for the third blank. Choice (I), *diligence*, can be eliminated because it doesn't match "recognition." While *compensation* can be a form of "recognition," it does not directly mean recognition, so eliminate (G), and the correct answer for the third blank is (H), *kudos*. Now look at the first blank, which refers to how the *young researcher . . . stated her findings*. As the researcher wanted to avoid accusations of unsupported conclusions, and was not seeking recognition, use "humbly" as a word for the first blank. Both (A), *eruditely*, which means scholarly, and also (B) can be eliminated, as they do not match "humbly." The correct answer for the first blank is (C), *diffidently*. The correct answer is (C), (D), and (H).

3. **B** The blank refers to the type of effort *flexing a muscle is viewed* as requiring. The clue for the blank is *involuntary*. The transition word *whereas* indicates the word for the blank is the opposite of *involuntary*, so use "voluntary" as a word for the blank. Choices (A), (C), and (E) can be eliminated because they do not match "voluntary." Choice (D), *thoughtful*, means considerate, which does not match "voluntary," so eliminate (D). The correct answer is (B), *conscious*.

4. **dubious of** and **lugubrious**

    The first blank is an easy place to start, and refers to how *the Ghost Hunters* felt about *the home-owner's claims of supernatural activity*. The clue for the blank is *indeed haunted*. The transition words *initially . . . soon* indicates that the word will be the opposite of the clue. If a *haunted* house is a contrast, then initially the Ghost Hunters must have been suspicious of the claims of supernatural activity, so use "suspicious of" as a word for the first blank. Choice (A), which means believing of, and (C) can be eliminated, because they do not match "suspicious of." The correct answer for the first blank is (B), *dubious of.* Now, look at the second blank, which refers to the type of *spirits* the Ghost Hunters *had encountered* elsewhere. The clue for the second blank is *playful.* The transition words *more . . . than* indicate that the word for the blank will be the opposite of *playful,* so use "not-playful" as a word for the second blank. Choice (E), which means merry, and (F) can be eliminated, because they do not match "not-playful." Choice (D), *lugubrious,* means mournful, so the correct answer for the second blank is (D). The correct answer is (B) and (D).

5.   **disinterested**, **proxy**, and **recuse**

The third blank is an easy place to start, and refers to an action taken by *some jurists.* The clue for the third blank is *strong opinions.* A jurist with a strong opinion about a case may feel that he or she cannot be impartial, so use "dismiss" as a word for the third blank. Choices (G) and (I) can be eliminated because they do not match "dismiss." The correct answer for the third blank is (H), *recuse.* Now look at the first blank, which refers to how *the judge was known for* treating cases. The clue for the first blank is *strong opinions.* The transition word *though* indicates that the blank is an opposite of the clue, so use "impartial" as a word for the first blank. Choices (A) and (B) can be eliminated because they do not match "impartial." The correct answer for the first blank is (C), *disinterested.* Now look at the second blank, which refers to what it was *rare for anyone . . . to request* on the judge's *cases.* The clue for the second blank is the correct answer for the first blank, *disinterested.* If the judge treats cases objectively, then it would be rare for someone to request a "replacement" *for his cases,* so use that as a word for the second blank. Choice (E) can be eliminated, as it does not match "replacement." Choice (D), *modification,* may seem tempting, but would imply asking the judge to change something else about the case, not for the judge to recuse himself. The correct answer for the second blank is (F), *proxy.* The correct answer is (C), (F), and (H).

6.   **exhaustive** and **precipitous**

The first blank is an easy place to start, and refers to a quality of *the study of a disease.* The clue for the first blank is *slow.* The transition word *and* indicates that the word for the first blank will match *slow,* so recycle "slow" as a word for the first blank. Eliminate (A) and (C) because they do not match "slow," and the correct answer for the first blank is (B), *exhaustive.* Now, look at the second blank. The second blank refers to the types of *breakthroughs* through which *cures for major diseases have often been found.* The clue for the second blank is *slow.* The transition word *however* indicates that the word for the blank will be the opposite of *slow,* so use "fast" as a word for the second blank. Choices (E) and (F) can be eliminated, because they do not match "fast." The correct answer for the second blank is (D), *precipitous,* which indicates a sudden change. The correct answer is (B) and (D).

Practice Drill #3

1. **definitively**, *sieve*, and **assaying**

   The second blank is an easy place to start, and refers to what *baleen* does with *prey* and *seawater*. The clue for the second blank is *filtering structure*, so use "filter" as a word for the second blank. Choices (E) and (F) can be eliminated, because they do not match "filter." The correct answer for the second blank is (D), *sieve*. Now look at the first blank, which refers to a relationship scientists do not have to the *date when whales evolved to feed using baleen*. The clue for the first blank is *does not conclusively prove age*, so recycle "conclusively" as a word for the first blank. Choice (A), which means relevantly, and (C), which means convincingly, can be eliminated because they do not match "conclusively." The correct answer for the first blank is (B), *definitively*. Now look at the third blank, which refers to an action *some researchers* have taken toward *skull modifications and formations*. The clue for the second blank is *attempted to date*, so use "examining" as a word for the third blank. Choices (G) and (I) can be eliminated, because they do not match "examining." The correct answer for the third blank is (H), *assaying*. The correct answer is (B), (D), and (H).

2. **routed**, **collaborator**, and **romance**

   The first blank is an easy place to start, and refers to what happened to *their armies . . . at the Battle of Actium*. The clue for the first blank is *defeat*, so recycle "defeat" as a word for the first blank. Choices (B) and (C)—*consoled, invigorated*—can be eliminated, because they do not match "defeat." The correct answer for the first blank is (A), *routed*. Now look at the third blank, which refers to a relationship *Antony* has to *Cleopatra*. The transition word *and* indicates that the word for the third blank is paired with *battle*, and the question previously groups *militarily and amorously*, so the clue for the third blank is *amorously*, which can be recycled as a word for the third blank. Choices (G) and (I) can be eliminated because they do not match "amorously." The correct answer for the third blank is (H), *romance*. Now look at the second blank, which refers to a relationship *Antony* has to *Cleopatra*. The structural agreement between *militarily and amorously* and *battle and romance* indicates that the clue for the second blank is allies, so use "ally" as a word for the second blank. Choice (E) can be eliminated, because it does not match "ally." Choice (F), *liaison*, may seem tempting, but can be eliminated since a *liaison* may establish a connection between hostile parties. The correct answer for the second blank is (D), *collaborator*. The correct answer is (A), (D), and (H).

3. **reduce** and **diminish**

   The second blank is an easy place to start, and refers to what happens to *risk factors*. The clue for the second blank is *heart-healthy*. The transition phrases *heart-healthy* and *risk factors* indicate that the word for the second blank will provide a contrast, so use "lessen" as a word for the second blank. Eliminate (D) and (E)—*attack, detach*—because they do not match "lessen," and the correct answer for the second blank is (F), *diminish*. Now, look at the first blank, which refers to what happens to *the risk of lung cancer*. The structural agreement between *lung cancer* and *various forms of cancer* indicates that clue for the first blank is also *heart-healthy*, and that the word for the first blank will also provide a contrast, so use "lessen" as a word for the first blank. Choices (A) and (C) can be eliminated, because they do not match "lessen." The correct answer for the first blank is (B), *reduce*. The correct answer is (B) and (F).

4. **C** The blank refers to the *administrator's job performance*. The clue for the blank is *accomplishments*. The transition word *despite* and *did not receive credit* provides the contrast which indicates that the word for the blank matches *accomplishments*. So, use "excellent" as a word for the blank. Choices (A), (B), and (E) can be eliminated because they do not match "excellent." Choice (D), *lugubrious*, means mournful, which does not match "excellent," so eliminate (D). The correct answer is (C), *effective*.

5. **E** The blank refers to the *nature* of *the message*. The clue for the blank is *calmly and without distress*. The transition word *although* indicates a contrast, so use "urgent" as a word for the blank. Choices (B) and (D) can be eliminated because they do not match "urgent." Choice (A), *facetious*, which means not serious, and (C), *puerile*, which means childish, do not match "urgent" and can be eliminated. The correct answer is (E), *dire*.

6. **C** The blank refers to what version *of the world . . . Shi-yu's art . . . creates*. The clue for the blank is *exaggerating*, so recycle "an exaggeration" as a phrase for the blank. Choice (B) can be eliminated because it does not match "an exaggeration." Choice (D), *a sublimation*, which means an improvement, and (A), *a mockery*, can be eliminated because the exaggeration is of both *beauty* and also *meanness and pettiness*, so neither extreme matches "an exaggeration." Choice (E), *an allegory*, means a symbolic representation, which may be tempting, but does not match "an exaggeration" and can be eliminated. The correct answer is (C), *a caricature*.

7. **unyielding** and **tenacity**

The second blank is an easy place to start, and refers to a quality *Bernie* possesses. The clue for the second blank is *admirable*. The transition word *though* indicates that the word for the second blank will be an opposite of *warm and magnanimous*. The combination of the clue and the contrast transition indicate to use "firm" as a word for the second blank. Eliminate both (D), *recalcitrance*, which means stubbornness, and also (E) because they do not match "firm," and the correct answer for the second blank is (F), *tenacity*. Now, look at the first blank, which refers to a quality Bernie possesses. The clue for the first blank is *tenacity*, and can be recycled as a word for the first blank. Choices (A) and (C) can be eliminated, because they do not match "tenacity." The correct answer for the first blank is (B), *unyielding*. The correct answer is (B) and (F).

Practice Drill #4

1. **paean** and **unreservedly**

    The second blank is an easy place to start, and refers to *the film*. The clue for the second blank is that *the new film* contained *shots of Toronto landmarks . . . and . . . even the actor's T-shirts, such as a Canadian coffee shop T-shirt and a Canadian indie-rock band shirt*. The blank is relating the film to *Canadian*, and because the film contained a large amount of Canadian culture, the film was obviously Canadian. Use a word like "obviously" for the blank. Eliminate (E) and (F)—*obscurely, cinematically*—because they do not match "obviously," and the correct answer for the second blank is (D), *unreservedly*. Now, look at the first blank, which also refers to the film. The clue for the first blank is what the film was *to Canada*, so use "homage" as a word for the first blank. Choices (A) and (B)—*breach, dearth*—can be eliminated, because they do not match "homage." The correct answer for the first blank is (C), *paean*. The correct answer is (C) and (D).

2. **E**   The blank refers to *certain human beings*. The clue for the blank is that certain humans *may be more . . . than others because they possess a gene that predisposes them toward aggressive behavior*. Therefore, a good word for the blank is "aggressive." Choices (A), (B), and (C)—*reserved, timorous, self-possessed*—can be eliminated because they do not match "aggressive." Choice (D), *uncouth*, means lacking good manners, which does not match "aggressive," so eliminate (D). The correct answer is (E), *quarrelsome*.

3. **prominence**, **autocratic**, and **loath**

    The third blank is an easy place to start, and refers to *districts*. The clue for the third blank is *experiment with new hiring methods* and that *through comprehensive comparative studies . . . we . . . will be serve the needs of students* but that these studies *are difficult to conduct*, so use "unwilling" as a word for the third blank. Choices (G) and (H) can be eliminated, because they do not match "unwilling." The correct answer for the third blank is (I), *loath*. Now look at the first blank, which refers to *the . . . debate over teacher tenure*. The clue for the first blank is *esoteric*, and the transition word *formerly* indicates that the word for the first blank will be an opposite of *esoteric*, so use "attention" as a word for the first blank. Choice (A), which means agreement, and (B), which means anger, can be eliminated because they do not match "attention." The correct answer for the first blank is (C), *prominence*. Now look at the second blank, which refers to *power*. The clue for the second blank is *preserve academic freedom*. The transition phrase *necessary to prohibit* describes *power*. If *tenure* is needed to *prohibit . . . power* and *preserve . . . freedom*, then the type of power in question is "centralized" power, so use "centralized" as a word for the second blank. Choices (E) and (F) can be eliminated, because they do not match "centralized." The correct answer for the second blank is (D), *autocratic*. The correct answer is (C), (D), and (I).

4. **neologisms** and **benighted**

The second blank is an easy place to start, and refers to the *speaker*. The clue for the second blank is *add meaning and richness*. The transition phrase *while some . . . others* indicates that the word for the second blank will be an opposite of the clue, so use "ignorance" as a word for the second blank. Eliminate (D) and (E) because they do not match "ignorance," and the correct answer for the second blank is (F), *benighted*. Now, look at the first blank, which refers to *some*. The clue for the first blank is *such as Lewis Carroll's lasting creation "chortle,"* so use "a new word" as a word for the first blank. Choices (A) and (C) can be eliminated, because they do not match "a new word." The correct answer for the first blank is (B), *neologisms*. The correct answer is (B) and (F).

5. **attributed, identical,** and **scourges**

The first blank is an easy place to start, and refers to *the modern concept of the robot . . . to the American science fiction writer*. The clue for the first blank is *the word was actually brought into use by Karel Čapek*, so use "credited" as a word for the first blank. Choices (A) and (C) can be eliminated, because they do not match "credited." The correct answer for the first blank is (B), *attributed*. Now look at the second blank, which refers to *a servant class of creatures*. The clue for the second blank is *looked almost . . . but were actually artificial clones*, so use "similar to" as a word for the second blank. Choice (E), which means open, and (F), which means attractive, can be eliminated because they do not match "similar to." The correct answer for the second blank is (D), *identical*. Now look at the third blank, which refers to *fascist dictatorships and mass production*. The clue for the third blank is *the horror of his current world*, so use "filled with" as a word for the third blank. Choices (G) and (H) can be eliminated, because they do not match "filled with." The correct answer for the third blank is (I), *scourges*. The correct answer is (B), (D), and (I).

6. **C** The blank refers to class. The clue for the blank is *purportedly an exhaustive study*. The transition word *yet* indicates the word for the blank is the opposite of the clue, so use "not exhaustive" as a word for the blank. Choices (A), (B), and (D)—*prudent, acceptable, adequate*—can be eliminated because they do not match "exhaustive." Choice (E), *authoritative*, means with authority, which does not match "exhaustive," so eliminate (E). The correct answer is (C), *comprehensive*.

7. **decorous** and **supervision**

The second blank is an easy place to start, and refers to *the well-behaved children*. The clue for the second blank is *their parents were always happy to take them on trips*. The transition phrase *required no* indicates that the word for the second blank is the opposite of what *well-behaved children* need, so use "looking after" as a word for the second blank. Eliminate (E) and (F)—*affluence, encumbrance*—because they do not match "looking after," and the correct answer for the second blank is (D), *supervision*. Now, look at the first blank, which refers to *the well-behaved children*. The clue for the first blank is *their parents were always happy to take them on trips*, so use "well-behaved" as a word for the first blank. Choices (B) and (C)—*finicky, exquisite*—can be eliminated, because they do not match "well-behaved." The correct answer for the first blank is (A), *decorous*. The correct answer is (A) and (D).

Practice Drill #5

1.	**quibble** and **paramount**

	The second blank is an easy place to start, and refers to *determining who was right*. The clue for the second blank is *no one else cared*. The transition word *but* indicates that the word for the second blank will be the opposite of the clue, so use "important" as a word for the second blank. Eliminate (D) and (F)—*irrelevant, didactic*—because they do not match important, and the correct answer for the second blank is (E), *paramount*. Now, look at the first blank, which refers to what the *English teachers* did *over small grammatical points*. The clue for the first blank is that *determining who was right was, for them, paramount*, so use "argue" as a word for the first blank. Choices (A) and (C)—*prevail, exult*—can be eliminated, because they do not match "argue." The correct answer for the first blank is (B), *quibble*. The correct answer is (B) and (E).

2.	**D**	The blank refers to what *one can often be . . . when one is too forthright*. The clue for the blank is that *it is not always appropriate*. The transition word *although* indicates the word for the blank should be the opposite of *trait to be valued* and the semicolon after *not always appropriate* suggests that the word will match with *not always appropriate*. Therefore, use "not always appropriate" as a phrase for the blank. Choices (A), (B), and (C)—*objective, equitable, deluded*—can be eliminated because they do not match "not always appropriate." Choice (E), *corrupt*, means to act dishonestly, which seems like a close match, but does not match "not always appropriate," so eliminate (E). The correct answer is (D), *tactless*.

3.	**prurient**, **pedestrian**, and **transformation**

	The first blank is an easy place to start, and refers to the *amorous relationships between men and women*. The clue for the first blank is *worthy of censure*, so use "inappropriate" as a word for the first blank. Choices (B) and (C)—*patronizing, sacrosanct*—can be eliminated, because they do not match "inappropriate." The correct answer for the first blank is (A), *prurient*. Now look at the third blank, which refers to something that happened in the culture. The clue for the third blank is that the reaction to the relationships *marks a profound shift*, so use "change" as a word for the third blank. Choice (H), which means to acquire the traits of another group, and (I), which means to have prejudice, can be eliminated because they do not match "change." The correct answer for the third blank is (G), *transformation*. Now look at the second blank, which refers to *the types of relationships Lawrence describes*. The clue for the second blank is the relationships *now seem to appear on film and television on a daily basis*, so use "normal" as a word for the second blank. Choices (D) and (F) can be eliminated, because they do not match "normal." The correct answer for the second blank is (E), *pedestrian*. The correct answer is (A), (E), and (G).

4.	**misrepresent** and **stigma**

	The first blank is an easy place to start, and refers to what responders may do to *their views to live pollsters*. The clue for the first blank is *if they believe those views may be considered socially unacceptable*. As a result, responders may hide their true views, so use "hide" as a word for the first blank. Eliminate (A) and (B) because they do not match "hide," and the correct answer for the first blank is (C), *misrepresent*. Now, look at the second blank, which refers to what *automated polling may minimize*. The clue for the second blank is what *these responders feel* and the transition phrase *in contrast* indicates that automated polling may do the opposite of what live polling does. If the automated polls minimize something, then what they minimize is *that responders sometimes misrepresent their views . . . if they believe those views may be considered socially unacceptable*, so use "bad feelings" as a word for the second blank. Choices (D) and (E)—*stagnation, relief*—can be eliminated, because they do not match "bad feelings." The correct answer for the second blank is (F), *stigma*. The correct answer is (C) and (F).

5. **neophyte**, **debut**, and **tenacity**

The first blank is an easy place to start, and refers to the *writer*. The clue for the first blank is *no previous experience*, so use "new" as a word for the first blank. Choices (A) and (C)—*seasoned, successful*—can be eliminated, because they do not match "new." The correct answer for the first blank is (B), *neophyte*. Now look at the third blank, which refers to how *she was . . . able to get a contract*. The clue for the third blank is *hard work*, so recycle "hard work" as a phrase for the third blank. Choice (G), which means laziness, and (I), which means shrewdness, can be eliminated because they do not match "hard work." The correct answer for the third blank is (H), *tenacity*. Now look at the second blank, which refers to the writer's *novel*. The clue for the second blank is *no previous publishing experience*, so use "first" as a word for the second blank. Choices (E) and (F)—*fictional, subsequent*—can be eliminated, because they do not match "first." The correct answer for the second blank is (D), *debut*. The correct answer is (B), (D), and (H).

6. **E** The blank refers to *Jeannie's . . . behavior*. The clue for the blank is *shy demeanor*. The colon indicates a transition that maintains the meaning of the clues, so use "shy" as a word for the blank. Choices (A), (B), and (C)—*unresponsive, supercilious, amenable*—can be eliminated because they do not match "shy." Choice (D), *acquiescent*, means ready to accept something, which does not match "shy," so eliminate (D). The correct answer is (E), *demure*.

7. **dubious**, **scrutinized**, and **substantiated**

The second blank is an easy place to start, and refers to what the *collector* did to *the bar*. The clue for the second blank is *he found that coral had grown*, so use "looked at" as a word for the second blank. Choices (D) and (E)—*briefed, assayed*—can be eliminated, because they do not match "looked at." The correct answer for the second blank is (F), *scrutinized*. Now look at the third blank, which refers to the effect of *this discovery* on *the woman's claim*. The clue for the third blank is *indicating that the bar had been underwater for years*. This is consistent with the woman's claim, so use "helped" as a word for the third blank. Choice (G), which means canceled out, and (I), which means betrayed, can be eliminated because they do not match "helped." The correct answer for the third blank is (H), *substantiated*. Now look at the first blank, which refers to what *the collector was* about *the woman's claims*. The clue for the first blank is that the woman's claims were substantiated and the transition phrase *at first* indicates that the collector was skeptical of her claims, so use "skeptical" as a word for the first blank. Choices (B) and (C)—*convinced, enamored*—can be eliminated, because they do not match "skeptical." The correct answer for the first blank is (A), *dubious*. The correct answer is (A), (F), and (H).

Chapter 4
Reading
Comprehension

THE TERRAIN OF THE MUNDANE

Practically every test taker in the world hates reading comprehension, and for a very good reason: It's incredibly boring. Well, take heart. Though we can't make the passages any less dull, we can try to make the time spent here a little less painful.

How can we do that? Well, let's talk about how the typical person approaches reading comprehension. First, he reads the passage. That means he reads the *entire* passage—each and every word. He tries to digest this information as much as possible as he reads, and then he moves on to the questions. For each question, he reads the question, goes back to the passage to find the answer, rereads the part of the passage that contains the answer, and only then goes on to the answer choices. Finally, after reading all of the answer choices, he picks the one he thinks is best.

What's wrong with this approach? There's too much reading going on. Basically, the typical person reads the passage at least twice—a big waste of time. Why is reading and rereading passages a bad idea? In order to do well on reading comprehension, you don't need to read that much. It's not *how much* you read that's important; it's *what* you read.

Types of Passages

Subject matter for reading comprehension is going to vary from test to test, but you can expect to see three major categories represented:

- Natural science
- Humanities
- Social science

In the end, it doesn't really matter what the subject matter of a passage is. The important thing is not to let a particular category scare you. For example, if you hate science and haven't taken a science class since high school, don't think that a science passage is necessarily going to be a killer. Often, a science passage is relatively easy. Though the jargon may be hard to get past, all the information contained in the passage is factual. Therefore, there's no need for you to do any interpreting or analyzing. The passages ETS selects are pretty cut-and-dried.

Politically Correct

That said, there is one type of passage in which subject matter may count—and that's when ETS uses what we call a PC (or politically correct) passage. Most of the time a PC passage falls into either the humanities or social studies category. We call it a PC passage because it deals with a topic such as women, African Americans, Native Americans, or even the environment.

What can you expect about a PC passage? Everything in the passage is going to be either neutral or positive (sometimes even inspirational) in tone. In no way can a correct answer for a question be un-PC. Consider this example: "Women should not work in the public sphere because they are not as rational as men." That sentence is *very* un-PC, and therefore could never be the right answer. So anytime you have a passage that has a subject matter such as women or minorities, you already know a little something. You know that every right answer must be PC and that any answer choice that is not PC must be wrong.

Keep in mind that ETS, for the most part, is always PC—obviously so on a PC passage, but also on other passages that aren't explicitly PC. Think of it this way: Does ETS want to say anything controversial? No. Why not? Lawsuit, lawsuit, lawsuit. ETS's whole goal is to make money. Lawsuits mean losing money. If anyone was in any way offended by anything, ETS could be subject to a lawsuit. Think of what the National Organization for Women might say if it read the sentence, "Women should not work in the public sphere . . ." on the GRE. ETS ain't stupid—so it's not going to do anything stupid.

Need Some Math Help?
Is all this verbal talk making you crave math problems? We can help! Check out *Math Workout for the GRE* for a perfectly balanced review.

What's the Big Idea?

During the course of the two Verbal sections, you are likely to see about 10 passages. Typically, eight of them will be *short*, meaning one or two paragraphs at most, and the other two will be *long*, meaning three or four paragraphs. One of the most common beginners' mistakes on the GRE, particularly on the long passages, is to read the entire passage, all at once, without a strategy. Otherwise logical, reasonable test takers who have memorized various strategies in the quantitative section often throw all process to the wind and read erratically.

Don't be that test taker.

Instead, think strategically about the different types of passages you will encounter.

First, for short passages, train yourself to carefully read every sentence and, while doing so, look at the *function* of each sentence. On your scratch paper, write down one of the following words to describe each sentence:

Claim
Evidence

Meaning, a statement of belief (claim) or a piece of proof that the claim is correct (evidence).

Trent Reznor is considered one of the greatest modern music composers. (CLAIM) His albums have sold 20 million copies and he has composed the music for several major Hollywood films. (EVIDENCE)

Typically the two will arrive in that order, claim-evidence, though it's possible to reverse them as well. Here's an example:

Trent Reznor's albums have sold 20 million copies and he has composed the music for several major Hollywood films. (EVIDENCE) He is considered one of the greatest modern music composers. (CLAIM)

About three-quarters of all the sentences can be classified as either claim or evidence. Occasionally, however, you may encounter sentences that don't easily fit either mold. You may encounter moments when it's better to use the following words:

Objection
Background

Meaning, a reason for disagreeing (objection) or the circumstances or situation underlying a particular event (background).

Before the modern era of streaming music arrived, the nineteen-nineties can be seen as the last decade of enormous music sales. (BACKGROUND) For example, during that time, it's been reported that Trent Reznor's albums sold 20 million copies. (EVIDENCE) However, it's possible that his album sales were inflated by the fact that many occurred before the arrival of Soundscan, the modern music sales tracking software, and are therefore untrustworthy. (OBJECTION)

Write all those words down on your scratch paper. Taken together, they constitute the *structure* of the passage.

Second, write down the *main idea*. No matter how difficult a passage is to understand, the main idea can always be written simply and quickly. We all have been finding main ideas since the beginning of elementary school, so the less said, the better.

Think of it this way: You should be searching for not only the content (main idea), but also the *way that the content is delivered* (structure). GRE often asks about both. To use a metaphor, be ready to describe the flavor of the lemonade—as well as the shape of the glass.

Third, ask yourself *whether the author agrees* with the topic at hand or not. You may be surprised that the author doesn't always agree with the theory that is being discussed, particularly in academic essays, so be ready to spot any little signs of disagreement. And we do mean *little*. Academic writing is notoriously sensitive, so be sure to keep your eyes peeled for tiny words that indicate an academic writer is trying to initiate a confrontation.

Though some music journalists have criticized Reznor's music for its excessively gloomy outlook and abrasive tone, it must be noted, however delicately, that minor chords don't necessarily indicate the presence of a tortured and depressive soul.

Did you see the objection? It's easy to miss. A structure such as *Though . . . don't necessarily . . .* tells us that the author disagrees with the music journalists' assessment of Reznor's soul.

To summarize, when dealing with Reading Comprehension passages, you want to write down

Structure
Main Idea
Author's Opinion

That is your process for understanding Reading Comprehension. Never again will you throw caution to the wind when you read a short passage. Consider yourself systematized.

The process for long passages is very similar, except for the first step. Instead of reading *every* sentence, begin by reading the *first* sentence of each paragraph. The initial goal is still the same: to find the structure. If there are no clues in the first sentence, rummage around the rest of the paragraph, looking for transition words (*but, however, furthermore,* etc.) or other sentences that may provide the function of the paragraph. Once you have found it, use the same four words to describe each paragraph: claim, evidence, objection, or background.

The point is not to memorize every detail in the text, since the GRE rarely asks such narrow and specific questions. Instead, try to see the big picture, which will yield a higher score.

After you have written down the structure, once again write down the main idea and the author's opinion.

Doesn't this take a fair amount of time? Why yes, yes it does—there's no getting around that. However, spending extra time up front can reduce total time spent on a question. This means that the questions will almost answer themselves—*if* you write down the correct structure, correct main idea, and correct author's opinion. In fact, a good rule of thumb should be that taken all together, you should be spending about *two minutes per reading comprehension question.* For example, for a passage with three questions, the entire process should take about six minutes.

With that in mind, always remember to take the easy test first and to make sure you are not wasting your time on individual questions. For example, a long four-paragraph passage that features only two or three questions may be best saved for last. More preferable would be a short one-paragraph passage with three questions, which minimizes the amount of up-front reading you need to do while maximizing the number of questions that appear.

No matter what part of the reading spectrum you fall on, remember that you aren't getting points for reading the passage. Therefore, don't get stuck in the passage. If you read a sentence and it doesn't make sense, don't keep rereading that same sentence over and over again. Move on to the next sentence or paragraph, or go to the questions themselves.

Read the passage briefly and quickly. Read the questions and answers slowly. Speaking of which . . .

The Questions

After you have the main idea in your head, you can move on to the questions. For the purpose of simplicity, we break down all questions into three types:

- General
- Specific
- Weird

Each of these question types will require a slightly different approach, which we'll go into a little later. Because we didn't spend much time reading the passage, we'll have to read each question carefully and try to answer a couple questions: Where in the passage is the answer to this question? What and how much will I need to read to answer this question? What do I think, in my own words, the answer is?

Make sure you read each question carefully. Compare these two questions:

1. Which of the following would most likely refute the author's assertion in line 12?
2. Which of the following would most likely support the author's assertion in line 12?

The answer to question 1 is going to be very different than the answer to question 2. Just that one little word change can completely change the question, and if you're not paying attention and assume that the question is asking something it's not, you could get burned. Here's one more:

3. All of the following would most likely refute the author's assertion in line 12 EXCEPT

Although the word *EXCEPT* is in capital letters, it's still easy to miss if you're reading the question quickly. So take your time. It's not worth it to save 5 seconds speed-reading the question if you end up getting that question wrong.

The Answers

You don't get points based on how well you read the passage or the questions, of course. You get points if you pick the correct answer. Thus, the answers are incredibly important. As with the questions, you'll have to read each answer carefully.

How do we find a right answer? Good question. We don't. Instead, we're going to use our old friend Process of Elimination to find four wrong answers. Whichever answer is left must be correct, no matter how awkward it is. POE is the most important part of Reading Comprehension, so we're going to spend a lot of time talking about what makes a wrong answer.

Why focus so much on the wrong answers? Because ETS doesn't write four good answers and then one best answer. If they did that, everyone would try to argue his or her particular answer as the best one. For instance, what is *Hamlet* about? Revenge, madness, obligation, power, religion, or something else? Everyone has a different opinion, each one valid and supported by different facts. That's great for studying the Danish prince, but not great for a standardized test. ETS needs clear right and wrong answers. So rather than write good answers and then a best answer, ETS writes one answer that actually answers the question and is supported by the passage, and four answers that do not answer the question, or are not supported by the passage.

POE

One of the dependable things about a standardized test such as the GRE is that ETS regularly follows a very specific pattern of types of wrong answers. You can depend on seeing all of the following:

1. Extreme Language
2. No Such Comparison
3. Reversals
4. Recycled Language and Memory Traps
5. Outside Knowledge
6. Emotional Appeal

Let's take a look at each one in a little more detail. First, though, let's work a sample passage.

> Because dendrites, the portions of a neuron
> which conduct the electrical impulses from
> other neural cells, do not actually process
> *Line* electrical signals, it was long believed that they
> (5) acted essentially as does an electrical cable.
> This theory, the passive cable theory, used
> the same basic equations for the transference
> of electricity by dendrites as are used for
> small lengths of cable. To a large extent, this
> (10) simplification still holds true; surprisingly
> complicated yet accurate models of
> neurological processes have been built using
> the passive cable theory as a mathematical
> basis. Recently, however, work has been done
> (15) analyzing the many different proteins within
> any given dendrite membrane. These proteins,
> rather than simply assisting in the transference
> of electrical signals, may selectively amplify
> certain signals. Because these effects are
> (20) still relatively mysterious at the microscale,
> it is still unknown how they may affect
> neurotransmission on the macroscale.

Ugh. Dense, neurological science stuff. Luckily, we don't have to understand everything about dendrites and what they do, we just need to know what isn't said in the passage. Let's look at the answers to a question. Even without the question itself, we can still eliminate some answers.

○ The passive cable theory gives incongruous results at the macroscale.

○ Dendrites may assist in processing electrical signals.

○ The proteins within the dendrite membrane are too miniscule to study.

○ Previously accurate models of neurological processes may now contain inaccuracies.

○ Certain aspects of dendrites may affect the usefulness of the passive cable theory in certain situations.

Let's go through each answer piece by piece. Choice (A) mentions that *passive cable theory gives incongruous results at the macroscale*. Where does the passage talk about the macroscale? At the very end, it says that *it is still unknown how they may affect neurotransmission on the macroscale*. The passage says we don't know the effect at the macroscale. Does that mean we'll have *incongruous results*, as the answer states? Not according to the passage. The passage says we don't know what will happen at the macroscale. Choice (A) states what will happen. This is a reversal of what's stated in the passage, so (A) isn't the answer. Eliminate (A).

Choice (B) is flatly contradicted by the passage, so it's another reversal. Look at the very first sentence of the passage: *Because dendrites . . . do not actually process electrical signals*. The passage never says they may help *process* signals, it says they may help *amplify* certain signals. The GRE will commonly change words like this to make a wrong answer seem correct. Sure, *dendrites* and the *processing of electrical signals* are both mentioned in the passage, but not in the way that the answer states. Many people gravitate towards answers that contain words they remember from the passage. Carefully read both the answer choice and the relevant portion of the passage.

Does the passage say why we don't know that much about *the proteins within the dendrite membrane*? Nope, it just says that scientists have been studying them recently. The reference to proteins within the dendrite membrane is taken directly from the passage. This is recycled language—reused words from the passage. The GRE loves to reuse words from the passage, because many test takers will see those words and pick that choice. When recycled language is used to say something that the passage didn't say, it's wrong! Eliminate (C).

Choice (D) contains more recycled language with *accurate models of neurological processes*. Does (D) match what is said in the passage? We know that scientists have built *surprisingly complicated yet accurate models of neurological processes*. We also know that recent research on proteins within the dendrite membrane may somehow change that. Do we know how that will be changed? Nope. We don't even know if those changes will affect the previous models. If those models are accurate now, there's nothing in the passage to indicate they won't be accurate later. Eliminate (D).

All we've got left is (E). Let's look it over and make sure that it matches the passage. The problem with this answer is that it is extremely vague, so let's try to make it more clear. What does the answer mean when it says *certain aspects of dendrites*? Well, we know the passage mentions the *proteins within any given dendrite membrane*. What do we know about those proteins? They actually amplify certain signals, rather than passively pass them on. That *may affect the usefulness of the passive cable theory in certain situations*. The passage states that we don't know yet if it will affect the passive cable theory, and if it does when, so the answer is deliberately left a little general.

Notice that with every single answer we went back to the passage to check to see if the answer was supported by the text. Although we understand the structure and main idea of the passage, when we go back through we'll have to read the question, the answers, and any specific information from the passage carefully.

Now, let's look at these POE tools in detail.

Extreme Language

Typically, extreme language in an answer choice will make that answer choice wrong. Take a look at the following sentence:

Everyone loves chocolate ice cream.

ETS would never have this sentence as part of the correct answer. Why? Because it's too easy to prove wrong. All you have to say is, "I hate chocolate ice cream."

The following provides a list of words that are usually extreme language in the land of ETS.

everyone

no one

only

never

always

must

impossible

Keep in mind that, at first glance, some words may not look as if they are extreme. For example, the word *is*. Consider the following sentence:

It is the answer.

Does ETS know for sure that it is? How can ETS prove it without a doubt? Or think about the word *will*:

The United States will buy more imports in the next ten years.

Is ETS capable of predicting the future? This isn't to say that, if an answer choice contains *is* or *will*, it's wrong. Just remember that, in certain contexts, words can take on extreme meanings. Here's a list of words that ETS uses on the Reading Comprehension section that can often be extreme:

resolve

reconcile

prove

define

trace

Well, if extreme language is bad, then guess what? Wishy-washy wording is good—words like *can, may, most, some, sometimes, possible, seldom, few*.

So, the general rule of thumb: Answer choices that contain extreme language are usually wrong. Answer choices that contain wishy-washy wording or are moderate in tone are usually right. Before you eliminate extreme language, look back at the passage to see if the extreme language is supported, because sometimes an author *does* say something extreme.

No Such Comparison

This type of wrong answer is easy to spot. ETS will often invent a comparison that didn't exist in the passage. Common words include any phrases used for comparisons: *more than, less than, similar to, better, worse*, etc. While it's possible that a legitimate comparison could be made in the passage, the chances are slim. ETS prefers to use comparisons to make wrong answers. Furthermore, judgmental words such as *better* and *worse* could lead to lawsuits by test takers who disagree with those assessments.

Reversals

This seems like an easy error to spot. Just find the answer that says the opposite of what you're looking for, right? It's not that easy, particularly if you're reading too fast. Consider this example:

B) to provide support for the contention that all cobalt mines in sub-Saharan Africa have experienced a certain degree of looting

B) to provide support for the contention that *not* all cobalt mines in sub-Saharan Africa have experienced a certain degree of looting

One word changed, and the answer becomes one hundred and eighty degrees different. It's very easy to miss. Similarly, ETS could change one or two words, as follows:

B) to provide *support for* the contention that all cobalt mines in sub-Saharan Africa have experienced a certain degree of looting

B) to provide *criticism* of the contention that all cobalt mines in sub-Saharan Africa have experienced a certain degree of looting

Lastly ETS might reverse the order of the words in such a way that utterly changes the meaning of the sentence. Read this one carefully:

In the late 15th century, Christopher Columbus sailed from the New World to Europe in search of spices.

Again, speed is the enemy. Your eye may glance over the sentence, see *New World*, *Europe*, and *Christopher Columbus*, then think, "Yep! Looks good!" Failing to notice, of course, that this sentence says the Genoese sailor actually traveled from the New World to Europe, not the other way around.

Recycled Language and Memory Traps

With rare exception, all of us believe that our memories are perfect. Yet the fact is that most people don't have perfect recall, and that we misinterpret regularly. Without outside interference, we carry those misinterpreted thoughts for minutes, hours, days, or until we eventually forget them.

ETS knows this about us, and so very cunningly lays memory traps designed to appeal to the part of our brains that pokes us in the rib cage and says, "Don't you remember reading that? You *just* read that!" The problem is that the answer choice will be describing the wrong portion of the passage.

Recycled language traps also literally recycle language. Therefore, if you remember seeing the phrase *pygmy internment camp* in the passage, and an answer choice uses the words *pygmy internment camp*, eliminate that choice. If ETS wants to refer to a pygmy internment camp in the correct answer, it will find a synonym for that phrase. Or it will refer to the category in which it is included, such as *wartime detention*.

Outside Knowledge

Less common than the other errors, an outside knowledge trap is going to be chosen by the most intellectually sure among us. In other words, just because something is true outside the exam doesn't make it the correct answer. The question may be asking something different, or the context of the knowledge may have changed. Regardless, try to forget everything you know when you read the passages. The text is everything, the alpha and the omega, the beginning and the end.

Emotional Appeals

Equally less common are answer choices that attempt to appeal to the general emotions in people, usually based on hot topics, but which are not discussed in the passage. An example might look like this:

> C) The continued injustice of discrimination in the housing market

This choice may appeal to certain test takers who believe this is true. And, its entirely possible that it is true. But, it's also entirely possible that that answer choice isn't the most specific or most accurate response to the question. In these cases, do your best to put aside any biases you may have and stay focused on the task at hand, which is determining whether or not the passage supports the answer choice.

GENERAL QUESTIONS

Okay—let's go back and talk about the question types. Let's start off with general questions. These are questions that ask you to provide "big picture" information about the passage. Below are some examples of how general questions can be worded:

- Main Idea
    The primary purpose of the passage is to
    The main idea of the passage is
    The passage focuses primarily on which of the following?
    The passage is primarily concerned with
    Which of the following best states the central idea of the passage?

- Organization/Structure
    Which of the following best describes the organization of the passage as a whole?
    Which of the following is the most accurate description of the organization of the passage?

- Other

    Which of the following titles best describes the content of the passage?

    Which of the following is the best title for the passage?

    The passage would most likely be found in

    The passage would be most likely to appear as part of

- Tone

    The author's attitude toward . . . can best be described as

    The author's attitude toward . . . is best described as which of the following?

To answer any general question, focus on the main idea. Typically, an answer to a general question contains some sort of paraphrased version of the main idea. Also, don't forget about your tools for POE. As mentioned earlier, be wary of answer choices that include any of these elements:

Extreme Language

No Such Comparison

Reversals

Recycled Language and Memory Trap

Outside Knowledge

Emotional Appeal

Also, watch out for answer choices that don't answer the question.

Special Note on Tone Questions

Tone questions are a gift. Occasionally, they can be specific questions—that is, they ask about how the author feels about a particular paragraph rather than how he or she feels about the entire passage. But the approach to tone questions, whether general or specific, is basically the same. Take a look at the following answer choices:

- ○ overwhelming support
- ○ unabashed admiration
- ○ qualified appreciation
- ○ profound ambivalence
- ○ deep-rooted hostility

What's the right answer? Without reading the passage, you know it has to be (C). Why? Think of extremes. ETS doesn't like extremes, right? Therefore, the right answer to a tone question is never going to be extremely positive or extremely negative. It's going to be somewhere in between. An author can be neutral or objective. He or she can be appreciative or slightly critical. But the author is never going to love something to death or hate something completely. Again, extreme is bad; moderation is good.

(Note that *apathetic* or *indifferent* are always wrong answers on tone questions. If the author didn't care about something, why would he or she write about it? These answer choices are extremely neutral.)

Quick Quiz #1

For the following passage, find the main idea. The answers are on page 100.

If my colleagues and I are right, we may soon be saying good-bye to the idea that our universe was a single fireball created in the big bang. We
Line are exploring a new theory based on a 15-year-old
(5) notion that the universe went through a stage of inflation. During that time, the theory holds, the cosmos became exponentially large within an infinitesimal fraction of a second. At the end of this period, the universe continued its evolution
(10) according to the big bang model. As workers refined this inflationary scenario, they uncovered some surprising consequences. One of them constitutes a fundamental change in how the cosmos is seen. Recent versions of inflationary theory assert that
(15) instead of being an expanding ball of fire the universe is a huge, growing fractal. It consists of many inflating balls that produce more balls, which in turn produce more balls, ad infinitum.

Cosmologists did not arbitrarily invent this rather
(20) peculiar vision of the universe. Several workers, first in Russia and later in the U.S., proposed the inflationary hypothesis that is the basis of its foundation. We did so to solve some of the complications left by the old big bang theory. In its standard form, the big bang theory
(25) maintains that the universe was born about 15 billion years ago from a cosmological singularity—a state in which the temperature and density are infinitely high. Of course, one cannot really speak in physical terms about these quantities as being infinite. One usually assumes
(30) that the current laws of physics did not apply then. They took hold only after the density of the universe dropped below the so-called Planck density, which equals about 10^{94} grams per cubic centimeter.

As the universe expanded, it gradually cooled.
(35) Remnants of the primordial cosmic fire still surround us in the form of the microwave background radiation. This radiation indicates that the temperature of the universe has dropped to 2.7 kelvins. The 1965 discovery of this background radiation proved to
(40) be the crucial evidence in establishing the big bang theory as the preeminent theory of cosmology. The big bang theory also explained the abundances of hydrogen, helium, and other elements in the universe.

As investigators developed the theory, they
(45) uncovered complications. For example, the standard big bang theory, coupled with the modern theory of elementary particles, predicts the existence of many super-heavy particles carrying magnetic charge—that is, objects that have only one magnetic pole. These
(50) magnetic monopoles would have a typical mass 10^{16} times that of the proton, or about 0.00001 milligram. According to the standard big bang theory, monopoles should have emerged very early in the evolution of the universe and should now be as
(55) abundant as protons. In that case, the mean density of matter in the universe would be about 15 orders of magnitude greater than its present value, which is about 10^{-29} grams per cubic centimeter.

1. Which of the following best expresses the main idea of the passage?

   ○ Scientists have proven the big bang theory to be inaccurate and replaced it with the concept that the universe inflated over time.

   ○ Because the big bang theory cannot account for the actual state of the universe, it is possible that the universe actually evolved through inflation.

   ○ The big bang theory cannot be discounted completely, but the inflationary theory is also plagued by inconsistencies.

   ○ The big bang theory is incorrect because of the absence of magnetic monopoles in the universe.

   ○ Cosmologists have combined the big bang theory with the inflationary theory to produce a new picture of the universe's evolution.

2. The tone of the passage can best be described as

   ○ largely nostalgic but also critical
   ○ largely concerned but also amused
   ○ largely indifferent but also cautious
   ○ largely informative but also hopeful
   ○ largely appreciative but also modest

3. Which one of the following best describes the organization of the passage as a whole?

○ A new theory is introduced, a reason for the proposal of that theory is generally described, and certain shortcomings of an older theory are discussed.

○ A new theory is introduced, a reason for the proposal of that theory is generally described, and an older theory is discarded.

○ A new theory is introduced, and the reasons for the discarding of an old theory are described.

○ A new theory is introduced; the evidence supporting that theory is described.

○ A new theory is introduced, criticism of that theory is considered, and the new theory is further refined.

SPECIFIC QUESTIONS

These are questions that ask about particular details in the passage. Like general questions, specific questions can be phrased in several ways. Here are some examples:

> The author suggests that . . .

> According to the passage, . . .

> The author mentions . . .

> According to the author, . . .

Since specific questions ask you about details from the passage, there's one thing you must do for every specific question:

> Refer back to the passage.

No ifs, ands, or buts. You must do this. Never, never, never rely on your memory. Your memory is your worst enemy. That being said, let's talk about the two major groups of specific questions: line reference and lead word.

Line Reference

Line reference questions are easy to identify because they always contain a line reference or a highlighted portion of the passage. Consider these examples:

> The author mentions T. H. White
> (line 40) in order to . . .

> Which of the following
> situations is most analogous to
> the situation described by the
> author as . . . (lines 15–19)?

You get the idea. Line reference questions are great because they tell you where you should go in the passage to find the information. But they're also a little tricky because the information you're looking for typically isn't contained exactly in the line reference. Rather, it's usually a little bit before the line reference or a little bit after. Therefore, here's your approach to any line reference question:

1. Use the line reference to guide you to the right area of the passage.
2. Read roughly five lines above the line reference and roughly five lines below.
3. Answer the question, based on what you've read, in your own words (i.e., paraphrase) before moving on to the answer choices.

Lead Word

Lead word questions are basically line reference questions without the line reference. Well, if you don't have the line reference, how do you know where in the passage to look for the information? The answer is the lead word.

The lead word is a word or phrase that's easy to skim for. Usually, the lead word stands out in the question because it's the most important or the most specific. What's the lead word in the following question?

> It can be inferred that, during the 1840s, the abolitionist movement did which of the following?

The lead word is *1840s*. *Abolitionist movement* could be a lead word(s), but only if the entire passage were not about the abolitionist movement. If the main idea were the abolitionist movement, would *abolitionist movement* be easy to skim for? Nope. *1840s* is a good lead word because it's specific and it's very easy to skim for. Numbers, words that have capital letters at the beginning, and italicized words are all good lead words because they're easy to skim for.

Once you've identified the lead word in a question, here's your approach:

1. Skim (don't read) the passage for the lead word.
2. Once you find the line that contains the lead word, read roughly five lines before and five lines after.
3. Based on what you've read, answer the question in your own words (i.e., paraphrase). Do this before moving on to the answer choices.

Keep in mind that the lead word may appear more than once in the passage. So if you read the lines surrounding the lead word and don't find the answer to the question, skim the rest of the passage for another appearance of the lead word.

Also keep in mind that the lead word in the question won't necessarily be perfectly represented in the passage. For example, if the lead word in the question is "governmental intrusion," you may find the passage talking about "intrusive actions by the government."

POE for Specific Questions

Paraphrasing is the key to specific questions. However, you also have some POE tools to help you out as well. As always, watch out for answer choices that contain any of these elements:

> Extreme Language
> No Such Comparison
> Reversals
> Recycled Language and Memory Trap
> Outside Knowledge
> Emotional Appeal

Also, watch out for answer choices that

1. Contain information that's true according to the passage but that doesn't answer the question
2. Misrepresent information found in the same area of the passage as the correct answer

Quick Quiz #2

For each of the following questions, locate the answer in the passage by using either a line reference or a lead word. Make sure you paraphrase the answer to the question before looking at the answer choices. The answers are on page 101.

The feminists of revolutionary France were not the only persons hoping that the current paroxysm of social change would bring about improvement of their state. A most singular category of men, the public
(5) executioners, had thought that the advent of a new regime would transform that peculiar disdain in which society held them. For hundreds of years, the post of Master of the High Works in France's major cities was held by men from ten or so dynastic families,
(10) members of an abominable elite that had developed as a consequence of social prejudice: Anyone who had ever been a *bourreau* could never hope to find another job, nor could he aspire to marry any woman not herself the daughter of a colleague. In this
(15) way the dreadful dynasties developed. The best known recipients of this peculiar distinction were the Sanson family, who operated in Paris and Versailles from 1688 to 1847; the diary kept by Charles Henri Sanson, executioner of Paris during the Terror,
(20) provides details of the deaths of many illustrious victims.

Several passages in the Sanson diary suggest that professional executioners did not particularly like having to kill women. This chivalrous repugnance
(25) later spread through the Court d'Assizes; while women were regularly condemned to death in the late nineteenth and early twentieth centuries, in fact they were almost always reprieved. A roughly contemporaneous reluctance to execute women
(30) in the United States has been explained by recent American feminists as evidence of women's almost nonexistent social status at that time; to compensate for legal inegality the men who were women's judges, prosecutors, and jurors adopted a "protective"
(35) stance, frequently acquitting women who, in modern retrospect, seem guilty. In France the egalitarian practices of earlier centuries were ultimately reinstated, which guillotined five women.

This temporary preservation of execution as an
(40) exclusively male domain—a thing too necessary and revolting to be inflicted on or endured by half the population—apparently did not strike legislators as being intolerably illogical, or as being rather a back-handed sort of compliment to men. Proper equality
(45) would have involved either equal rights and equal punishment for men and women, or else abolition. However, arguments against the death penalty tend rather to develop from general humanitarian principles, and less from the putative equality of women.
(50) Chivalry, indeed, would seem to have been the nineteenth century's solution to the problems posed to the authorities by "female" executions. But more importantly, chivalry enabled society to observe a version of that logic set forth in 1791 by Olympe de
(55) Gouges, a logic echoed later in the United States by Wendell Phillips, who bluntly declared, "You have granted that women may be hung; therefore you must grant that woman may vote." In not executing women, the judiciary body was able to sidestep these
(60) irritating formulations: If women did not receive equal punishment under law, perhaps they need not be assured of equal rights.

1. Which of the following best describes the author's attitude toward the formation of public executioner dynasties?

   ◯ Qualified appreciation
   ◯ Studied neutrality
   ◯ Tempered disapproval
   ◯ Vehement condemnation
   ◯ Resigned acceptance

2. According to the passage, the unwillingness of men to condemn women to death in the United States during the late nineteenth century was

   ◯ a reflection of the influence of the Court d'Assizes on the judicial system in the United States
   ◯ in accordance with women's low standing in society and their lack of legal rights
   ◯ a result of a popular movement promoting the chivalrous idea that women should be protected from harm
   ◯ a misinterpretation on the part of modern historians, who believed many of the women to be guilty
   ◯ a reaction to the excesses of the French Revolution and the large number of women who were guillotined

3. The passage suggests that, during the French Revolution, popular arguments against the death penalty did which of the following?

○ Emphasized the failure of the death penalty to suppress dissent

○ Asserted that the defense of the death penalty was based upon faulty logic

○ Supported indirectly the notion that men were equal to women

○ Addressed only the needs of men, at the expense of those of women

○ Failed to employ the reasoning that men and women should have equal rights

WEIRD QUESTIONS

Finally . . . weird questions. We call these questions weird because they have special formats. They're also weird because they tend to be more time-consuming than usual. The types of weird questions are as follows:

- All That Apply

    For the following question, consider each of the answer choices separately and select all that apply.

    > Which of the following can be inferred from the passage about the earliest observations of Mars?

    > ☐ Though Aristotle correctly placed Mars farther from the Earth than the Moon, he drew this conclusion from a faulty assumption.

    > ☐ Ptolemaeus's writings were based in large part on the work done by Hipparchus, though the two disagreed on the relationship of the Earth to the universe.

    > ☐ The recognition of Mars as a planet and not simply a star could not be confirmed until the development of the telescope.

- Except/Least/Not

    All of the following are stated by the author as the advantages of hydroponics EXCEPT

    According to the passage, neutrinos are NOT

    It can be inferred from the passage that which of the following is LEAST compatible with Graham's approach to dance?

- Select-in-Passage

    Select the sentence that offers evidence to support the author's claim about superposition.

- Vocab in Context

    In the context in which it appears, "startling" (line 7) most nearly means

- Argument

    Which of the following, if true, most seriously weakens the argument?

All That Apply

All That Apply questions will give you three possible answer choices and ask you to select all of the answers that apply. Other than that, approach these questions exactly like you would a normal, five-answer Reading Comprehension question. Read the question carefully, write down A B C on your scratch paper, and POE. Focus on one answer at a time. If you're not sure whether that answer is correct or not, move on to the next answer choice and come back to it later.

A couple important notes about these questions: There can be one, two, or three correct answers to these questions. There will always be AT LEAST one answer that is correct. So never leave these blank, but don't be surprised if you eliminate two of the three answers.

Except/Least/Not

Often these questions are not that difficult, but they tend to consume a lot of time. Also, they can be a little tricky. What makes these questions easy to miss is the fact that you're trying to find information that's *incorrect* according to the passage—and usually, it's your job to find out the correct information. To sidestep this pitfall, here's how to approach EXCEPT/LEAST/NOT questions.

1. For each answer choice, ask yourself if it is true according to the passage or false.
2. If the answer choice is true, put a Y next to it; if the answer choice is false, put an N next to it.
3. After going through all the answer choices, you should have four Ys and one N. The answer is the one that doesn't belong—the N.

As long as you follow these steps, you should be okay. Just remember, you're looking for information that's *not* true.

Select-in-Passage

Select-in-Passage questions will ask you to click on a sentence from the passage which answers the question. These questions often involve finding the support for an argument, or a specific detail from the passage.

The trick with these questions is to use your scratch paper. Start by figuring out what the question is asking. Where do they talk about that in the passage? Use lead words and what you know from your breakdown of the passage to narrow down which sentences could work. Look through the passage to find two to five sentences that could work, and write down the line number of the first part of each sentence. Pretend each sentence is an answer choice to the question. Does it answer the question? Use POE until you only have one sentence that could be the answer.

Vocab in Context

Vocab in Context questions will ask you for the definition of a word. It may be a simple word; it may be a harder word. The key here, however, is that ETS is not necessarily asking for the standard definition of the word. Instead, they want to know what the word means in the context of the passage.

Consider this sentence: I decided to approach the task more cautiously than usual. The word *approach* in this case doesn't mean to physically walk up to the task. Instead, it's being used metaphorically to imply "getting ready to begin."

Because these questions want to know how a word is used in context, treat them as you would a Text Completion question. *Ignore* the actual word at first, and focus instead on what the passage tells you about that word. What clues are there in the sentence, or in the sentence previous, or in the sentence following, that suggest how the word is being used? Are there any transitions? Come up with your own simple word or phrase to replace the word. Then, POE. Check each answer choice and see if it kind of matches your word.

Remember that although sometimes these questions will ask for the primary definition of a word, they will also often ask for a secondary (or tertiary, et cetera) definition. So if the question asks about the word "table," the passage may be using one of the definitions of table as a verb, such as "to put aside consideration."

Argument

Argument questions typically appear by themselves, as the only question for a short passage. These questions will often contain the word "argument" in them. The passages for these questions are very similar to the passages supplied for the Argument prompt of the Analytical Writing section.

Start by reading through the passage and identifying the conclusions, premises, and assumptions. (For more help with identifying the parts of an argument, check Chapter 6, which explains what to look for in an argument prompt.)

Say the argument reads as follows:

> Music publishing companies have pointed to their decreased revenues as evidence that illegal music downloads have hurt their business at a time when it should be thriving. Although people listen to music more frequently now than ever before, music publishing company revenues continue to decline. Furthermore, more people downloaded music illegally in the past year than in any years previous.

Argument questions come in several varieties. For each type, we've given a typical correct answer to that style of question, were it to be asked about the argument above.

- **Strengthen** questions ask how best to support or strengthen the argument. With these, the correct answer will show that the argument's assumptions are valid. Eliminate any answers that weaken the argument, or don't support the conclusion.

  ○ Those who downloaded music illegally have reported downloading albums which they would have purchased if the illegal downloads were unavailable.

- **Weaken** questions ask how to undermine or weaken the argument. Because your goal is to show that the argument sucks, the correct answer will make it clear that the argument's assumptions are invalid, and therefore the conclusion does not follow from the premises. Eliminate any answers that support the argument, or don't weaken the conclusion.

  ○ Those who downloaded music illegally would not have purchased the same music if the option to illegally download it were not available.

- **Assumption** questions ask what the authors' assumption(s) are in the argument. If you've already written down the conclusion and the premises, then you just need to look for something that links the conclusion and the premises. Eliminate any answers that, if true, would weaken the argument.

  ○ The decreases in revenue are entirely due to fewer music purchases by illegal music downloaders.

- **Structure** questions are similar to main idea questions in other Reading Comprehension questions. These questions ask about the purpose of certain portions of the argument. Treat these as you would a main idea question: Eliminate any answers that are too specific, too broad, or only half right yet half wrong.

  ○ The first part states a conclusion, while the second part offers support for the conclusion.

- **Explain** questions require you to select an answer that resolves some apparent contradiction or paradox in the original passage. Wrong answers for this type of question won't address the argument's apparent contradiction, or will make the contradiction worse.

  ○ Most people primarily listen to a few albums they had previously purchased, rather than constantly buy new music.

IN SUMMARY . . .

For reading comprehension, it's the approach that counts. Break bad habits. Don't rely on your memory. Always paraphrase. The bottom line is that reading comprehension is an open-book test. All of the answers are in the passage. It's your job to hunt them down, and you can do that most effectively through POE—that is, getting rid of bad answer choices first.

Finally, don't forget that reading a lot isn't necessarily a good thing. It's not how much you read; it's what you read. We hope that with our approach you're not reading as much as you were before. However, just because you're reading less doesn't mean you can afford to read quickly. You're not reading a lot anymore, so take the time to make sure you understand what you do read.

1. Before you answer any questions, always find the main idea. You can find the main idea by reading the first two sentences of the first paragraph, the first sentence of each succeeding paragraph, and the last sentence of the entire passage. Be sure to state the main idea in your own words.

2. Don't forget that POE is the best way to get the right answer on Reading Comprehension. Be wary of any answer choice that contains
   a) Extreme Language
   b) No Such Comparison
   c) Reversals
   d) Recycled Language and Memory Traps
   e) Outside Knowledge
   f) Emotional Appeal
3. General questions: These questions ask about "big picture" information such as "what's the main idea" or "how is the passage organized" or "what's the author's tone." To answer general questions, focus on the main idea. Watch out for answer choices that
   a) mention something you haven't read,
   b) are too detailed or specific, or
   c) are too general or go beyond the scope of the passage.
4. Specific questions: These questions ask about particular details in the passage. Use either line references or lead words to guide you to the part of the passage that contains the answer. Always remember to read five lines before and five lines after. Watch out for answer choices that
   a) contain information that's true according to the passage but that doesn't answer the question, or
   b) misrepresent information found in the same area of the passage as the correct answer.
5. Weird questions: These questions are the most time-consuming.
   a) All That Apply: Focus on one answer choice at a time, and use POE.
   b) EXCEPT/LEAST/NOT: Play the Y/N (or T/F) game.
   c) Select-in-Passage: Use lead words to come up with some possible sentences that will answer the question. Treat each sentence as if it were an answer choice, and POE.
   d) Vocab in Context: Answer these questions as you would a Text Completion question. Use the passage to find clues and transitions to come up with your own word for the blank, and then POE.
   e) Arguments: Identify the conclusion and premises. POE.
6. Above all . . . never rely on your memory. Always refer back to the passage. And always, always paraphrase. Paraphrasing helps you see which answer choices are bad because it makes sure you understood what you just read.

Do You Deserve a Break?

Before you dive into these Practice Drills, how about a quick break to clear your head and reenergize you?

Practice Drill #1

<u>Directions:</u> The passage below is followed by questions based on its content. After reading the passage, choose the best answer to each question. Answer all questions on the basis of what is <u>stated</u> or <u>implied</u> in that passage. The answers are on page 102.

Political parties today are consciously non-ideological, but in the 1840s and 1850s ideology made its way into the heart of the political system. Political sociologists have pointed out that the stable
(5) functioning of a political democracy requires a setting in which parties represent broad coalitions of varying interests, and that the peaceful resolution of social conflict takes place most easily when the major parties share fundamental values. Such a view implies
(10) that the peaceful operation of the political system is the highest social value, an implication which, under certain circumstances, may be justly questioned. But it does contain important insights about the normal functioning of the American polity. Government by
(15) majority rule, Carl Becker observed many years ago, works best when political issues involve superficial problems, rather than deep social divisions. The minority can accept the victory of the majority at the polls, because both share many basic values, and
(20) electoral defeat does not imply "a fatal surrender of ... vital interests."

Before the 1850s, the second American party system conformed to this pattern—largely because sectional ideologies and issues were consciously
(25) kept out of politics. In this sense, the party system had a certain artificial quality. Its divisions rarely corresponded to the basic sectional divisions which were daily becoming more and more pronounced. The two decades before the Civil War witnessed
(30) the development of conflicting sectional ideologies, each viewing its own society as fundamentally well-ordered, and the other as both a negation of its most cherished values and a threat to its existence.

The development of the two ideologies was
(35) in many ways interrelated; each grew in part as a response to the growth of the other. Thus, as southerners were coming more and more consciously to insist on slavery as the very basis of civilized life, and to reject the materialism and lack of cohesion in
(40) northern society, northerners came to view slavery as the antithesis of the good society, as well as a threat to their own fundamental values and interests. The existing political system could not contain these two irreconcilable ideologies, and in the 1850s each
(45) national party—Whigs, Know-Nothings, and finally Democrats—disintegrated. And in the end the South seceded from the Union rather than accept the victory of a political party whose ideology threatened everything Southerners most valued.

(50) At the center of the Republican ideology was the notion of "free labor." This concept involved not merely an attitude toward work, but a justification of antebellum northern society, and it led northern Republicans to an extensive critique of southern
(55) society, which appeared both different from and inferior to their own. Republicans also believed in the existence of a conspiratorial "slave power" which had seized control of the federal government. Two profoundly different and antagonistic civilizations,
(60) Republicans thus believed, had developed within the nation, and were competing for control of the political system.

1. The primary purpose of the passage is to

   ○ discuss the requirements for a stable political system, in particular, a democracy
   ○ present a cause for the breakdown in relations between North and South that led, ultimately, to the Civil War
   ○ explain the reason why political parties seek to avoid introducing ideology into their platforms
   ○ analyze the effect of the Civil War on the political party system in the United States
   ○ propose the theory that the Republican party was responsible for the South's secession from the Union

2. It can be inferred from the passage that political parties today

   ○ do not differ from each other markedly in terms of interests
   ○ consider freedom from conflict the most important social concern
   ○ keep their distance from ideology because of its potential to divide
   ○ look to the Civil War as a lesson on how to maintain national unity
   ○ address only problems of little weight and rarely dispute one another

3. The author mentions Carl Becker in order to

⭘ challenge the position popularly held by political sociologists regarding the power of ideology

⭘ argue that a democracy is characterized by the peaceful transition of power from one party to another

⭘ promote the notion that it is better for a democracy to address only issues that are not divisive

⭘ suggest that, in order for a democracy to flourish, the political system must represent diverse interests

⭘ lend credence to the assertion that political stability is founded upon the absence of ideological confrontation

4. Consider all of the choices separately and select all that apply.

The author implies that Republicans in the 1850s would be likely to believe that:

☐ slaves were going to win many federal elections.

☐ their ideas were incompatible with those of their political rivals.

☐ Northern society was superior to Southern society.

5. Select the sentence that provides a practical illustration of why a non-ideological political party system may function well in America.

6. The passage suggests which of the following about politics in America prior to the Civil War?

☐ Growing divisions between the political parties became increasingly ideological, resulting in the eventual end of the existing political parties.

☐ While Southern Americans knew slavery was wrong, they were too economically dependent on slave labor to give up slavery.

☐ Republicans supported Southern Americans in their belief that slaves should not be paid for their labor.

7. The author's attitude toward the Republican party of the mid-nineteenth century can best be described as

⭘ admiring
⭘ appreciative
⭘ sympathetic
⭘ objective
⭘ vehement

Practice Drill #2

<u>Directions:</u> The passage below is followed by questions based on its content. After reading the passage, choose the best answer to each question. Answer all questions on the basis of what is <u>stated</u> or <u>implied</u> in that passage. The answers are on page 103.

In Anglo-American formalism, surrealism was considered a deviant art movement: improperly visual and impertinently literary, relatively inattentive to the imperatives of form, and mostly indifferent (5) to the laws of genre, a paradoxical avant-garde concerned with infantile states and outmoded forms, not properly modernist at all. For neo–avant-garde artists who challenged this hegemony three decades ago, its very deviance might have made surrealism (10) an attractive object. But such was not the case. Since this formalist model of modernism was staked on the autonomy of modern art as separate from social practice and grounded in visual experience, its antagonist, the neo–avant-garde account of (15) modernism, stressed the two movements, dada and constructivism, that appeared most opposed to this visualist autonomy—that sought to destroy the separate institution of art in an anarchic attack on its formal conventions, as did dada, or to (20) transform it according to the materialist practices of a revolutionary society, as did constructivism. Again surrealism was lost in the shuffle. To the neo–avant-gardists who challenged the formalist account in the 1950s and 1960s, it too appeared corrupt: technically (25) kitschy, philosophically subjective, hypocritically elitist. Hence when artists involved in pop and minimalism turned away from the likes of Picasso and Matisse, they turned to such figures as Duchamp and Rodchenko, not to precedents like Ernst and (30) Giacometti.

1. Select the sentence that suggests a point of view that, while reasonable to anticipate, was not embraced.

2. Consider each of the choices separately and select all that apply.

The passage suggests which of the following about surrealism as an art movement?

☐ Through its lack of attention to form and indifference to genre, surrealism is understood as an impertinent, but sometimes infantile, form of modernism.

☐ Although surrealism did not always follow the very rules of form opposed by some critics of formal conventions, surrealism was rejected by those critics as dishonest.

☐ Those in the neo-avant-garde movement believed that artists such as Duchamp succeeded in a way that surrealist artists had not.

3. The passage suggests that those sharing a neo-avant-garde point of view objected to which of the following about the formalist model of modernism?

○ its overly cautious approach to modern art
○ its use of deviant states and forms
○ its view of art as a distinct institution
○ its embrace of materialist practices
○ its representation of antiquated ideals

Practice Drill #3

<u>Directions:</u> The passage below is followed by questions based on its content. After reading the passage, choose the best answer to each question. Answer all questions on the basis of what is <u>stated</u> or <u>implied</u> in that passage. The answers are on page 104.

E. M. Forster is an Edwardian in point of time, and he is equally so in spirit. His outlook on the world and his literary manner were already thoroughly
Line developed in that epoch and have passed through the
(5) subsequent years of turbulence and cataclysm with remarkably little modification. The various modern revolutions in physics, in psychology, in politics, even in literary style, have not escaped his intelligent notice, but they can scarcely be said to have
(10) influenced him deeply. His response to the explosion of the Victorian dream of benevolent progress has been a modest and orderly retreat to safer ground— to a tolerant individualism now unmixed with Utopian dreams, but nevertheless closer to Victorian ideals
(15) than to any of the popular creeds of today. Rather than conform to bad times, Forster prefers to remind us cheerfully that his views are atavistic.
The strength of Forster's resistance to the twentieth century is especially apparent when we place him
(20) beside some of his fellow writers. If Joyce, Lawrence, Pound, and the early Eliot represent the main current of the modern literary movement in English, we must admit that Forster's private stream runs in an older channel. These others were radical iconoclasts whose
(25) rejection of bourgeois-democratic life was violent and shattering. Equally shattering was their fragmentation of the polite cadences of Victorian literature. In seeing the falseness of the old psychology, they conceived a scorn for the *hypocrite lecteur*; their role
(30) as apocalyptic prophets, as naysayers to the boredom and specious rationality of modern life, demanded that they be obscure and idiosyncratic. Forster, in contrast, unashamedly calls himself a bourgeois and remains faithful to the tradition of calm intelligibility.
(35) He is anti-apocalyptic in both his politics and his literary sense. To some degree his novels return us to the congenial Victorian relationship between writer and reader, with its unspoken agreement over the usefulness of the sociable virtues and its apotheosis
(40) of the happy family. Though Forster's heroes struggle against "society" as a body of inhibitions, their revolt is never truly radical. And Forster's ironical style, though it is unsparing in its probing at shams and half-truths, presupposes a confidence in the reader's
(45) sympathy and good judgment—a confidence that seemed quite archaic to the other writers named.
Forster's resistance to modernity may account for the fact that his novels, though they are almost universally esteemed, have never won him a cult of
(50) fanatical disciples. With a few exceptions, critics have tended to explicate and admire his works without becoming heated over the possible merit of his ideas. Yet Forster decidedly *is* a novelist of ideas, and didactic moral content is hardly less conspicuous
(55) in his work than in Lawrence's. Forster's persistent "moral" is that the life of affectionate personal relations, disengaged from political and religious zeal by means of a tolerant eclecticism, is supremely valuable. This is not a stirring creed; in fact, it is a
(60) warning against allowing oneself to be stirred by any creed.

1. The author's primary purpose in this passage is to

   ○ discuss E. M. Forster and his writing, particularly in the context of his reaction to modernity
   ○ compare E. M. Forster to other writers of the twentieth century such as Joyce and Lawrence
   ○ affirm that E. M. Forster is as much a novelist of ideas as other modern writers
   ○ suggest that E. M. Forster's writing is a reflection of not only Victorian ideals but also Edwardian
   ○ analyze E. M. Forster's response to the revolutions in science and art and how it affected his work

2. According to the passage, Forster's relationship to Victorianism is which of the following?

   ○ He believed Victorian ideals were preferable to those of modernity.
   ○ He did not believe in Victorian ideals but nevertheless clung to them.
   ○ He considered Victorian ideals to be not only oppressive but also false.
   ○ He rejected Victorian ideals, but not so completely as other modern writers.
   ○ He incorporated Victorian ideals into his own personal ideals.

3. The author most likely refers to Forster saying his "views are atavistic" (line 17) in order to

○ make a case for the importance of individualism to Forster and his work
○ isolate Forster as a writer unconnected to the revolutions of the modern world
○ emphasize that Forster was an atypical modern writer
○ suggest that Forster was an ardent supporter of the popular beliefs of his time
○ point out Forster's inherent belief in Victorianism

4. Select the sentence that proposes an explanation for the lack of passion among some readers for the ideas often put forth by Forster.

5. Consider each of the choices separately and select all that apply.

The passage suggests which of the following about other writers who produced works in the same period as did Forster?

☐ These writers, like Forster, rejected bourgeois values and directed their writing away from a style of polite veneer toward peculiar and individualized voices.
☐ These writers showed a greater willingness to embrace modernity than did Forster, who did not give up his belief in the importance of certain societal virtues.
☐ These writers, much like Forster, used their writing to instruct readers about their moral viewpoint, even if their styles differed from that of Forster.

6. The author's reaction to Forster's novels can best be described as one of

○ disparagement
○ skepticism
○ neutrality
○ appreciation
○ enthusiasm

7. Consider each of the choices separately and select all that apply.

It can be inferred from the passage that Joyce, Lawrence, Pound, and Eliot in his early period were all writers who

☐ wrote in a style ahead of the spirit of their time.
☐ were often rude and offensive.
☐ lacked confidence in their audiences' sympathy.

Practice Drill #4

<u>Directions:</u> The passage below is followed by questions based on its content. After reading the passage, choose the best answer to each question. Answer all questions on the basis of what is <u>stated</u> or <u>implied</u> in that passage. The answers are on page 105.

Natural selection is an immensely powerful yet beautifully simple theory that has held up remarkably well, under intense and unrelenting scrutiny and testing, for 135 years. In essence, natural selection locates the mechanism of evolutionary change in a "struggle" among organisms for reproductive success, leading to improved fit of populations to changing environments . . .

Yet powerful though the principle may be . . . natural selection is not fully sufficient to explain evolutionary change. First, many other causes are powerful, particularly at levels of biological organization both above and below the traditional Darwinian focus on organisms and their struggle for reproductive success. At the lowest level of substitution in individual base pairs of DNA, change is often effectively neutral and therefore random. At higher levels, involving entire species or faunas, punctuated equilibrium can produce evolutionary trends by selection of species based on their rates of origin and extirpation, whereas mass extinctions wipe out substantial parts of biotas for reasons unrelated to adaptive struggles of constituent species in "normal" times between such events.

Second . . . no matter how adequate our general theory of evolutionary change, we also yearn to document and understand the actual pathway of life's history. Theory, of course, is relevant to explaining the pathway . . . But the actual pathway is strongly *underdetermined* by our general theory of life's evolution. This point needs some belaboring . . . Webs and chains of historical events are so intricate, so imbued with random and chaotic elements, so unrepeatable in encompassing such a multitude of unique (and uniquely interacting) objects, that standard models of simple prediction and replication do not apply.

History can be explained—with satisfying rigor if evidence be adequate—after a sequence of events unfolds, but it cannot be predicted with any precision beforehand . . . History includes too much chaos, or extremely sensitive dependence on minute and unmeasurable differences in initial conditions, leading to massively divergent outcomes based on tiny and unknowable disparities in starting points. And history includes too much contingency, or shaping of present results by long chains of unpredictable antecedent states, rather than immediate determination by timeless laws of nature.

Homo sapiens did not appear on the earth, just a geologic second ago, because evolutionary theory predicts such an outcome based on themes of progress and increasing neural complexity. Humans arose, rather, as a fortuitous and contingent outcome of thousands of linked events, any one of which could have occurred differently and sent history on an alternative pathway that would not have led to consciousness . . .

Therefore, to understand the events and generalities of life's pathway, we must go beyond principles of evolutionary theory to a paleontological examination of the contingent pattern of life's history on our planet—the single actualized version among millions of plausible alternatives that happened not to occur. Such a view of life's history is highly contrary both to conventional deterministic models of Western science and to the deepest social traditions and psychological hopes of Western culture for a history culminating in humans as life's highest expression and intended planetary steward.

1. The primary purpose of the passage is to

   ○ suggest that the natural selection theory is no longer applicable to today's world
   ○ point out the limitations of natural selection at the lower and higher levels
   ○ propose changes to the natural selection theory to improve its accuracy
   ○ discuss the reasons why natural selection is not a complete evolutionary theory
   ○ expose problems with the natural selection theory in light of recent historical studies

2. Consider each of the choices separately and select all that apply.

   In the first two paragraphs, the author implies that

   ☐ there is strong reason to believe in the accuracy of Darwin's theory of evolutionary change
   ☐ some biological changes are more complex than Darwin's theory allows for
   ☐ biological changes are not necessarily the result of adverse conditions

3. Consider each of the choices separately and select all that apply.

   The passage suggests that the author views the existence of human beings as

   ☐ inevitable, although it may have come about in a different manner

   ☐ a circumstance that began a brief time ago when compared to the existence of the earth itself

   ☐ the result of a linear sequence of related events

4. The author mentions *Homo sapiens* primarily in order to

   ◯ highlight the short period during which humans have lived on the earth

   ◯ suggest the notion that the pathway to consciousness was a long-term process

   ◯ support the idea that the pathway of life is determined, in large part, by random events

   ◯ explain evolution through natural selection by employing a specific species as an example

   ◯ emphasize the intricacy of events that leads to the evolution of an organism or species

5. Select the sentence that explains that the intermingling of highly detailed occurrences makes the prediction of evolution problematic.

6. Which of the following statements is supported by information given in the passage?

   ◯ The study of history will never be completely satisfactory.

   ◯ The theory of natural selection addresses the possibility of random events.

   ◯ The evolution of life does not follow a fixed or determined path.

   ◯ It is possible to determine with a fair degree of accuracy historical events.

   ◯ Theories will always be inadequate because they are at best predictions.

7. Which of the following best describes the organization of the passage?

   ◯ A theory is rejected, and new theories are suggested to replace it.

   ◯ A theory is considered, and conditions are stated under which the theory can apply.

   ◯ A theory is explained, and observations are made that both support and contradict it.

   ◯ A theory is described, and its limitations are noted and then further explored.

   ◯ A theory is outlined, and its relevance questioned by employing it in a different field of study.

Practice Drill #5

Directions: The passage below is followed by questions based on its content. After reading the passage, choose the best answer to each question. Answer all questions on the basis of what is stated or implied in that passage. The answers are on page 107.

Occupations foster gender differences among workers in a variety of ways, one of the most pervasive being "internal stratification." That is,
Line men and women in the same occupation often
(5) perform different tasks and functions. Even in those occupations that appear sexually integrated, the aggregate statistics often mask extreme internal segregation. Although the proportion of female bakers increased from 25 percent in 1970 to 41 percent in
(10) 1980, for example, the majority of female bakers are found in highly automated baking industries, while their male counterparts are located in less automated bakeries. The same phenomenon has been detected among pharmacists, financial managers, and bus
(15) drivers—all groups where the influx of women workers suggests a diminution of sex segregation.

Another strategy used to maintain gender differences in supposedly integrated occupations is the use of sumptuary and etiquette rules. When
(20) women enter male-dominated occupations, certain rules are often introduced to govern their dress and demeanor. In office settings, for instance, dress codes—either formal or implicit—are not unusual; female employees may be required to wear
(25) dresses, nylons, and high-heeled shoes to enhance their femininity. So it is for female marines and male nurses, both of whom are required to dress differently from their male and female counterparts. Male nurses never wear the traditional nursing cap;
(30) female marines never sport the standard Marine Corps garrison cap.

Informal practices also play a role in constituting femininity in female marines and masculinity in male nurses. As members of visible minority groups, they
(35) stand out at work and receive far more than their fair share of attention. This phenomenon was first documented by Rosabeth Moss Kanter, who found that women in corporations, simply by virtue of their numerical rarity, were noticed and scrutinized more
(40) than their male counterparts. This added pressure may actually result in different job performances from men and women in nontraditional occupations and exacerbate gender differences. Kanter's corporate women, for example, became more secretive, less
(45) independent, and less oppositional in response to their greater visibility—all traits that have traditionally been associated with femininity.

Another informal technique that enhances gender differences is practiced by supervisors who evaluate
(50) men and women differently. The very qualities that are highly praised in one sex are sometimes denigrated in the other. Thus, a man is "ambitious," a woman, "pushy"; a woman is "sensitive," a man, "wimpy."

(55) But it would be a mistake to claim that all gender differences are forced on people. In addition to the external pressures I have just described, male nurses and female marines actively construct their own gender by redefining their activities in terms of
(60) traditional masculine and feminine traits. For example, women in the Marine Corps insist that their femininity is intact even as they march cadence in camouflage units. Likewise, male nurses contend that their masculinity is not at all threatened while they care for
(65) and nurture their patients.

1. The author is primarily concerned with

   ○ explaining how femininity and masculinity can be reconstructed for specific careers
   ○ examining jobs that, at first glance, seem to be nontraditional for men and women
   ○ proving that discrimination based on gender is pervasive in all workplaces
   ○ exploring the reasons why gender differences cannot be ignored in any occupation
   ○ discussing practices that serve to perpetuate gender differences in the workplace

2. Select the sentence that best strengthens the author's claim that informal workplace codes regarding aesthetics can preserve gender disparities.

3. The author suggests which of the following about internal stratification?

○ Although women now work in industries once dominated by men, they find it difficult, if not impossible, to be promoted to managerial positions.

○ As women enter the work force in greater numbers, men feel their jobs are threatened and their hostility results in increased tension on the job.

○ Because men and women rarely engage in the same activities on the job, certain specialties can be feminine-identified and others masculine-identified.

○ Since men and women are segregated in the workplace, men tend not to value the work carried out by women.

○ Even when men and women are given the same tasks to perform, women continue to receive less pay than do their male counterparts.

4. The primary purpose of the last paragraph is to

○ emphasize the importance of outside forces in establishing gender differences

○ point out that men and women act to enforce gender differences themselves

○ provide an example of men and women who defy the typical perceptions of masculinity and femininity

○ demonstrate that, even in a nontraditional context, conventional definitions of "masculine" and "feminine" are preserved

○ describe the tension that men and women feel when their sexuality is questioned

5. Consider each of the choices separately and select all that apply.

Which of the following statements about men in the labor force cannot logically be inferred from the passage?

☐ In many previously male-dominated industries, men have been displaced by a new generation of female employees.

☐ Men are more adept than women at performing tasks that require a high degree of manual effort.

☐ In certain industries, men have been forced to disregard convention, thereby encouraging gender disparities.

6. The author specifically mentions all of the following as methods to maintain gender differences in the workplace EXCEPT

○ a manager's use of particular words for men and particular words for women although describing the same quality

○ the designation of dress codes so that the physical differences between men and women are highlighted

○ the internal pressure men and women feel to be traditionally masculine or feminine

○ pressure from coworkers to behave in a conventionally masculine or a feminine way

○ the assignation of different duties for men and women in the same occupation

7. Select the sentence which theorizes that unofficial habits regarding gender in the workplace can influence employee behavior.

Practice Drill #6

Directions: The passage below is followed by questions based on its content. After reading the passage, choose the best answer to each question. Answer all questions on the basis of what is <u>stated</u> or <u>implied</u> in that passage. The answers are on page 109.

Although meningitis clone III-1 has caused hundreds of thousands of meningitis cases, it does not appear to be uniquely virulent. Now that it is possible to
Line perform clonal analysis of meningococcal strains, it is
(5) clear that other clones have caused similar epidemics in Africa and Asia. These findings do suggest, however, that the introduction of a potentially epidemic clone under the right circumstances can be devastating. Two explanations have been given for
(10) this process: Epidemic clones randomly expand as they progress through a population, or they survive by escaping herd immunity. As an analogy to influenza outbreaks, it has been proposed that epidemics might result from what are called antigenic shifts.
(15) Although all serogroup A meningococci share the same polysaccharide, individual clones differ in the other antigens exposed on the cell surface. Once immunity to the shared antigens wanes, a new clone with sufficiently different surface antigens might
(20) escape immune surveillance and start an epidemic. Epidemiologists following disease patterns will then see an "antigenic shift" as new clones supersede older clones.

1. Select the sentence that best expresses the author's conclusion regarding the limitations of the usefulness of identifying a similar antigen through clonal analysis.

2. Consider each of the choices separately and select all that apply.

   The passage supplies information for answering which of the following questions?

   ☐ How can we be certain that different epidemics originated in the same cell?
   ☐ Is it possible to develop a method of identifying all clones?
   ☐ Is the mutation of meningitis strains a previously unstudied phenomenon?

3. According to the passage, an antigenic shift takes place when

   ⬭ an epidemic causes specific clones to alter their surface antigens so that they are undetectable
   ⬭ shared antigens begin to be outnumbered by different antigens, thus allowing certain clones to pass through a population
   ⬭ certain clones are able to sidestep a weakened herd immunity and advance through a population
   ⬭ clones no longer randomly progress through a population but rather direct themselves toward the weakest elements
   ⬭ certain clones build resistance to herd immunity and share this ability with other clones through their antigens

Practice Drill #7

<u>Directions:</u> The passage below is followed by questions based on its content. After reading the passage, choose the best answer to each question. Answer all questions on the basis of what is <u>stated</u> or <u>implied</u> in that passage. The answers are on page 109.

New York stood at the center of the momentous processes that recast American society in the nineteenth century. Once a modest seaport, the city early took the lead in developing new forms
(5) of commerce and mass production; by 1860 it was both the nation's premier port and its largest manufacturing city. The appearance of new social classes was both cause and result of industrial development and commercial expansion. Wealth from
(10) investments in trade and manufacturing ventures supported the emergence of an urban bourgeoisie; the expansion of capitalist labor arrangements brought into being a class of largely impoverished wageworkers. The resulting divisions fostered, on
(15) each side, new and antagonistic political ideas and social practices.

We know most about the male participants in these conflicts, workingmen and employers. Politically, bourgeois men upheld their right to protect, improve
(20) upon, and increase the private property on which rested, they believed, their country's welfare. In return, many workingmen affirmed a belief in the superior abilities of those who worked with their hands—as opposed to the idle, acquisitive, parasitical
(25) owners of property—to direct American society in accordance with republican values of social equality, civil virtue, and yeomanry that they inherited from the Revolution.

Class transformation was related to, but not
(30) synonymous with, the thorough-going transformation of the gender system in the first half of the nineteenth century: that is, the changes in all those arrangements of work, sexuality, parental responsibilities, psychological life, assigned social
(35) traits, and internalized emotions through which the sexes defined themselves respectively as men and women. Women of the emerging bourgeoisie articulated new ideas about many of these aspects of their lives. Designating themselves moral guardians
(40) of their husbands and children, women became the standard-bearers of piety, decorum, and virtue in Northern society. They claimed the home as the sphere of society where they could most effectively exercise their power. In their consignment to the
(45) household as the sole domain of proper female activity, women suffered a constriction of their social engagements; at the same time, they gained power within their families that also vested them with greater moral authority in their own communities.

(50) While the cult of domesticity spoke to female interests and emerged from altered relations between men and women, it also contained within it conflicts of class. As urban ladies increased their contacts with the working poor through Protestant missions
(55) and charity work, they developed domestic ideology as part of a vision of a reformed city, purged of the supposed perfidies of working-class life. Domesticity quickly became an element of bourgeois self-consciousness. In confronting the working poor,
(60) reformers created and refined their own sense of themselves as social and spiritual superiors capable of remolding the city in their own image. From the ideas and practices of domesticity they drew many of the materials for their ideal of a society that had put
(65) to rest the disturbing conflicts of class.

1. The author of the passage is primarily concerned with discussing

   ○ the authority possessed by middle-class women in New York both in public and in private
   ○ the transformation of New York into an industrial and commercial center of activity
   ○ social conflict in New York, in terms of class and gender, as a result of economic expansion
   ○ the social values of the middle class in New York, particularly the cult of domesticity
   ○ the attempt of the middle class in New York to reform the working class

2. The author states, "We know most about the male participants in these conflicts" (lines 17–18) primarily in order to

   ○ challenge past studies because they have largely ignored the female participants
   ○ preface a debate over the motivating factors for class conflict
   ○ propose possible reasons as to why only men's roles have been examined
   ○ emphasize the impact that class conflict had on industrial development
   ○ allude to a later discussion of the women who were active in such conflicts

3. According to the passage, middle-class men were similar to working-class men in that each group

  ⌔ perceived the other to be an obstruction to industrial and commercial expansion
  ⌔ placed a great deal of weight on private ownership and the entrepreneurial spirit
  ⌔ responded to the changing economy with both excitement and aversion
  ⌔ felt threatened by the activity of women who sought to lay claim to the home
  ⌔ considered itself responsible for the well-being and prosperity of the country

4. According to the passage, bourgeois women did which of the following by taking charge of the home?

  ⌔ Both enlarged the scope of their authority and circumscribed their power
  ⌔ Portrayed their challenge to male authority as an act necessary to preserve morality
  ⌔ Reconstructed the duties of parents as well as the role of children
  ⌔ Increased their missionary activity intended to assist the working class
  ⌔ Set out to reform the city, in particular the working class

5. Consider each of the choices separately and select all that apply.

According to the passage

  ☐ certain Americans felt that property ownership was in the best interest of the whole country
  ☐ some men who engaged in manual labor believed that those in wealthier classes did not contribute to society
  ☐ the Republican party, which was formed after the American Revolution, believed strongly in social equality

6. Select the sentence that gives a specific arena where the two major social changes discussed in the passage became integrated.

7. Consider each of the choices separately and select all that apply.

Based on the facts about social change described in the passage, which of the following could be an accurate characterization of someone living in New York City in the nineteenth century?

  ☐ A wealthy woman who believes in service to the poor as an important element in leading a truly virtuous life
  ☐ A factory worker who is able to find friends who respect his belief in old-fashioned values
  ☐ A woman, married to a successful investor, who is validated after questioning unethical choices her husband makes

Practice Drill #8

Directions: The passage below is followed by questions based on its content. After reading the passage, choose the best answer to each question. Answer all questions on the basis of what is <u>stated</u> or <u>implied</u> in that passage. The answers are on page 111.

The societies in which shamanism has flourished have been small, relatively self-sufficient social systems which see themselves as coping directly
Line with their natural worlds. Like all human beings,
(5) the members of such groups lived in a world of uncertainty. The presence of a person who could maintain contact with the cosmic forces of the universe directly, who could make sense of both the measured order of ordinary times and the
(10) catastrophes of drought, earthquake, or flood, was of incalculable value.

More complex social systems tend to have "institutionalized" specialists who transmit information without explicit recourse to the supernatural. Such
(15) societies have priests and prophets, not shamans, at the overt level. But the line between shaman and prophet is tenuous. The prophet usually does not enjoy the legitimacy within his society that is granted the shaman. His is a voice crying in the
(20) wilderness, not that of the legitimate curer and philosopher. Despite these differences, the prophet can be seen as a kind of shaman, and thus the study of shamanism illuminates some of the obscurities in religious traditions.

1. The primary purpose of the passage is to

   ◯ explain the differences between shamans in small and large societies
   ◯ describe the reasons why shamans are esteemed in certain societies
   ◯ discuss the roles of shamans as well as prophets in social systems
   ◯ compare religious leaders in small social systems to those in complex social systems
   ◯ argue that the power of the shaman is derived from the supernatural

2. Consider each of the choices separately and select all that apply.

   The author puts the word *institutionalized* in quotation marks in order to

   ☐ support his later statement that such specialists are often not trusted in their societies
   ☐ emphasize that such specialists can only be a part of more advanced societies
   ☐ indicate his lack of belief in the legitimacy of such specialists

3. The passage suggests that shamans and prophets differ because

   ◯ shamans are more powerful because they have a mandate from their deity
   ◯ shamans possess a higher social status, due to their ability to call upon the supernatural
   ◯ shamans are revered as demigods while prophets are considered mortal
   ◯ shamans are less likely to be challenged by members of their society
   ◯ shamans maintain greater authority because they live in isolated social systems

4. Consider each of the choices separately and select all that apply.

   The passage provides evidence for which of the following statements about shamans?

   ☐ A shaman is unlikely to be well-received in a socially sophisticated community.
   ☐ There are certain aspects of a shaman that are similar to those of an institutionalized specialist.
   ☐ The benefits of a shaman extend beyond assistance in times of need.

5. Select the sentence in the passage in which the author's word choice reveals a degree of irony in the roles of some spiritual specialists.

Practice Drill #9

The importance of a well-balanced diet high in fiber and low in saturated fat is understood by most shoppers in Arcadia County. Moreover, food
Line nutrition labels clearly display important nutritional
(5) information. As a result, sales of high-fiber foods in Arcadia County have risen dramatically during the last decade, while sales of foods high in saturated fat have dropped by a similar magnitude. Even so, during the last decade the number of shoppers in
(10) Arcadia County who are overweight has increased substantially.

The more the residents of a city exercise, the lower the average number of heart attacks in that city. Likewise, the less the residents of a city exercise,
(15) the greater the average number of heart attacks in that city. Therefore, people who wish to reduce the chance of suffering a heart attack should exercise more.

1. Which of the following, if true, most helps explain why during the last decade more shoppers in Arcadia are overweight?

   ○ Many people who buy food in Arcadia County do not actually live in Arcadia County.

   ○ Shoppers in Arcadia County who maintain a healthy weight do not all read nutritional labels when purchasing food.

   ○ People who reduce their intake of saturated fat often increase the number of calories they consume.

   ○ The obesity rate in Arcadia County has decreased steadily over the past decade.

   ○ During the past decade, most of the fruits and vegetables grown in Arcadia County were shipped out of the state.

2. Which of the following, if true, most seriously undermines the argument?

   ○ Heart attacks are a common cause of death in cities with high exercise rates.

   ○ The cities with low exercise rates are often those with the highest standards of living.

   ○ A particular resident of a city whose population has a high exercise rate may not exercise at all.

   ○ The cities with high exercise rates are also the cities with the lowest number of cigarette smokers.

   ○ The differences in exercise rates among cities often result from the availability of conveniently located gyms.

In a study, scientists dissected the brains of 10,000 recently deceased people who were all of similar ages and backgrounds. To minimize the risk *Line* of contamination and ensure optimal visual analysis *(5)* of the brain tissue, the scientists washed the tissue before staining it for analysis. The scientists found that the brain tissue of deceased patients with Alzheimer's disease contained unusually high concentrations of aluminum. The aluminum was *(10)* found in tissues that had lesions containing amyloid protein, a protein that damages nerve cells and has previously been shown to cause Alzheimer's. The scientists hypothesized that Alzheimer's disease results when amyloid protein grows in lesions caused by excess aluminum in the brain.

3. Which of the following, if true, would strengthen the scientists' hypothesis?

   ○ The brains of some of the deceased people who did not have Alzheimer's disease had unusually low concentrations of aluminum.
   ○ Some frequently prescribed medications used to control the symptoms of Alzheimer's disease cause stomach irritation, for which patients often take antacids containing high concentrations of aluminum.
   ○ Amyloid protein has also been shown to play a role in Huntington's disease and Type 2 Diabetes.
   ○ When the scientists washed the brain tissue, they used water that came from the Stefl Reservoir, a source known to contain water with high concentrations of aluminum.
   ○ Patients undergoing kidney dialysis sometimes experience disorientation similar to that of Alzheimer's patients due to a decrease in their ability to excrete aluminum.

Some economists have argued that market regulation is antithetical to the ideal functioning of a democratic society because it interferes with *Line* the individual's right to make decisions in his own *(5)* financial interest. In a regulated market, the citizen is not always at liberty to choose where or how to build his house or whom to hire for his business. If all individuals do not have complete freedom to make economic decisions purely with respect to their own *(10)* self-interest, then a society is not a true democracy. Yet this perspective overlooks the fact that the democratic ideal encompasses two separate, but not mutually exclusive goals: 1) to ensure individual liberty and 2) to promote the overall health and well-*(15)* being of the population. Some degree of market regulation may be necessary to fulfill the latter goal, for an individual's exercise of his own liberty can in some instances interfere with the liberty of others.

4. Which one of the following most accurately expresses the main conclusion of the argument?

   ○ Market regulation ensures individual liberty and promotes the overall health and well-being of the population.
   ○ Market regulation is not automatically at odds with the ideals of a democratic society.
   ○ Market regulation does not allow individuals to make choices.
   ○ Market regulation is a necessary precondition for democracy.
   ○ Market regulation is antithetical to the ideals of a democratic society.

ANSWERS AND EXPLANATIONS

Quick Quiz #1

1. **B** To find the main idea, here's all you need to read:

   - "If my colleagues and I are right, we may soon be saying good-bye to the idea that our universe was a single fireball created in the big bang. We are exploring a new theory based on a 15-year-old notion that the universe went through a stage of inflation."
   - "Cosmologists did not arbitrarily invent this rather peculiar vision of the universe."
   - "As the universe expanded, it gradually cooled."
   - "As investigators developed the theory, they uncovered complications."
   - "In that case, the mean density of matter in the universe would be about 15 orders of magnitude greater than its present value, which is about 10^{-29} grams per cubic centimeter."

   Given these sentences, how might you paraphrase the main idea? That the big bang theory may be wrong and that the inflationary theory may be right? Now you can go to the answer choices.

   Eliminate (A) because it's too extreme. Scientists haven't *proven* the big bang theory wrong. Leave (B) in because it's a good match for your paraphrase. Also, note how moderate (B) is. Eliminate (C) because it says the inflationary theory is bad. Remember, it's the big bang theory that's problematic, not the inflationary theory. Eliminate (D) because it mentions stuff (magnetic monopoles) you didn't read about. Eliminate (E) because it suggests the big bang theory is okay. The best answer, then, is (B).

2. **D** Most of the passage provides information about the big bang and complications that arise from the theory. However, in the beginning of the first two paragraphs, the authors express hope that their new theory will resolve these complications. Thus, (D) is correct. Choices (A) and (C) are wrong because the authors are not nostalgic or indifferent. While the authors may be concerned about the problems associated with the big bang, the overall tone of the passage is not one of concern. In any event, the authors are not amused, eliminating (B). While the authors do appear to appreciate their new theory of inflation, (E) is too strong: The passage as a whole is not largely appreciative, but, rather, mostly informative.

3. **A** Rather than dealing with one answer at a time, start by looking at the first statement of each answer. They are all the same, and they are accurate: The first paragraph introduces the recent theory of inflation. Next, look at the second statement of each answer. Choices (A) and (B) work best: The beginning of the second paragraph explains that the inflation theory was developed to address complications arising from the big bang theory. Choice (C) is wrong because the authors did not say that the big bang theory was discarded, (D) is wrong because no supporting evidence is provided, and (E) is wrong because the authors do not discuss criticism of the inflation theory. Finally, look at the last statement in (A) and (B). Choice (A) is correct because the remainder of the passage describes the big bang theory and shortcomings of that theory. Choice (B) is too strong; the authors seek to supplement, not discard, the big bang theory.

Quick Quiz #2

1. **C** This tone question is specific, not general. Regardless, for any tone question, extreme answer choices are bad. What answer choices are too extreme here? Definitely (D), so cross it out. The other answer choices are fairly moderate, so leave them in for now. What now? Use "dynasties" as your lead word. That takes you to the first paragraph. How does the author feel about the formation of the dynasties? Not too good: She calls them an "abominable elite that had developed as a consequence of social prejudice." So what's the best answer? Something that's slightly negative. Eliminate (A) because it's positive. Eliminate (B) because it's not negative at all. Keep (C) for now because it's slightly negative. Finally, leave in (E) because it's slightly negative.

   The remaining answer choices are (C) and (E). Which one is better? Well, does the author dislike the formation of the dynasties or is she resigned to it? She dislikes it, right? So the best answer is (C).

2. **B** This is a specific question. Use "United States" as your lead words. Once you find the lead words, remember to read about five lines above and five lines below. So where is "United States"? In the second paragraph. What does the passage say about men in the United States? That they took a "'protective' stance" toward women to compensate them for their "nonexistent social status." Always make a paraphrase of the answer before moving on to the answer choices.

   Eliminate (A) because who cares about the Court d'Assizes. Keep (B) because it looks like a pretty good match for your paraphrase. Eliminate (C) because you didn't read anything about a popular movement. Eliminate (D) because who cares about the modern historians. Eliminate (E) because you didn't read anything about lots of French women being guillotined. The best answer is (B).

3. **E** This is a specific question. Use "death penalty" as your lead words. Once you find the lead words, don't forget to read about five lines above and five lines below. So where is "death penalty"? In the third paragraph. What does the passage say about popular arguments against the death penalty? That they focus on humanitarian principles and that they don't focus on equal rights. In other words, men and women are equal, so if women aren't subject to capital punishment, then men shouldn't be either. It's important that you paraphrase the answer to the question before moving on to the answer choices.

   Eliminate (A) because it doesn't talk about humanitarian principles or equal rights. Eliminate (B) for the same reason. Eliminate (C) because it misinterprets information in the passage. Popular arguments *failed* to incorporate equal rights. Eliminate (D) because it also misrepresents information in the passage. It's the men that are getting killed, not the women. Keep (E) because it's a good match for your paraphrase. Choice (E) is the best answer.

Practice Drill #1

1. **B** The support for the answer to this primary purpose question is provided by the statement in the passage that "the two decades before the civil war witnessed the development of conflicting . . . ideologies . . . each viewing . . . the other as . . . a threat to its existence." Choice (A) can be eliminated because the word "requirement" is extreme language that is not supported by the text, which states that such a view "may be justly questioned." Choice (C) is a memory trap, referencing "consciously non-ideological . . . political parties," and can be eliminated because the passage does not spell out the reason this choice is made. Choice (D) is a reversal, as the passage focuses on "the two decades before the Civil War." Choice (E) is a reversal, as the passage provides support that each party "grew in part as a response to the growth of the other." The correct answer is choice (B).

2. **C** The support for the answer to this inference question is provided by the statement in the passage that "political parties today are consciously non-ideological." Choice (A) can be eliminated, because the phrase "do not differ" is extreme language that is not supported by the text, which states that each party represents groups of "varying interests." Choice (B) is a memory trap, referencing the statement in the passage that "peaceful operation of the political system is the highest social value," which is stated as an implication, and the members of the parties may not agree with that implication. Choice (D) is recycled language, as the passage provides no connection between modern political parties and the Civil War. Choice (E) can be eliminated, because the word "only" is extreme language that is not supported by the text, which states "consciously non-ideological" without indication of what the parties address. The correct answer is choice (C).

3. **E** The support for the answer to this purpose question, indicated by the phrase "in order to," is provided by the statement in the passage that the view that "peaceful resolution . . . takes place most easily when the major parties share fundamental values" contains "important insights about the normal functioning of the American polity." Choice (A) is a reversal, as Becker is referenced in order to support the view of the sociologists. Choice (B) can be eliminated, because the word "characterized" is extreme language that is not supported by the text, which only provides for a reason "the minority can accept the victory of the majority." Choice (C) is a reversal, as the passage provides support for the idea that political parties may wish to discuss only issues that are not divisive, but not that the democracy as a whole should do so. Choice (D) is recycled language, as the point in the passage about varying interests is distinct from the reason that the author mentioned Becker. The correct answer is choice (E).

4. **B and C**

   The support for the answer to this inference question is provided by the statement in the passage that Republicans in the 1850s supported free labor, critiqued southern society, believed in a conspiratorial "slave power," and that antagonistic civilizations . . . were competing for control. Choice (A) is a memory trap, confusing the reference to a slave power with the idea that slaves would win . . . federal elections. The correct answer is (B) and (C).

5. **"The minority can accept the victory of the majority at the polls, because both share many basic values, and electoral defeat does not imply 'a fatal surrender . . . of vital interests.'"** *(Lines 17–21)*

This select the sentence question references a practical illustration of why a non-ideological political party system may function well in America. Possible sentence choices may be narrowed to the first paragraph, which provides the only examples of something that may function well. The final sentence of the first paragraph provides the only practical illustration, as the rest of the paragraph discusses the topic in general terms. The correct answer is the final sentence of the first paragraph.

6.   **A**   The support for the answer to this inference question is provided by the statement in the passage that the "existing political system could not contain the two irreconcilable ideologies [of the northerners and southerners] and in the 1850s each national party . . . disintegrated." Choice (B) is a reversal, as the passage states that southerners saw slavery as the very basis of civilized life. Choice (C) is a memory trap, referencing the statement in the passage that the Republican ideology centered on the notion of "free labor," altering the meaning of that phrase. The correct answer is (A).

7.   **D**   This is a tone question, which requires analyzing the author's choice of language toward the subject. The author discusses the Republican party only in the final paragraph, and careful analysis of the language in that paragraph shows that the author provides no indication of his or her own opinion. The author states only the beliefs of the Republicans and does not provide his or her own judgements. Thus, the author's attitude is neutral, eliminating (A), (B), (C), and (E). The correct answer is choice (D).

Practice Drill #2

1.   **"For neo-avant-garde artists who challenged this hegemony three decades ago, its very deviancy might have made surrealism an attractive object."** *(Lines 7–10)*

This select the sentence question references a point of view that both is reasonable to anticipate and also was not embraced. The phrase "its very deviancy might have made surrealism an attractive object" provides support for a point of view that is reasonable to anticipate, and the sentence "But such was not the case" indicates that this view was not embraced. The correct answer is the second sentence.

2.   **B and C**

The support for the answer to this inference question is provided by the statements in the passage that "surrealism was . . . inattentive to the imperatives of form," and that the neo-avant-gardists who challenged the formalist account saw surrealism as hypocritically elitist. Additionally, the neo-avant-gardists referenced in the final sentence turned to such figures as Duchamp and not to surrealist artists. Choice (A) is a reversal, as the recycled language it contains refers to the perspective of Anglo-American formalism, which considers surrealism not properly modernist at all. The correct answer is (B) and (C).

3. C   The support for the answer to this inference question is provided by the statement in the passage that the "formalist model of modernism was staked on the autonomy of modern art as separate from social practice," and further clarified by the phrase "separate institution of art." Choice (A) is a memory trap, referencing the passage's characterization of formalism as considering surrealism through such descriptive words as "improperly," "impertinently," and "inattentive to . . . imperatives." Choice (B) is a reversal, as surrealism—not formalism—is referred to with the recycled language deviant. Choice (D) is a reversal, as the recycled language "material practices" is referenced as an aspect of constructivism, not formalism. Choice (E) is a reversal, as the memory trap antiquated ideals refers to the phrase "outmoded forms" used by formalism to reference surrealism. The correct answer is choice (C).

Practice Drill #3

1. A   The support for the answer to this primary purpose question is provided by the statement in the passage regarding "Forster's resistance to the twentieth century." Choice (B) is recycled language, as the passage does compare Forster to Joyce and Lawrence but focuses on characteristics of Forster rather than continuing to discuss Joyce and Lawrence. Eliminate (C), as the passage provides no such comparison between the degree to which Forster versus other modern writers are equally novelists of ideas. Choice (D) is recycled language, as the passage does describe Forster as Edwardian, but does not describe his writing as Edwardian or explain what Edwardian writing would entail. Choice (E) is a reversal, as the passage states that Forster noticed revolutions in physics and literary style, but they did not influence him deeply. The correct answer is (A).

2. D   The support for the answer to this retrieval question is provided by the statement in the passage that Forster's "response to the explosion of the Victorian dream . . . has been a modest and orderly retreat to safer ground . . . but nevertheless closer to Victorian ideals" than to other ideals. Choices (A), (B), and (E) are reversals, as the passage distinguishes between Forster's beliefs and Victorian ideals. Choice (C) can be eliminated as the word "oppressive" is extreme language that is not supported by the statement in the text that Forster's beliefs are "unmixed with Utopian dreams." The correct answer is (D).

3. C   The support for the answer to this purpose question is provided by the statement in the passage that Forster's beliefs are "closer to Victorian ideals than to any of the popular creeds of today." Choice (A) is recycled language as "individualism" is used to describe Forster, not to describe something important to Forster's work. Choice (B) can be eliminated, because "isolate" and "unconnected" are extreme language that is not supported by the text, which states that "modern revolutions . . . have not escaped his intelligent notice." Choice (D) can be eliminated, because "ardent supporter" is extreme language that is not supported by the text, which claims that Forster's beliefs are in line with Edwardian ideals, but makes no statement about Forster's political actions. Choice (E) can be eliminated, because inherent belief in Victorianism is extreme language that is not supported by the text, which states that Forster's beliefs are "now unmixed with Utopian dreams," and differ from Victorianism. The correct answer is (C).

4. **"Forster's resistance to modernity may account for the fact that his novels, though they are almost universally esteemed, have never won him a cult of fanatical disciples."** *(Lines 47–50)*

This select the sentence question references a sentence that proposes an explanation for the lack of passion among some readers for the ideas put forth by Forster. This subject refers to the statement in the passage that Forster's "novels . . . have never won him a cult of fanatical disciples" due to "Forster's resistance to modernity." While the next sentence continues to discuss reactions to Forster, it provides no explanation. The correct answer is the first sentence of the third paragraph.

5. **B and C**

The support for the answer to this inference question is provided by the statements in the passage that "Forster's didactic moral content is hardly less conspicuous in his work than Lawrence's," that Forster's novels promote "the usefulness of the sociable virtues," and that "the strength of Forster's resistance to the twentieth century is especially apparent when we place him beside some of his fellow writers." Choice (A) is a reversal, as the passage states that Forster "unashamedly calls himself a bourgeois." The correct answer is (B) and (C).

6. **D** This is a tone question, which requires analyzing the author's choice of language toward the subject. The author references Forster's novels with such language as congenial, heroes, ironical, unsparing in its probing at shams and half-truths, and almost universally esteemed. Thus, the author's attitude toward Forster's novels is positive, eliminating (A), (B), and (C). Choice (E) can be eliminated, as enthusiasm is extreme language that is not supported by the text and contradicts the author's statement that Forster's novels do not present a stirring creed. The correct answer is (D).

7. **A and C**

The support for the answer to this inference question is provided by the statements in the passage both that Forster's "ironical style . . . presupposes a confidence in the reader's sympathy and good judgment" in contrast to "the other writers named," and also that in referring to Forster's style as older while naming his "spirit . . . Edwardian," the passage implies that the other writers are ahead of the Edwardian spirit. Choice (B) can be eliminated, as "rude and offensive" are extreme language that is not supported by the text, which refers poetically to the "polite cadences of Victorian literature." The correct answer is (A) and (C).

Practice Drill #4

1. **D** The support for the answer to this primary purpose question is provided by the statement in the passage that "natural selection is not fully sufficient to explain evolutionary change." Choices (A), (C), and (E) can be eliminated as a reversal, as the passage refers to many other causes as powerful and also refers to natural selection as an adequate general theory. While the author holds that natural selection does not explain the entirety of evolutionary change, the author sees natural selection as an effective single piece among many pieces. Choice (B) is recycled language as the discussion of lower and higher levels serves to introduce the author's more primary points. The correct answer is (D).

2. **A, B, and C**

A series of statements in the passage provide the support for the answer to this inference question. Choice (A) is supported by the statement in the passage that "natural selection . . . has held up remarkably well, under intense and unrelenting scrutiny and testing, for 135 years." Choice (B) is supported by the statement in the passage that "mass extinctions wipe out substantial parts of biotas for reasons unrelated to adaptive struggles of constituent species in 'normal' times." Choice (C) is supported by the statement in the passage that substitution in individual base pairs of DNA involves change that is often "effectively . . . random." The correct answer is (A), (B), and (C).

3. **B** The support for the answer to this inference question is provided by the statements in the passage that *Homo sapiens* appeared just a geologic second ago. Choice (A) is a reversal, as the passage credits "fortuitous . . . events," rather than an outcome predicted by evolutionary theory. Choice (C) is a reversal as the passage states that "random and chaotic . . . elements" are a crucial part of historical outcomes. The correct answer is choice (B).

4. **C** The support for the answer to this purpose question is provided by the statement in the passage that "to understand the events in generalities of life's pathway we must go beyond principles of evolutionary theory." The author presents the discussion of *Homo sapiens* as an example in support of this primary point. Choice (A) is recycled language, as the reference to a geologic second ago serves as an aside. Choices (B) and (E) are reversals, as the author's point is stated as "contrary . . . to conventional . . . western science" and natural selection, which allow for both a long-term process and intricacy of events. Choice (D) is a reversal, as the author explains a process that he or she contrasts against natural selection. The correct answer is (C).

5. **"Webs and chains of historical events are so intricate, so imbued with random and chaotic elements, so unrepeatable in encompassing such a multitude of unique (and uniquely interacting) objects, that standard models of simple prediction do not apply."** *(Lines 32–37)*

This select the sentence question references a sentence that explains that the intermingling of highly detailed occurrences makes the prediction of evolution problematic. The reference to prediction provides an easy place to start, indicating the final sentence of the third paragraph. This sentence is further supported by its reference to "uniquely interacting . . . objects." The correct answer is the final sentence of the third paragraph.

6. **C** The support for the answer to this retrieval question is provided by the statement in the passage that humans arose from the outcome of events, any one of which could have occurred differently and sent history on an alternate pathway. Additionally, the passage states that the "pattern of life's history is the single actualized version among millions of plausible alternatives that happened not to occur." Choice (A) can be eliminated, as "never" is extreme language that is not supported by the text. Choice (B) is a reversal, as the passage contrasts natural selection from change that is random. Choice (D) is a reversal, as the passage states that "history . . . cannot be predicted with any precision." Choice (E) can be eliminated, because the phrase "always be inadequate" is extreme language that is not supported by the text, which refers to natural selection as adequate. The correct answer is (C).

7. **D** This is a structure question, so evaluate the answer choices and eliminate choices that contradict the text. Choices (A), (C), and (E) are reversals, as the passage supports natural selection, and merely refers to it as "not fully sufficient." Choice (B) can be eliminated, as the phrase "conditions are stated" is extreme language that is not supported by the text, which indicates that natural selection is not the only cause, but does not specify precisely in which situations natural selection applies. The correct answer is (D).

Practice Drill #5

1. **E** The support for the answer to this primary purpose question is provided by the statement in the passage that "occupations foster gender differences among workers in a variety of ways." Choice (A) is a reversal, as the passage notes that "male nurses and female marines actively construct their own gender." Choice (B) is recycled language, as the passage focuses on gender-oriented practices, not nontraditional jobs. Choices (C) and (D) can be eliminated, as the words "all" and "cannot be ignored" are extreme language that is not supported by the text, which uses qualifiers like often, majority, and not unusual. The correct answer is (E).

2. **"In office settings, for instance, dress codes—either formal or implicit—are not unusual; female employees may be required to wear dresses, nylons, and high-heeled shoes to enhance their femininity."** *(Lines 22–26)*

   This select the sentence question references the sentence that best strengthens the author's claim that informal workplace codes regarding aesthetics can preserve gender disparities. The phrase "informal workplace codes" provides an easy place to start. The third sentence of the second paragraph indicates that dress codes may require specifics designed to enhance femininity, which satisfies the subject of the question. The correct answer is the third sentence of the second paragraph.

3. **C** The support for the answer to this inference question is provided by the statement in the passage that "internal stratification" refers to that "men and women in the same occupation often perform different tasks and functions." Choice (A) can be eliminated, as the word "impossible" is extreme language that is not supported by the text, which references ambition as a quality denigrated in a woman. Choice (B) is a memory trap, as the passage references both the influx of women workers and that women in corporations may be noticed and scrutinized more than their male counterparts simply by virtue of their numerical rarity. Choice (D) is a memory trap, as the passage references extreme segregation and refers to different evaluations of men and women with the qualities "that are highly praised in one sex are sometimes denigrated in the other." Choice (E) is a memory trap, as the passage refers to the majority of female bakers as "found in highly automated baking industries, while their male counterparts are located in less automated bakeries," which does not necessarily indicate a difference in pay. The correct answer is (C).

4.   **B**   The support for the answer to this purpose question is provided by the statement in the passage that "it would be a mistake to claim that all gender differences are forced on people," as "male nurses and female marines actively construct their own gender." Choice (A) is a reversal, as the author is emphasizing the importance of internal forces in the last paragraph. Choice (C) is a reversal, as the passage uses the example of male nurses and female marines earlier as an example of unusual gender roles, and as a counterexample in favor of traditional gender roles in the final paragraph. Choice (D) is a memory trap, as the author discusses the preservation of conventional gender roles in a nontraditional context in the majority of the passage, while the last paragraph focuses on self-made gender roles. Choice (E) is a memory trap, as the passage states "male nurses contend that their masculinity is not at all threatened," but provides no reference for tension. The correct answer is (B).

5.   **A and B**

The support for the answer to this inference question is provided by the statement in the passage that "male nurses never wear the traditional nursing cap," which is part of a series of examples used to illustrate a strategy used to maintain gender differences. Because this question specifies "cannot logically be inferred," (C) is eliminated because it is supported by the passage. Choice (A) is not supported because the influx of women workers does not indicate a displacement of male jobs. Choice (B) is not supported because the denigrating term "wimpy" does not indicate different capabilities for manual effort. The correct answer is (A) and (B).

6.   **D**   The support for the answer to this retrieval question is provided by a series of statements in the passage. The word "except" indicates that the correct answer is the choice not supported by the text. Choice (A) is supported with the reference to "the very qualities . . . highly praised in one . . . sometimes denigrated in the other." Choice (B) is supported with the reference to dress codes to "enhance . . . femininity." Choice (C) is supported by the phrase "actively construct their own gender . . . in terms of traditional masculine and feminine traits." Choice (E) is supported with the reference to "men and women in the same occupation who perform different tasks and functions." Choice D is recycled language, as the passage provides no support for pressure from coworkers. The correct answer is (D).

7.   **"The added pressure may actually result in different job performances from men and women in nontraditional occupations and exacerbate gender differences."** *(Lines 40-43)*

This select the sentence question references a sentence that theorizes that unofficial habits regarding gender in the workplace can influence employee behavior. An easy place to start is the phrase "employee behavior" as opposed to requirements imposed on employees. The phrase "informal practices" at the beginning of the third paragraph further leads to the final two sentences of the third paragraph. While the final sentence provides an example, the second-to-last sentence of the third paragraph provides a theory with the statement "added pressure may result in different job performances." The correct answer is the second-to-last sentence of the third paragraph.

Practice Drill #6

1.   \   **"Once immunity to the shared antigens wanes, a new clone with sufficiently different surface antigens might escape immune surveillance and start an epidemic."** *(Lines 17–19)*

This select the sentence question references a sentence that best expresses the author's conclusion regarding the limitations of the usefulness of identifying a similar antigen through clonal analysis. As clonal analysis depends on the similarity of surface antigens, find the sentence that expresses that different antigens provoke a different response. In the second-to-last sentence, the phrase "sufficiently different surface antigens might escape immune surveillance" provides the support for the subject of this question. The correct answer is the second-to-last sentence.

2.   A and C

The support for the answer to this retrieval question is provided by the statements in the passage that "individual clones differ in the . . . antigens exposed on the cell surface" and that "it is . . . now . . . possible to perform clonal analysis of meningococcal strains." Choice (B) can be eliminated, as the word "possible" is extreme language that is not supported by the text, which indicates difficulty in identifying different clones with a single method, but cannot support whether or not it is possible to do so. The correct answer is (A) and (C).

3.   C   The support for the answer to this retrieval question is provided by the statement in the passage that "once immunity to the shared antigens wanes, a new clone might escape immune surveillance and start an epidemic," which links back to the author's statement that such clones "survive by escaping herd immunity." Choice (A) can be eliminated, as the word "causes" is extreme language that is not supported by the text, which states that an antigenic shift happens, but not that it is caused by an epidemic. Choice (B) is a reversal, as the weaker "immunity to shared antigens" depends on their prevalence in the population. Choice (D) is recycled language, as the two options of randomly expand and escaping herd immunity are provided as possibilities not as mutually exclusive. Choice (E) is recycled language, as the means of escaping herd immunity is "different . . . antigens," not resistance. The correct answer is (C).

Practice Drill #7

1.   C   The support for the answer to this primary purpose question is provided by the statements in the passage that "wealth from investments in trade . . . supported . . . the expansion of capitalist labor arrangements" and that "the resulting divisions fostered . . . new and antagonistic political ideas and social practices." Choice (A) is recycled language, as the public and private activities of middle-class women are one of the aspects the author discusses, but do not fully express the author's purpose. Choice (B) is recycled language, as the transformation of New York is only the background of the elements the author discusses. Choice (D) is recycled language, as "the social values

of the cult of domesticity" are one of the aspects the author discusses, but do not fully express the author's purpose. Choice (E) is a memory trap, as the attempts at reform are a source of tension, but do not fully express the author's purpose. The correct answer is (C).

2. E   The support for the answer to this purpose question is provided by the statement in the passage that "class transformation was related to . . . the thorough-going transformation of the gender system," which leads into the discussion of women of the emerging bourgeoisie. Choices (A) and (C) can be eliminated, as the words "ignored" and "only" are extreme language that are not supported by the text, which states only that "we know most about the male participants." Choices (B) and (D) are reversals, as the author indicates greater knowledge about the male participants in order to foreshadow a discussion of female participants. The correct answer is (E).

3. E   The support for the answer to this retrieval question is provided by the statement in the passage that "bourgeois men upheld their right to . . . improve upon . . . private property and in return, many workingmen affirmed a belief in the . . . abilities of those who worked with their hands . . . to direct . . . society in accordance with . . . values." Choice (A) is recycled language, as the passage does not provide support that working-class men felt that bourgeois men were an obstruction to . . . expansion. Choice (B) can be eliminated, as the claim that each group valued private ownership is extreme language that is not supported by the text, which credits bourgeois men with the value for private property. Choice (C) is a memory trap, as the events in the passage may have provoked both excitement and aversion, but these qualities are not indicated by the text. Choice (D) is a memory trap, as the phrase "gain power within their families" does not indicate that the men were threatened by this power. The correct answer is (E).

4. A   The support for the answer to this retrieval question is provided by the statement in the passage that "in their consignment to the household . . . women suffered a constriction of their social engagements and that at the same time, they gained power within their families that also vested them with greater moral authority in their own communities." Choice (B) can be eliminated, as the phrase "challenge to male authority" is extreme language that is not supported by the text, which does not indicate that the activities of women were designed to challenge male power. Choice (C) is a memory trap, as the reconstruction referenced in the passage did not specifically apply to parent-child roles. Choice (D) is a memory trap, as the reference to Protestant missions does not indicate missionary activity. Choice (E) can be eliminated, as the phrase "set out to reform the city" is extreme language that is not supported by the text, which states that the women had the vision of a reformed city. The correct answer is (A).

5.   A and B

The support for the answer to this retrieval question is provided by the statements in the passage that "bourgeois men upheld their right to . . . increase the private property on which rested . . . their country's welfare," and that workingmen believed themselves superior to the "parasitical owners of property." Choice (C) is a memory trap, as the republican values referenced in the passage are not the same as the republican party. The correct answer is (A) and (B).

6. **"As urban ladies increase their contacts with the working poor through Protestant missions and charity work, they developed domestic ideology as part of a vision of a reformed city, purged of the supposed perfidies of working-class life." (Lines 53–57)**

This select the sentence question references a specific arena where the two major social changes discussed in the passage became integrated. As the passage discusses changes in the male world and the female world, and the female element is not discussed in the first half of the passage, look for a sentence that incorporates the male perspective in the female sphere. In the final paragraph of the passage, the second sentence discusses the development of "a vision of a reformed city, purged of the supposed perfidies of working-class life." This sentence incorporates the concepts from the first half the passage. The correct answer is the second sentence of the final paragraph.

7. **B and C**

This evaluate question requires applying the concepts from the passage to a new situation. Choice (A) is recycled language, as service to the poor in order to lead a truly virtuous life is not supported as the motivation of the women in the passage. The correct answer is choices (B) and (C).

Practice Drill #8

1. **C** The support for the answer to this primary purpose question is provided by the statement in the passage that "despite . . . differences, the prophet can be seen as a kind of shaman." Choice (A) is a reversal, as the passage states that "more complex social systems" tend not to have shamans. Choice (B) is a memory trap, as the passage does discuss the value of the shaman, but the author's focus is broader. While the passage discusses the recycled language religious and complex social systems in choice (D), it provides no such comparison between the leaders in different systems. Choice (E) is a memory trap, as the reference to the supernatural is designed as a contrast not as a primary point. The correct answer is (C).

2. **A** The support for the answer to this purpose question is provided by the statement in the passage that "the prophet usually does not enjoy the legitimacy within his society that is granted the shaman." The author places the word "institutionalized" in quotation marks in order to indicate that these prophets are not necessarily accepted. Choice (B) can be eliminated, as the word "only" is extreme language that is not supported by the text, which references these specialists as a tendency in more complex social systems. Choice (C) can be eliminated, as the phrase "his lack of belief" is extreme language that is not supported by the text, because the author states that the prophet is not given legitimacy, not that the author personally believes there is a lack of legitimacy. The correct answer is (A).

3. **D** The support for the answer to this inference question is provided by the statement in the passage that "the prophet usually does not enjoy the legitimacy within his society that is granted the sha- man." Choice (A) can be eliminated, as the passage provides no such comparison between whether the shaman or the prophet is more powerful. Choice (B) is a memory trap, as the contrast of the

supernatural is provided as a difference in means, not ability. Choice (C) is a memory trap, as the phrase "of incalculable value" does not provide support for "revered as demigods." Choice (E) can be eliminated as the word "isolated" is extreme language that is not supported by the text, which refers to such systems as relatively self-sufficient. The correct answer is (D).

4.   **B and C**

The support for the answer to this retrieval question is provided by the statements in the passage that "the prophet can be seen as a kind of shaman," and the specialists referred to earlier in the paragraph are the prophets, as well as that the shaman "could make sense of . . . ordinary times." Choice (A) can be eliminated, as the word "unlikely" is extreme language that is not supported by the text, which indicates only "the societies in which shamanism has flourished." The correct answer is (B) and (C).

5.   **"His is a voice crying in the wilderness, not that of the legitimate curer and philosopher."** *(Lines 19–21)*

This select the sentence question references the sentence in which the authors word choice reveals a degree of irony in the roles of some spiritual specialists. As the author's tone is primarily objective, look for poetic language. In the second-to-last sentence, the author uses the poetic phrase "voice crying in the wilderness," which is a religious reference. By using this phrase to indicate the lack of legitimacy given to the prophet, the author makes an ironic choice. The correct answer is the second-to-last sentence.

Practice Drill #9

1.   C   This Resolve/Explain question requires a resolution of the conflict that elements of nutrition are understood by most shoppers in Arcadia County, yet the number of shoppers in Arcadia County who are overweight has increased substantially. The correct answer must allow both facts to be true, and provide an explanation that incorporates both facts. Choice (A) can be eliminated as out of scope, as the passage refers to "shoppers in Arcadia County," not people who live there. Choice (B) can be eliminated as out of scope, as "shoppers . . . who maintain a healthy weight" cannot help explain "overweight . . . shoppers." Choice (D) is a reversal, as a decrease in the obesity rate would make the increase in overweight shoppers require additional explanation. Choice (E) is out of scope, as the passage refers to rising sales, and provides no indication that the desired foods are restricted to fruits and vegetables. The correct answer is (C).

2.   D   This weaken question addresses the conclusion of the passage, which states that "people who wish to reduce the chance of suffering a heart attack should exercise more." The argument presents a causal pattern, assuming that the correlation between average number of heart attacks and exercise rates is not a coincidence. If this correlation is a coincidence, then the argument's conclusion is weakened. Choice (A) can be eliminated as out of scope, as the passage discusses raising and lowering the risk of heart attack not whether heart attacks are a common cause of death. Choice

(B) can be eliminated, as high standards of living cannot be supported to have an impact on the conclusion. Choice (C) is a reversal, as a resident who personally has a high exercise rate may not see a benefit from additional exercise, but one who does not exercise is more likely to see a benefit from exercise. Choice (E) is out of scope, as the reason for different exercise rates does not impact the conclusion. The correct answer is (D).

3. **E** This strengthen question addresses the conclusion of the passage, which states that "the scientists hypothesized that Alzheimer's disease results when amyloid protein grows in lesions caused by excess aluminum of the brain." The argument presents a causal pattern, assuming that the correlation between Alzheimer's and aluminum is not a coincidence. If this correlation is not a coincidence, then the argument's conclusion is strengthened. Choice (A) is out of scope, as an unusually low concentration of aluminum in other people does not address the correlation. Choice (B) is out of scope, as the argument concludes about a cause of Alzheimer's and choice (B) reverses the cause and effect. Choice (C) is out of scope, as other diseases do not support a cause for Alzheimer's. Choice (D) is out of scope, as a high concentration of aluminum in the water would impact both sets of brains, not only those of the Alzheimer's patients. The correct answer is (E).

4. **B** This main point question asks for the conclusion of the passage. In order to identify the conclusion of an argument, ask "why does the author believe this to be true?" The reference to some economists indicates that the author may disagree with those economists, which is stated as that "this perspective overlooks the fact that the democratic ideal encompasses two separate but not mutually exclusive goals." This indicates that some degree of market regulation may be acceptable, and is the conclusion of the argument. Choices (A) and (D) are extreme language that is not supported, as the author does not conclude that market regulation is necessary or ensures anything. Choices (C) and (E) are reversals, as the author indicates that market regulation may be acceptable. The correct answer is (B).

Chapter 5
Sentence
Equivalence

THE GOAL: FILL IN THE BLANK

Sentence Equivalence questions are very similar to Text Completion questions, and we will approach them in a manner similar to the way we did one-blank Text Completion questions. Sentence Equivalence questions will give you a sentence with one blank, and you need to find the two words that could fill in the blank. Inserting either word into the blank will result in equivalent sentences. Here's an example:

Although he had inherited a large fortune, his _____ spending quickly drained his family's coffers, leaving him in poverty.

- ☐ timorous
- ☐ extravagant
- ☐ pernicious
- ☐ provident
- ☐ frugal
- ☐ profligate

The steps for solving a Sentence Equivalence question are as follows:

1. Write down A B C D E F vertically on your scratch paper.
2. Read the sentence. For now, do not read the answers.
3. Locate clues and transitions in the sentence. Use these to figure out your own word or phrase to fill in the blank. Write down this word or phrase on your scratch paper.
4. Compare each answer choice to your word or phrase. If they kind of match, put a check mark next to that answer choice on your scratch paper. If they don't, cross off that answer. If you don't know a word, put a question mark next to it and leave it.

Vocabulary

Sentence Equivalence questions are basically a way to test your vocabulary. Because of this, make sure you're studying GRE vocabulary words every day. As you do POE, remember that you can't eliminate any answer you don't know. If you come across an unknown (or barely remembered) vocabulary word, put a question mark next to that answer on your scratch paper. Later, you should look up and learn all the words you didn't know.

Once again: *Never cross off words if you don't know what they mean.*

Clues and Transitions

When you read a Sentence Equivalence question, look for clues and transitions. Remember that clues tell us what must go in the blank. The clues are generally the most descriptive words or phrases in the sentence, and can be used to prove what the meaning of the blank has to be. There will always be a clue in the sentence. A transition tells us whether the blank goes in the same or opposite direction as the clue. (For more about clues and transitions, see Chapter 3: Text Completions.)

Quick Quiz #1

In the following sentences, find any clues or transitions. Then, use the clues and transitions to help you determine what word should go in the blank. Remember the clue is typically the most descriptive part of the sentence. Also, don't forget you can often repeat a part of the clue as the word that goes in the blank. Suggested answers are on page 132.

1. The house had been abandoned in the 1920s, and years of disuse and _____ had left it in severe disrepair.

2. Rather than shift the company's focus immediately, a series of initiatives were implemented to apply the new directive _____.

3. Contemporary critics _____ Keaton's *The General*, although later audiences and critics would eventually hail it as a masterpiece.

4. Smith's friends, dismayed at his avarice, soon abandoned him to his _____ and self-centered pursuit of profit.

5. They were nearly polar opposites: he sociable, she insular, he garrulous, she _____.

6. In contrast to Newton's formulation of light as a series of discrete particles, Goethe viewed light as a _____ stream.

Time for POE

Once you've filled in your own word or phrase in the blank, it's time to eliminate wrong answers. As always, using your scratch paper is important. Compare each answer choice to your word or phrase. If the two kind of match up, put a check mark. If they don't, cross off that answer.

Proven Techniques

Let's look at some scratch paper possibilities, and talk about what to do for each one. Say that your scratch paper looks like this:

14.		15.		16.		17.	
	A ✓		A̶		A̶		A ✓
	B̶		B ✓		B̶		B̶
	C ?		C ✓		C ?		C ?
	D ?		D̶		D̶		D ?
	E ✓		E̶		E ?		E̶
	F̶		F ✓		F̶		F ?

Look at the work you did on question 14. Although you didn't know what the words from (C) or (D) meant, they don't matter. Why? You've got two words that you know work. In that case, pick (A) and (E) and move on.

How about question 15? Now we've got 3 checks, which is a problem because we should only have 2 words. No problem. If that happens, it just means your word or phrase was a little too vague. See if you can change your word or phrase to match the clue more closely, and try each remaining answer choice again. Look to eliminate any word whose meaning can not be *proven* by the information in the sentence.

Question 16 is the type of question that freaks most people out, but it shouldn't. Whatever question 16 was, you knew you could cross off (A), (B), (D), and (F). Sure, (C) and (E) were apparently tough vocab words you didn't know, but who cares? They're the only words left, which means that they must be the answers. Choose (C) and (E) and move on.

One Foot in the Door

Look at the scratch paper for question 17 above. One of the answers is definitely (A), but it looks like you've got three words you didn't know: (C), (D), and (F). What should you do now?

If you don't know any of those three words at all, then guess one of them and move on. Hey, it's not great, but you've got a much better shot at getting that question right than most people do. If you guess quickly, the time you saved by not staring blankly at those hard vocab words can be used on Reading Comprehension questions.

On the other hand, if you sort of recognize the words with question marks, then you've got a couple of options.

- **Positive/Negative**

  Is your original word a positive or negative word? Put a + or − next to your word and the answer you picked. Look at the words you didn't know. Are they positive or negative words? If your original word was positive, cross off any negative words. If your original word was negative, then cross off any positive words.

- **Word Association**

  Look at the words you didn't know. Do you remember where you've heard any of them? Can you think of a phrase that uses them? If so, then ask yourself whether that same association could apply to the word you did know (or your original word or phrase). If not, then cross off that answer. But if it sort of fits, then pick it and click Next.

Speechless?

Finally, let's look at the worst-case scenario: You have no idea what word goes in the blank. You've read the sentence several times, but you can't find the clue or any transitions. If that happens, then the first thing you should do is click Mark so you can return to that question later, and then click Next. Once you've worked on two or three other Sentence Equivalence questions in that section, you can come back and possibly see something you missed the first time.

However, if when you return to that question you still can't think of a word to go in the blank, then it's time to match up some answers.

Let's say we couldn't figure out what the blank had to mean, but the answers were

☐ manifest
☐ arduous
☐ graceful
☐ elegant
☐ grueling
☐ eloquent

Look through the answers. Are there any words that match up? They don't have to be synonyms; they just have to have roughly similar meanings. Choices (C) and (D), *graceful* and *elegant*, mean sort of the same thing. Draw a line connecting those two letters on your scratch paper. Now check to see whether there are more matches (there are often two pairs of matching words). Choice (B), *arduous*, is similar in meaning to choice (E), *grueling*. Draw a line connecting those two letters as well. The only words we have left are choice (A), *manifest*, and choice (F), *eloquent*, which do not even come close to meaning the same thing. Cross off (A) and (F). Now we've got two options: Either pick (C) and (D), or pick (B) and (E). Choose one of those pairs of words and move on to the next question.

In Summary

Sentence Equivalence questions are, like Text Completion questions, basically a way to test your vocabulary. Use your scratch paper, and keep studying that Key Terms list!

1. **Write down A B C D E F** vertically on your scratch paper.
2. **Read the sentence.** For now, do not read the answers.
3. Locate clues and transitions in the sentence. Use these to **figure out your own word or phrase to fill in the blank.** Write down this word or phrase on your scratch paper.
4. **Compare each answer choice to your word or phrase.** If they kind of match, put a check mark next to that answer choice on your scratch paper. If they don't, cross off that answer. If you don't know a word, put a question mark next to it and don't eliminate it.

   If you're left with one check and multiple question marks, use Positive/Negative or Word Association to figure out which question-marked answer you should pick.
5. If you can't come up with your own word or phrase for the sentence, then try to match up pairs of similar answer choices. If you can find only one match, choose those two words. If you can find two sets of matching words, choose one of those pairs.

Study Break
After you wrap up these drills on the next pages, reward yourself with a study break. Go grab a coffee or call a friend or listen to a good song—give yourself a pat on the back for your hard work!

Practice Drill #1

Directions: For each sentence, select the two answer choices that when used to complete the sentence blank, fit the meaning of the sentence as a whole and produce completed sentences that are alike in meaning. Remember to use your scratch paper and POE. The answers are on page 132.

1. After successfully conning the investors out of millions of dollars, the crook _____ with the money in the middle of the night and managed to avoid arrest.

   - ☐ indicted
   - ☐ absconded
   - ☐ squandered
   - ☐ converged
   - ☐ divested
   - ☐ decamped

2. Because there is now such a _____ of vampire novels on the market, the excitement they once evoked has been deadened by their sheer number.

   - ☐ lack of
   - ☐ dogma
   - ☐ glut
   - ☐ inundation
   - ☐ dearth
   - ☐ deviance

3. Although the accusations against the politician were _____, they were believed by enough voters to seriously damage his bid for office.

   - ☐ credible
   - ☐ specious
   - ☐ ephemeral
   - ☐ presumptuous
   - ☐ spurious
   - ☐ transient

4. Even though the curator actually spent several months arranging the exhibit, the paintings seemed as if they had been hung with _____.

   - ☐ guile
   - ☐ haste
   - ☐ deliberateness
   - ☐ creativity
   - ☐ celerity
   - ☐ slowness

5. The critical analysis of the works of Shakespeare is not, as yet, _____; the sheer volume and complexity of his writings ensure that there will always be more to analyze.

   - ☐ abstruse
   - ☐ pedantic
   - ☐ comprehensive
   - ☐ elaborate
   - ☐ learned
   - ☐ exhaustive

6. Both Darius and Xerxes continued the Persian tradition of showing leniency to beaten foes who showed themselves to be _____, while punishing ruthlessly those who chose to remain defiant.

   - ☐ bellicose
   - ☐ complaisant
   - ☐ obeisant
   - ☐ prolix
   - ☐ turbulent
   - ☐ venerated

7. Most historians credit the influence of Clovis's deeply religious wife, Clotild, for his decision to _____ paganism in favor of Christianity.

   - ☐ desiccate
   - ☐ abjure
   - ☐ exacerbate
   - ☐ legitimize
   - ☐ espouse
   - ☐ renounce

Practice Drill #2

Directions: For each sentence, select the two answer choices that when used to complete the sentence blank, fit the meaning of the sentence as a whole and produce completed sentences that are alike in meaning. Remember to use your scratch paper and POE. The answers are on page 133.

1. Widely disseminated since its publication during the reign of Caesar Augustus, Virgil's *Aeneid* has served as the _____ of perfect Latin expression for hundreds of generations of students.

   ☐ paragon
   ☐ epithet
   ☐ anomaly
   ☐ epitome
   ☐ nadir
   ☐ epitaph

2. The analyst's report indicated that Gaines Corp. had significantly underreported its capital depreciation; rather than remaining steady, the company's value had actually _____.

   ☐ grown
   ☐ declined
   ☐ underestimated
   ☐ diminished
   ☐ augmented
   ☐ amortized

3. Elements of the author's work are undeniably autobiographical; however, the piece as a whole has been _____ to such an extent that it cannot properly be called a historical record.

   ☐ narrated
   ☐ inscribed
   ☐ documented
   ☐ fabricated
   ☐ contrived
   ☐ catalogued

4. The obligation to perform charitable acts is a central _____ of many world religions that promulgate magnanimity toward the less fortunate among us.

   ☐ tenet
   ☐ paradigm
   ☐ model
   ☐ idyll
   ☐ precept
   ☐ sanctity

5. Words rely on their contexts as well as their texts to create meaning, but this does not mean that language is inherently incapable of possessing _____ definitions; after all, many words have only one meaning that can be reasonably inferred regardless of the situation in which they are uttered.

   ☐ concrete
   ☐ hermetic
   ☐ definitive
   ☐ heterogeneous
   ☐ iconoclastic
   ☐ diverse

6. Charitable appeals often feature a single individual, whether animal or human, because people tend to react more _____ to individuals than to groups.

   ☐ magnanimously
   ☐ quietly
   ☐ discreetly
   ☐ perniciously
   ☐ nefariously
   ☐ benevolently

7. Dean always seemed to go along with the group and change his opinion to complement those around him, and this _____ nature often irritated his friends.

   ☐ vociferous
   ☐ indelible
   ☐ malleable
   ☐ tractable
   ☐ strident
   ☐ immutable

Practice Drill #3

<u>Directions:</u> For each sentence, select the <u>two</u> answer choices that when used to complete the sentence blank, fit the meaning of the sentence as a whole <u>and</u> produce completed sentences that are alike in meaning. Remember to use your scratch paper and POE. The answers are on page 135.

1. The members of the team were already upset that they were losing, but their anger escalated when the _____ members of the opposing team boasted about their considerable lead in points.

   ☐ fortunate
   ☐ vigorous
   ☐ haughty
   ☐ incensed
   ☐ humble
   ☐ arrogant

2. The president of the company was shocked when he arrived at the quiet boardroom the day after the stock market crash; rather than exhibiting outrage, the members of the board were completely _____.

   ☐ impassive
   ☐ histrionic
   ☐ stoic
   ☐ impassioned
   ☐ empathetic
   ☐ fetid

3. The law student was bent on augmenting his transcript with challenging classes; as a result he was completely vexed by the involute, _____ tax law textbooks.

   ☐ transparent
   ☐ luculent
   ☐ convocational
   ☐ labyrinthine
   ☐ byzantine
   ☐ perspicuous

4. In the new age of the Internet, blogs and chat rooms have become forums for some normally _____ people to say what they might not otherwise have the intrepidity to utter out in the real world.

   ☐ pusillanimous
   ☐ mettlesome
   ☐ ingenious
   ☐ plucky
   ☐ recreant
   ☐ impudent

5. While her neighbors found her new lawn decorations absurdly _____, Josie thought they were tasteful, even sophisticated.

   ☐ cosmopolitan
   ☐ unkempt
   ☐ meretricious
   ☐ tawdry
   ☐ viridian
   ☐ svelte

6. The newly appointed chief financial officer had saved millions for the company in the last year; unfortunately, his _____ attitude was making the employees miserable, as they were forced to give up some of the luxuries afforded to them in previous years.

   ☐ magnanimous
   ☐ penurious
   ☐ prodigal
   ☐ parsimonious
   ☐ dispassionate
   ☐ hedonistic

7. When the town's water supply ran low during the summer drought, the residents received an earnest missive from the mayor that _____ them to take heed of the dearth of water and avoid any water-related activities that weren't necessary.

☐ lambasted
☐ beseeched
☐ wheedled
☐ inundated
☐ castigated
☐ importuned

Practice Drill #4

<u>Directions</u>: For each sentence, select the <u>two</u> answer choices that when used to complete the sentence blank, fit the meaning of the sentence as a whole <u>and</u> produce completed sentences that are alike in meaning. Remember to use your scratch paper and POE. The answers are on page 136.

1. Although the president had been accused of reducing defense spending, the new report revealed that during his administration military _____ had actually increased.

   ☐ adventurism
   ☐ outlays
   ☐ successes
   ☐ gaffes
   ☐ expenditures
   ☐ efficiencies

2. The government assistance program provided both subsidized and free meals to children from _____ families.

   ☐ imperious
   ☐ imperturbable
   ☐ impecunious
   ☐ impious
   ☐ impertinent
   ☐ impoverished

3. The _____ of available housing units meant that supply surpassed demand and drove down the price that renters were willing to pay.

   ☐ dearth
   ☐ glut
   ☐ paucity
   ☐ decrepitude
   ☐ surfeit
   ☐ temerity

4. Supported as it was by legislators from across the ideological spectrum, the recently enacted parks bill was rightly labeled a successful _____ of bipartisanship.

   ☐ rostrum
   ☐ exemplar
   ☐ antithesis
   ☐ illustration
   ☐ forum
   ☐ tenet

5. Many Britons were surprised by the results of the ethnographic survey, which revealed that nearly five percent of the population of England and Wales were of South Asian _____.

   ☐ extraction
   ☐ pretense
   ☐ arbitration
   ☐ affectation
   ☐ descent
   ☐ antecedence

6. While the film critic was _____ in her conviction that sequels are generally inferior to their predecessors, she did acknowledge occasional exceptions such as *The Godfather Part II*, a film she considered superior to the original.

   ☐ wavering
   ☐ vacillating
   ☐ adamant
   ☐ perturbed
   ☐ disconsolate
   ☐ resolute

7. After decades of stability, the past fifteen years have borne witness to a remarkably _____ period for airlines, during which virtually every airline has been part of a merger, filed for bankruptcy, or both.

   ☐ fallow
   ☐ avionic
   ☐ erratic
   ☐ malignant
   ☐ volatile
   ☐ desolate

Practice Drill #5

Directions: For each sentence, select the <u>two</u> answer choices that when used to complete the sentence blank, fit the meaning of the sentence as a whole <u>and</u> produce completed sentences that are alike in meaning. Remember to use your scratch paper and POE. The answers are on page 138.

1. Despite its _____ as a plot device in films and television programs, multiple-personality disorder is in reality remarkably rare.

   ☐ simplicity
   ☐ coincidence
   ☐ pervasiveness
   ☐ correlation
   ☐ ubiquity
   ☐ facility

2. Psychologists define "confirmation bias" as a fallacy whereby facts that _____ one's previously held beliefs are emphasized and those that diverge are downplayed.

   ☐ calibrate
   ☐ corroborate
   ☐ facilitate
   ☐ extrapolate
   ☐ qualify
   ☐ substantiate

3. While the ascent of online classified advertising has coincided with the _____ of newspapers, the journalist was reluctant to attribute the diminution of the latter to the rise of the former.

   ☐ appropriation
   ☐ concatenation
   ☐ wane
   ☐ ubiquity
   ☐ aggregation
   ☐ dwindling

4. Aspirant writers may take _____ in the example of Frank Herbert, whose magnum opus *Dune* was, at the outset, rebuffed by every publishing house in the country.

   ☐ consolation
   ☐ insinuation
   ☐ succor
   ☐ allusion
   ☐ solstice
   ☐ instruction

5. In an era in which mass media is but a thrall of its corporate masters, the amateurish _____ of commercials for local businesses provide a tonic for the slick homogeneity of most advertising.

   ☐ amalgamations
   ☐ eccentricities
   ☐ synergies
   ☐ conglomerations
   ☐ syllogisms
   ☐ idiosyncrasies

6. Though the futurist conceded that Apple's iPhone was a revolutionary device, she was adamant that it would not be immune to the same forces that caused such previous "game changing" products as Ford's Model T and Sony's Walkman to be considered _____.

   ☐ avant-garde
   ☐ electronic
   ☐ circuitous
   ☐ antediluvian
   ☐ superannuated
   ☐ radical

7. Unlike Lacey, who is nearly emaciated due to her eating habits, Marty's other cat, Marco, has _____ appetite.

   ☐ an edacious
   ☐ a meager
   ☐ a spurious
   ☐ a scanty
   ☐ a sporadic
   ☐ a voracious

Practice Drill #6

<u>Directions</u>: For each sentence, select the <u>two</u> answer choices that when used to complete the sentence blank, fit the meaning of the sentence as a whole <u>and</u> produce completed sentences that are alike in meaning. Remember to use your scratch paper and POE. The answers are on page 139.

1. The economics professor had a plan to discourage her _____ students who thought blandishments would get them higher grades: any wheedling student would have to complete an additional 15-page research paper by the end of the semester.

   ☐ lumbering
   ☐ viable
   ☐ fawning
   ☐ candid
   ☐ obsequious
   ☐ ingenuous

2. Most singers of a style of Portuguese music called "Fado" sound and appear appropriately _____ as they sing lyrics about lost love and regret.

   ☐ fatuous
   ☐ morose
   ☐ buoyant
   ☐ melancholy
   ☐ nonplused
   ☐ discordant

3. The horse trainer thought her newest clients had a penchant for picking ironic names for their _____ steeds; one example was Tractable, a horse who definitely did not live up to his name.

   ☐ auspicious
   ☐ compliant
   ☐ obdurate
   ☐ serendipitous
   ☐ tranquil
   ☐ recalcitrant

4. The guileless politician's responses at the debate disconcerted some of her potential voters, and she was worried that her opponent's _____ statements would encompass a wider range of voters' interests.

   ☐ affable
   ☐ ambiguous
   ☐ conspicuous
   ☐ benevolent
   ☐ equivocal
   ☐ candid

5. When Becca brought home the irascible puppy, her more quiescent dogs were rattled by their new _____ housemate.

   ☐ pugnacious
   ☐ languid
   ☐ bellicose
   ☐ juvenile
   ☐ diminutive
   ☐ phlegmatic

6. When Howard began his career as a professional mediator, he had no idea that some of his clients would be so _____; he thought that having a job that requires one to deal with disputing parties would entail placating their enmity.

   ☐ acquiescent
   ☐ indignant
   ☐ churlish
   ☐ disparate
   ☐ amenable
   ☐ distinct

7. The newspaper's humor columnist, while talented, puts off writing her columns until the last minute; as a result, she submits pieces that are so _____ that her editor emails her after almost every deadline to remind her of the minimum line requirement.

☐ fallacious
☐ terse
☐ jocular
☐ waggish
☐ laconic
☐ erroneous

Practice Drill #7

Directions: For each sentence, select the <u>two</u> answer choices that when used to complete the sentence blank, fit the meaning of the sentence as a whole <u>and</u> produce completed sentences that are alike in meaning. Remember to use your scratch paper and POE. The answers are on page 141.

1. In the summer of 1911, merchant Nathan Steinberg beamed in anticipation of large profits as he placed his order for 3,000 pairs of stylish high-button shoes; little did he know that they would be _____ come that fall!

   ☐ outmoded
   ☐ passé
   ☐ chic
   ☐ inapplicable
   ☐ repulsive
   ☐ disagreeable

2. The port city of Galveston, Texas, was once a great _____ of economic activity, but though great effort went into its reconstruction after the floods of 1900, it never returned to its former prosperity.

   ☐ bounty
   ☐ maritime
   ☐ abundance
   ☐ hub
   ☐ chronicle
   ☐ locus

3. Anthony's dauntless approach to life led him to blithely undertake risky enterprises that less _____ men would think twice about.

   ☐ lethargic
   ☐ audacious
   ☐ torpid
   ☐ exotic
   ☐ aggrandized
   ☐ intrepid

4. The misapprehension that lemmings commit mass suicide by jumping off cliffs has been fostered by legends, films, and television commercials; one reason people believe the myth may be that lemmings are _____ to Scandinavia, a region with an unusually high suicide rate.

   ☐ tantamount
   ☐ organic
   ☐ endemic
   ☐ prodigious
   ☐ indigenous
   ☐ titanic

5. An exceptionally sophisticated predator, the platypus uses the electroreceptors on its bill to locate _____, resulting in a remarkably efficient and effective hunting practice.

   ☐ iniquity
   ☐ quarry
   ☐ quintessence
   ☐ pith
   ☐ prey
   ☐ lassitude

6. Though Salsa takes its roots from various countries in Central and South America, it is fundamentally and essentially Cuban: its development was a _____, but ultimately the music belongs to one country.

   ☐ collaboration
   ☐ synergism
   ☐ feat
   ☐ coup
   ☐ lyric
   ☐ denouement

7. The praise the students received for their flashy presentation and detailed handouts was utterly unwarranted, for their apparent diligence was motivated merely by _____.

- ☐ prepossession
- ☐ cronyism
- ☐ assiduity
- ☐ sycophancy
- ☐ torpidity
- ☐ obsequiousness

ANSWERS AND EXPLANATIONS

Quick Quiz #1

These answers are just suggestions. You may have come up with similar different words.

1. *neglect*

2. *gradually*

3. *harshly criticized*

4. *greedy*

5. *not talkative*

6. *continuous*

Practice Drill #1

1.   **B and F**

Because the clue tells you the crook *managed to avoid arrest*, write something down like "escaped" for the blank. *Absconded* and *decamped* both mean to leave secretly or to sneak out, so (B) and (F) are the correct answer choices. Watch out for distractor answer choices like *indicted* (related to criminals, but not to escaping) and *squandered* and *divested* (related to money, but not to escaping).

2.   **C and D**

The blank is about *vampire novels [now] on the market,* so look for a clue that describes the current status of those books. Although such novels *once evoked excitement,* that response *has been deadened by [the books'] sheer numbers,* so there must now be a lot of them on today's market. Write down "a lot" and cross off answers that don't match. The clue in this sentence is *sheer number.* Both *glut* and *inundation* match the predicted answer, and are thus the credited responses. Watch out for distractor choices that also refer to quantity, but mean the opposite of the required word, such as *lack of* and *dearth.*

3.   **B and E**

The sentence says that *the accusations against the politician . . . were believed by enough voters to seriously damage his bid for office.* The *although* transition lets you know that the blank should contrast with the clue, so the accusations should not have been believed. Write down something like "false" for the blank. *Specious* and *spurious* both mean *false,* so (B) and (E) are correct. Watch out for trap answers such as *credible* (believable), which has the correct context, but the opposite of the correct meaning for the blank.

4.   **B and E**

Even though is a transition that changes direction, so the paintings must have been hung in a way contrary to what one would expect from the clue. Since the curator *spent several months arranging the exhibit,* one might expect the paintings to appear *as if they had been hung with* great care over a long period; write down the opposite, such as "sloppiness and speed." Now look to eliminate words that don't match. *Haste* and *celerity* both match "speed," so (B) and (E) are the credited responses. Beware of distractor answers *deliberateness* and *slowness,* which reflect the clue without the contrast required by the transition *even though.*

5.   **C and F**

Because *there will always be more to analyze,* the *critical analysis of the works of Shakespeare* must not be complete. Write down "complete" and look to eliminate words that don't match. *Comprehensive* and *exhaustive* both mean "complete," so choices (C) and (F) are the correct answers. Be sure to write down your own answer first, so as to avoid being tempted by distractor choices such as *pedantic* and *learned;* both refer to scholarly endeavors, but neither matches the meaning of the blank that is indicated by the clue.

6.   **B and C**

The transition *while* and the juxtaposition of *showing leniency* and *punishing ruthlessly* indicate that *leniency* (mercy) was shown to those who did the opposite of *remain defiant,* so write down "not defiant" for the blank, and cross off answer choices that don't match. Both *complaisant* and *obeisant* mean submissive (i.e. "not defiant"), so answer choices (B) and (C) are correct. Watch out for the distractor answer *bellicose* (warlike), which describes foes, but continues the direction of the clue (*defiant*) instead of changing it (as required by the transition *while*).

7.   **B and F**

The clue tells you that whatever Clovis did to paganism, he did it *in favor of Christianity,* so he must have rejected the former. Look to eliminate words that don't match "reject" or "give up." Both *legitimize* and *espouse* mean the opposite of what you're looking for, so eliminate (D) and (E). Neither *desiccate,* which means to dry out, nor *exacerbate,* which means to make worse, means "reject" or "give up," so eliminate choices (A) and (C). Only *abjure* and *renounce* match the predicted answer, so (B) and (F) are correct.

Practice Drill #2

1.   **A and D**

The clue tells you that the *Aeneid* has been *widely disseminated since its publication,* so write down a word like "model" for the blank. *Anomaly* (exception) and *nadir* (lowest point) can be eliminated, as can (B) and (F): An *epithet* can be a descriptive word or phrase or an expression of contempt, and an *epitaph* is an inscription on a grave marker. Both *paragon* and *epitome* mean "a perfect example," so (A) and (D) match the predicted answer and are the correct responses.

2.   **B and D**

If the company *underreported its capital depreciation*, then its actual value was lower than reported; instead of remaining steady, its value must therefore have decreased. Both *grown* and *augmented* are the opposite of what you're looking for, so eliminate answer (A) and (E). Neither *underestimated* nor *amortized*, which means paid off in installments, matches the predicted answer, so eliminate (C) and (F). Only *declined* and *diminished* match the word "decreased," so (B) and (D) are the correct answers.

3.   **D and E**

The sentence states that parts of the work are *autobiographical*, but the transition *however* indicates that the second part of the sentence goes in a different direction; that fact, combined with the assertion that *the piece as a whole cannot properly be called a historical record*, indicates that the work must have been "fictionalized." Write that down for the blank, and eliminate answer choices that don't match. Only *fabricated* and *contrived* match "fictionalized," so (D) and (E) are the correct answers. Watch out for *documented* and *catalogued*, synonyms that might be attractive because they are words that can be associated with *historical records*, but they don't contrast with *autobiographical*.

4.   **A and E**

The world *religions . . . promulgate magnanimity toward the less fortunate among us*, so *the obligation to perform charitable acts is a central* idea of those religions. Write down "idea" for the blank, and eliminate answer choices that don't match. *Tenet* and *precept* both match the predicted answer, so (A) and (E) are the credited responses. Watch out for the distractor answers *idyll* (which looks like "ideal," but actually refers to a quaint piece of literature or music) and *sanctity* (which is related to religion, but means "sacredness" rather than "belief" or "idea"). *Paradigm* and *model* are synonyms that also don't match the predicted answer.

5.   **A and C**

The transition *but* indicates that the sentence changes direction after the first comma. The initial clue states that words *rely on their contexts . . . to create meaning*, which suggests that their definitions sometimes change; however, the shift in direction required by the transition *but* dictates that we can expect *language* to have at least some words with *only one meaning . . . regardless of the situation in which they are uttered*. Write down "unchanging" for the blank and eliminate answer choices that don't match. Only *concrete* and *definitive* describe things that are not subject to change; thus, (A) and (C) are the credited responses.

6.   **A and F**

The goal of *charitable appeals* is to collect charitable donations, so if such appeals *often feature a single individual*, it must be true that *people tend to react more* "generously" *to individuals than to groups*. Write down "generously" and look for answers to eliminate. Both *perniciously* and *nefariously* are nearly the opposite of the predicted answer, so eliminate (D) and (E). Choices (B) and (C) give roughly synonymous meanings, but they don't match "generously." Both *magnanimously* and *benevolently* match the predicted answer, so (A) and (F) are correct.

7.   **C and D**

The clue states that *Dean always seemed to go along with the group and change his opinion to complement those around him*, which demonstrates that Dean has a "flexible" *nature [that] often irritated his friends.* Look to eliminate words that don't match "flexible." The correct answers are (C) and (D), *malleable* (easily changed) and *tractable* (easily led). Incorrect choices *vociferous* and *strident* both could mean *loudly crying out*, and incorrect choices *indelible* and *immutable* are near synonyms that go in the opposite direction of the missing word.

Practice Drill #3

1.   **C and F**

The clue in this sentence is *boasted*, so recycle the clue and write down "boastful" for the blank. Now look for answers to eliminate. Only *haughty* and *arrogant* match the predicted answer, so (C) and (F) are the correct choices. It is important to write down your own answer first, so as to avoid distractors like *fortunate* and *vigorous* (which are possible descriptions for winners), as well as *incensed* and *humble* (which describe the losing team's members).

2.   **A and C**

The transition in this sentence is *rather than*, and the clues are *shocked*, *quiet boardroom*, and *exhibiting outrage*. The day after a *stock market crash, members of the board* might be expected to be *exhibiting outrage*, which is why *the president of the company was shocked when he arrived at the quiet boardroom.* Write down "not outraged" for the blank, and eliminate answer choices that don't match. *Histrionic* and *impassioned* mean roughly the opposite of the predicted answer, so cross them off. *Empathetic* (understanding another's feelings) and *fetid* (foul-smelling) can also be eliminated. Only *impassive* and *stoic*, which both mean "showing no emotion," have the correct meaning. The answers are (A) and (C).

3.   **D and E**

There are three clues in this sentence: *challenging*, *vexed*, which means confused, and *involute*, which means complicated. Write down something like "challenging" for the blank. Choice (A), *transparent*, is the exact opposite of the predicted answer; cross it off. *Luculent* (clear or cogent) and *perspicuous* (lucid) also contradict "challenging," but don't eliminate them if you don't know what they mean. *Labyrinthine* and *byzantine* both mean extremely complex and intricate, which are qualities likely to be "challenging," so (D) and (E) are the credited responses.

4.   **A and E**

The clues here, *intrepidity* (the noun form of intrepid, meaning brave) and *normally*, along with the transition, *might not otherwise*, indicate that the word in the blank means the opposite of brave. Write down "cowardly" and look for incorrect answers to eliminate. *Mettlesome* and *plucky* mean brave—the opposite of the predicted answer—so cross off (B) and (D). *Ingenious* (brilliant) and *impudent* (rude) also don't match "cowardly;" eliminate (C) and (E) as well. That leaves the synonyms *pusillanimous* and *recreant* (both of which mean "cowardly") as the correct answers; (A) and (E) are the credited responses.

5.   **C and D**

The clue in this sentence is the phrase *tasteful, even sophisticated;* the word *absurdly*, and the transition, *while*, let you know that the word in the blank means the opposite of *tasteful*. Write down "tasteless" and look for incorrect choices to cross off. *Cosmopolitan* and *svelte* both mean sophisticated, the opposite of the predicted answer; eliminate (A) and (F). *Unkempt* (messy) and *viridian* (green) may describe a lawn, but they don't match "tasteless;" cross off (B) and (E) as well. You are now left with *meretricious* and *tawdry*, which match the predicted answer, making (C) and (D) the credited responses.

6.   **B and D**

The *newly appointed chief financial officer [has] saved millions for the company*, so he is good at saving money. However, the fact that the employees *were forced to give up some of the luxuries afforded to them in previous years*, along with the words *unfortunately* and *miserable*, suggest that the employees think the manager is overly penny-pinching. Write down "stingy" for the blank and look for incorrect answers to eliminate. Choices (A) and (C) are opposites of *stingy*. *Hedonistic* describes someone who loves luxury, which also goes in the wrong direction. *Dispassionate* (showing no emotion) doesn't match the predicted response either. That leaves *penurious* and *parsimonious* (both of which mean "stingy") as the credited responses; the correct answers are (B) and (D).

7.   **B and F**

The *earnest missive from the mayor* indicates that he or she is (understandably) very concerned about the serious *dearth of water* caused by the *summer drought*. Accordingly, write down a word like "urged" for the blank. Now look to eliminate words that don't match the predicted answer. *Lambasted* and *castigated* both mean "harshly criticized," but there is no support in the sentence for the mayor's message being critical. *Inundated* (flooded) is a trap answer because it relates to water, but doesn't match "urged." *Wheedled* (cajoled) is close, but it implies the use of flattery, which is not supported. Only *beseeched* and *importuned* match the predicted answer; hence, (B) and (F) are correct.

Practice Drill #4

1.   **B and E**

Since the sentence begins with the transition *although*, you know that the first and second parts of the sentence will be different. The first part says that *the president had been accused of reducing defense spending*, so the second part must state that the *spending . . . actually increased*. Write down "spending" and look to eliminate choices that don't match. Only *outlays* and *expenditures* mean "spending," so (B) and (E) are correct.

2. **C and F**

The sentence states that *the purpose of the program was to provide both subsidized and free meals;* logically, such assistance must be offered to *children from families* with limited resources. Write down "poor" and look for incorrect answers to cross off. Only *impecunious* and *impoverished* match the predicted answer, so (C) and (F) are correct.

3. **B and E**

The sentence states that *supply surpassed demand,* meaning that there were "too many" *available housing units.* Check the choices. Both *glut* and *surfeit* match "excess," so (B) and (E) are correct. Watch out for trap answers *dearth* and *paucity* (both mean "lack," the opposite of the meaning required by the clue).

4. **B and D**

The sentence says that the bill *was supported . . . by legislators from across the ideological spectrum,* so it received votes from politicians with diverse perspectives. Since *bipartisanship* means cooperation from both sides, the bill *was rightly labeled a successful* "example" of such cooperation. Check the choices. Only *exemplar* and *illustration* match "example," so the correct answers are (B) and (D). Be sure to write down the predicted answer first, so as to avoid the trap answers *rostrum* (podium or dais) and *forum,* which are both reminiscent of political discourse, but which don't match the meaning required by the clue.

5. **A and E**

The sentence states that many Britons were surprised by the results of the *ethnographic survey,* so the results of this study of ethnic and cultural backgrounds must have been unexpected. Since *England and Wales* are part of Europe, it might be unexpected that *five percent of the population . . . were of South Asian* "heritage." Of the choices, only *extraction* and *descent* match the predicted answer, so the correct responses are (A) and (E).

6. **C and F**

The sentence begins with the transition *while,* indicating a change or contrast in the sentence, so the word in the blank describes her normal *conviction that sequels are generally inferior to their predecessors.* If her willingness to *acknowledge occasional exceptions* to that rule contrasts with her normal stance, she must usually be "firm" *in her conviction.* Both *wavering* and *vacillating* mean roughly the opposite of "firm," so eliminate (A) and (B). Neither *perturbed,* which means disturbed, nor *disconsolate,* which means gloomy, match the predicted answer, so eliminate (D) and (E). That leaves *adamant* and *resolute,* both of which match "firm," so (C) and (F) are the credited responses.

7. **C and E**

The time transition *after decades* indicates that something has changed; the first part of the sentence states that the airlines had previously enjoyed *decades of stability,* so the most recent *fifteen years must have borne witness to a remarkably* "unstable" *period for airlines.* (Indeed, being *part of a merger* and filing for *bankruptcy* are both examples of significant change, and one or both of these are true for *virtually every airline.*) Write down "unstable" and cross off choices that don't match. Both *erratic* and *volatile* match "unstable," so (C) and (E) are correct. *Avionic* (with its linguistic similarity to "aviation") is a trap answer that refers to electronic devices used in aircraft.

Practice Drill #5

1.   C and E

The transition *despite* indicates that the two parts of the sentence are different; the second part of the sentence states that *multiple-personality disorder is in reality remarkably rare,* so the contrast must be that the disorder is often used *as a plot device in films and television programs.* Write down something like "frequentness" for the blank, and cross off words that don't match. Only *pervasiveness* and *ubiquity* match the predicted answer, so (C) and (E) are correct.

2.   B and F

The sentence includes the transition *and,* which means that the two parts of the sentence agree; the second half of the sentence states that facts that *diverge are downplayed,* so, in order for the rest of the sentence to be consistent (as required by the continuation transition *and*), it makes sense that *facts that* "confirm" *one's previously held beliefs are emphasized.* Look for words that don't match "confirm" and cross them off. The only words that match the predicted answer are *corroborate* and *substantiate,* so (B) and (F) are correct. Watch out for trap answers like *calibrate* and *extrapolate,* which are commonly associated with data (*facts*), but don't have the meaning required by the clues.

3.   C and F

The sentence begins with the transition word *While,* which signals that the second part of the sentence is different from the first. The second part states that the journalist was *reluctant to attribute the diminution of the latter [newspapers] to the rise of the former [online advertising].* Thus, the first part must convey that some relationship actually exists between the *ascent* and the *diminution;* recycle the clue and write down "diminution" (decrease) for the blank. Only *wane* and *dwindling* match the predicted answer, so (C) and (F) are correct.

4.   A and C

The sentence states that a novel now considered a *magnum opus* (masterpiece) was at first *rebuffed [rejected] by every publishing house in the country.* Aspirant [*hopeful* or *beginning*] *writers* are likely to take "comfort" *in [this] example,* since it suggests that perseverance in the face of rejection may ultimately lead to an author's success. Write down "comfort" and cross off choices that don't match. Only *consolation* and *succor* match "comfort." The correct answers are (A) and (C).

5.   **B and F**

The sentence sets up a juxtaposition between *commercials for local businesses* and *most advertising,* with the former described as *amateurish* and *a tonic* (cure) for *the slick homogeneity* (sameness) that characterizes the latter. Even if you don't know the word *tonic,* the fact that *amateurish* is the opposite of *slick* indicates that the word in the blank must mean the opposite of *homogeneity;* write down "non-sameness" and eliminate answers that don't match. Both *eccentricities* and *idiosyncrasies* describe peculiar qualities or quirks, which match the predicted answer; the correct answers are thus (B) and (F).

6.   **D and E**

The sentence begins with the transition word *though* and the time transition *previous,* indicating a shift in meaning within the sentence. In the first part, the futurist *conceded that Apple's iPhone was a revolutionary device,* so the second part must refer to a contrasting idea, such as "old-fashioned." Be aware of the phrase *it would not be immune,* which creates a sort of double negative that cancels itself out and keeps the blank going in the opposite direction of the clues. Additional support for a contrasting word in the blank comes from the mention of *products* like *Ford's Model T* and *Sony's Walkman;* if they were only *previous[ly]* "game changing," they must now be *considered* "old-fashioned." Eliminate *avant-garde* and *radical,* which reflect the clues (*revolutionary* and *"game changing"*) without the contrast required by the transitions (*though* and *previous*). *Electronic* and *circuitous* are trap answers, as they sound related to devices like the iPhone (which have electronic circuits), but don't match "old-fashioned." Only *antediluvian* and *superannuated* match the predicted answer, so (D) and (E) are the credited responses.

7.   **A and F**

Marty's other cat, Marco, is unlike Lacey, who is nearly *emaciated [abnormally thin] due to her eating habits.* If Lacey's *eating habits* make her so thin, she must not eat very much; if Marco is *unlike Lacey,* he must have "a large" appetite. Cross off answers that don't match "a large." *Edacious* and *voracious* both mean "devouring," so answer (A) and (F) are correct. *Meager, scanty,* and *sporadic* echo the clue (*emaciated due to her eating habits*) without the contrast required by the transition (*unlike*), so they are on the wrong side of the fence, and *spurious* means false, so it has no relation to the clue.

Practice Drill #6

1.   **C and E**

There are two clues in this sentence to describe the students: *blandishments* and *wheedling.* Both are words with negative connotations that describe people who use flattery to try to manipulate or find favor with others. Write down "flattering (bad)" and look to eliminate choices that don't match. *Fawning* and *obsequious* both mean flattering (with negative connotations), so answer (C) and (E) give you appropriate, equivalent sentences. *Candid* (honest) and *ingenuous* (innocent or sincere) go in the wrong direction of the blank; *lumbering* (ponderous or clumsy) and *viable* (feasible) are also not supported by the sentence.

2.   **B** and **D**

The clue is *lyrics about lost love and regret*, which indicates that the word in the blank must be something like "sad." Write this word down and cross off answers that don't match. Eliminate *fatuous* (foolish), *buoyant* (cheerful), *nonplused* (perplexed) and *discordant* (incongruous or harsh-sounding). The remaining choices, *morose* and *melancholy*, match the predicted answer. The credited responses are (B) and (D).

3.   **C** and **F**

The first clue is the phrase *ironic names*, which indicates that the clients' horses had names that did not match the animals' individual qualities. The second clue, *Tractable*, means obedient, and this horse definitely *did not live up to his name*, so he must have been disobedient. Since Tractable is *one example* of the ironically named horses, the other animals can be assumed to have similarly stubborn personalities. Write down "disobedient" for the blank. Cross off *auspicious* (promising), *compliant* (obedient), *serendipitous* (lucky), and *tranquil* (calm). The remaining choices, *obdurate* (stubborn) and *recalcitrant* (resisting authority) match the predicted answer, making (C) and (F) the correct responses.

4.   **B** and **E**

The first politician is described as *guileless*, which means she was honest and straightforward in her speech; since *she was worried that her opponent's statements would encompass a wider range of voters' interests*, those statements must have been dishonest or not straightforward in a way that might appeal to voters with varying interests. Write down "deceptive/appealing" and look to eliminate words that don't match. *Ambiguous* and *equivocal* both mean "open to more than one interpretation," which matches both parts of the predicted answer; keep these choices. Cross off *affable* (easygoing), *conspicuous* (noticeable), *benevolent* (kind), and *candid* (honest). The correct answers are (B) and (E).

5.   **A** and **C**

You have two clues about the puppy: He is described as *irascible* (quick to anger), and Becca's *more quiescent [passive] dogs were rattled* by him. Write down something like "aggressive" for the blank. Eliminate *languid* and *phlegmatic*, both of which mean sluggish or inactive (good descriptors for the mellower dogs); cross off *juvenile* and *diminutive* as well (these are trap answers that reference the puppy's youth and small size, rather than his quick temper). That leaves *pugnacious* and *bellicose*, which match "aggressive." The credited responses are (A) and (C).

6.   **A** and **E**

The most important transition in this sentence is a time transition: *When Howard began his career* (at the beginning of the sentence) and *he thought* (after the semicolon) which indicate that Howard eventually realized he was wrong. He *thought* that his clients would be *disputing parties . . . [full of] enmity*, so he expected them to be hostile. Since he was wrong, *some of his clients* must actually have been "not hostile." *Indignant* and *churlish* mean roughly the opposite of the predicted answer (they reflect the clue without the contrast required by the time transition), so cross them off. *Disparate* (different) and *distinct* (separate) may describe two disputing parties, but they don't match "not hostile" either. *Acquiescent* and *amenable* both mean "agreeable," which matches the predicted answer, so (A) and (E) are the credited responses.

7.   **B and E**

Since the columnist's *editor . . . [has to] remind her of the minimum line requirement*, her columns must not be long enough. Write down "short" and cross off choices that don't match. *Terse* and *laconic* both mean "using few words"; keep these choices. None of the other answers even comes close to matching "short," so (B) and (E) are the correct responses.

Practice Drill #7

1.   **A and B**

The clue states that Steinberg is a *merchant . . . [who] beamed in anticipation of large profits*, but the phrase *little did he know* acts as a transition that indicates the word in the blank will be the opposite of the clue. Therefore, Steinberg will not make large profits from selling the shoes; for some reason that he does not expect, the shoes will be hard to sell *that fall*. Speaking of *that fall,* the mention of the changing seasons and the assertion that the shoes are *stylish* in the summer of Steinberg's purchase act as additional clues, indicating that the reason for poor sales may be related to fashions (which typically change with the seasons). Write down "unsellable/out of style" for the blank. *Chic* is a trap answer, as it means "stylish" (the opposite of one half of the predicted answer). *Inapplicable* doesn't match either half of the predicted answer. *Repulsive* or *disagreeable* shoes would probably be hard to sell, but those words have nothing to do with changing styles. Both *outmoded* and *passé* mean "out of style," so (A) and (B) are the correct answers.

2.   **D and F**

The clue, *former prosperity,* indicates that Galveston was once prosperous, so it used to be a place with a lot of *economic activity.* Write down something like "center" for the blank. *Maritime* (related to the sea) is a distractor choice because Galveston is a *port city*, but this answer doesn't match the predicted one. Similarly, *bounty* and *abundance* are trap answers, as they describe a state of plenty; however, these choices lack a reference to Galveston as a "center" *of economic activity. Chronicle* (account) doesn't match the predicted answer at all, and can be eliminated. That leaves *hub* and *locus,* both of which describe centers of activity; hence, (D) and (F) are the credited responses.

3.   **B and F**

Even if you don't know the definitions of *dauntless* or *blithely,* there is enough of a clue in the second part of the sentence to determine the meaning of the word in the blank. *Men [who] would think twice* about joining Anthony's *risky enterprises* are probably not overly bold; hence, they must be *less* "bold" than Anthony. *Lethargic* and *torpid* both mean "sluggish," which doesn't match "bold" at all; cross off (A) and (C). *Exotic* and *aggrandized* don't match the predicted answer either, so eliminate (D) and (E). This leaves only *audacious* (bold) and *intrepid* (fearless), making the correct answers (B) and (F).

4.   **C and E**

The sentence states that *people believe the myth* that *lemmings commit mass suicide*, and speculates that this belief has something to do with the relationship between lemmings and Scandinavia, where there is *an unusually high suicide rate.* If people believe something about lemmings that is true of Scandinavia, the blank must describe a connection between the animals and the region. Write down "connected to" and look for incorrect answers to eliminate. Cross off *tantamount* (equivalent), because although this word could match "connected to," lemmings and Scandinavia cannot be the same thing. *Organic* is a trap answer, as it is often misinterpreted to mean "natural," but actually refers to chemical composition, bodily organs, or chemical-free agriculture. Eliminate *prodigious* (large) and *titanic* (huge) as well. All that remain are *endemic* and *indigenous*, which mean "native;" the correct answers are (C) and (E).

5.   **B and E**

The platypus is a *sophisticated predator* that uses an *effective hunting practice.* Since the clues indicate only that the platypus is a hunter, it must try to locate "food." Only *quarry* and *prey* match the predicted answer, so (B) and (E) are the credited responses.

6.   **A and B**

Keep track of the transitions in this sentence. The *but* means that the *development [of Salsa]* had a characteristic inconsistent with *belongs to one country*, so the blank means something like "belongs to more than one country." This predicted answer is echoed by the first half of the sentence, with the transition *[t]hough* changing the direction from the clue that *Salsa takes its roots from various countries*; the second half of the sentence parallels the contrast (from multiple sources to a single source) in the first half. *Feat* and *coup* are synonyms meaning "achievement," which doesn't match "belonging to more than one country." *Lyric* is a distractor that looks attractive because of its association with music, but also strays far from the predicted answer. *Denouement* (final outcome) can also be eliminated. That leaves *collaboration* and *synergism*, which both describe teamwork among various actors; the correct answers are thus (A) and (B).

7.   **D and F**

If the students' diligence was only *apparent* and the praise they received was *unwarranted*, then their motivation must have been *merely* to receive *the praise* they did not deserve. Write down "desire for praise" and cross off words that don't match. *Assiduity* is a near synonym for *diligence*, so that word is the opposite of what should go in the blank. Eliminate *prepossession* (favorable bias), *cronyism* (giving preference to friends in hiring or appointment decisions), and *torpidity* (sluggishness). *Sycophancy* and *obsequiousness* both describe insincere behaviors designed to gain favor with superiors, so (D) and (F) are the credited responses.

Chapter 6
Analytical Writing

WELCOME TO ANALYTICAL WRITING

So, as you are aware, one of the tasks that ETS has deemed essential for evaluating your grad school potential is writing two short essays. You won't be writing these essays on a topic in your graduate field. In fact, you won't be writing these essays on any academic topic at all. There will be no research involved, no careful consideration of evidence, no peer review, no faculty supervision. In short, it's about as far away from the type of academic writing you'll be doing in grad school as you can imagine. But don't worry. With the right knowledge and some practice, you can learn to score higher on the Analytical Writing section. It's no different from the rest of the GRE in that regard.

How Much Does Analytical Writing Matter?

We asked this question about the GRE as a whole in the Introduction chapter, and the answer here is fundamentally the same: It depends. However, it's probably safe to say that right now the Analytical Writing section will matter the least of the three sections. It doesn't distinguish between candidates as well as the multiple-choice sections do. About 60 percent of test takers score between 4 and 5.5 on the Analytical Writing section, which means most people get a 4, 4.5, 5, or 5.5.

The best way to be certain, however, is to call the schools you're interested in, and ask them directly. Some will tell you that they don't really care about the Analytical Writing section at all, and some will tell you that they want a minimum score of 5. It's important to find out what the situation is at the schools you intend to apply to, so you can determine how much time and effort to devote to this chapter.

Structure

First, let's review the basics of the Analytical Writing section. This section contains two parts. The first part lasts 30 minutes and is officially titled "Present Your Perspective on an Issue." The second part also lasts 30 minutes and is officially titled "Analyze an Argument." For ease of reference, we'll continue to refer to the two tasks as the Issue essay and the Argument essay. The Analytical Writing section will always be the first section on your test, and will never be experimental.

Scoring

Each essay will receive two scores, ranging from 0 to 6. If the scores are within one point of each other, they will be averaged. If the scores are not within one point of each other (this is rare), then an expert reader will be brought in to read and score the essay. The final scores for the two essays are then averaged and rounded to the nearest half point.

More Great Books
Word Smart
Word Smart for the GRE
More Word Smart

For example, your Argument essay may receive a 5 from both readers, so your average for that essay would be a 5. Your Issue essay may receive a 5 from one reader and a 4 from the other, so your average for that essay would be a 4.5. The average of 5 and 4.5 is 4.75, which rounds up to 5. Thus, you would get a 5 as your Analytical Writing score.

The essays are scored "holistically," which means the readers assign a score based on their overall impression of the essay. There's no checklist that they use to sum up the points (e.g., half a point for good grammar, one point for a good conclusion, etc.). It's okay to make minor grammatical or spelling errors as long as the essay as a whole is strong. The readers aren't going to examine your essays carefully enough or long enough to notice all the details. They have a lot of essays to grade and are probably not going to spend more than two or three minutes reading each one. Later, we'll talk about how to make your essay cater to a short attention span.

Think of the scores for the Analytical Writing section as 0–3: bad, 4–6: good. A score from 4–6 means that you, to a varying degree of success, answered the question asked. It was clear what your position was, and your support clearly connected to your position. A score from 0–3 means that you did not actually answer the question asked. Maybe your position wasn't clear, or your support didn't seem to connect to your position, or maybe you just wrote about something only tangentially related to the question asked.

Consequently, your goal for your essay should be to make sure you answer the question. If you have a free minute at the end of your essay, it's always helpful to look over the prompt and then look over your essay. Did you do what they asked you to do? If so, you'll probably get a 4, 5, or 6.

What You'll See on the Screen

Don't expect to get a fancy word processor on the Analytical Writing section. In fact, what you get barely deserves the name "word processor." There's no spell check, no grammar check, no italics, no underlining—basically no formatting features at all. Here's what your screen will look like:

IBT Client

GRE® Practice Test Section 1 of 5   Quit w/ Save | Exit Section | Help ? | Next ▷

Question 1 of 2   Hide Time 00 : 29 : 52

A community should first and foremost educate its citizens in how to properly aid the community as a whole.

Write a response in which you discuss the extent to which you agree or disagree with the claim. In developing and supporting your position, be sure to address the most compelling reasons or examples that could be used to challenge your position.

Cut | Paste | Undo | Redo

As you can see, it's not much. The essay prompt will stay in front of you the whole time at the left side of your screen. You type your essay into the field at the right. You'll have to scroll eventually to see everything you've written, because the field isn't very big. To navigate in the text field you can use the arrow keys or click with the mouse. There are also four editing buttons on the right side of your screen: Cut, Paste, Undo, and Redo. By highlighting text in your essay, you can move it around with the cut-and-paste feature. You shouldn't need to use these buttons, however. In fact, if you're using the cut-and-paste feature heavily, it's already a bad sign: a pretty clear indicator that your essay isn't well planned. By the way, you have to type your essays—no writing them by hand—so brush up on your typing if it's a little rusty.

Topics

The topics are about issues of general interest and don't require any special knowledge. Make sure to read the directions for each essay prompt. The directions sometimes have subtle differences. Visit the ETS website at www.ets.org/gre for a complete list of all the potential essay topics and directions. (Yes, you really get to see this information in advance of the test!) Practice responding to these essay prompts. Practicing with a variety of these essays will prepare you for whatever comes your way on test day.

There are nearly 250 topics listed for each essay, so the point isn't to memorize them to be ready for your actual GRE topic in advance. Rather, by browsing through the lists, you'll get an idea of what kinds of topics you'll be asked to write about.

Understanding the Two Tasks

The two essays that ETS requires you to write have distinct features, and it's important to know exactly how they differ. The simplest way to understand the distinction is that the Issue essay requires you to present your own opinion and support it with examples, while the Argument essay requires you to evaluate someone else's opinion without giving your own. Another way to put it is that the Issue essay requires you to develop your own argument by making claims and providing evidence to support and explain those claims, while the Argument essay requires you to critique another person's argument by analyzing its claims and judging the evidence it presents.

This distinction is important, because if you don't understand clearly the task you're being asked to perform, you're not likely to do a good job on the essay. In particular, many people get confused about the Argument essay because they're not accustomed to breaking down an argument and analyzing its logic. Many people simply give their own opinion on the argument, which is a sure way to score poorly. We'll be covering all the details of how to break down arguments and write a strong Argument essay later in this chapter.

Essay Writing Basics

It's important to understand that the essays you write for the GRE are not going to be masterpieces. We're not redefining the craft of writing here. You have limited time to write and revise, so what we're talking about is a quickly produced first-draft essay.

In order to score well, there are several components your essay should have. The following are some of the most important:

Proven Techniques

- **Length.** This is a good example of the difference between GRE writing and real writing. In the real world, good, vigorous writing is concise. Unnecessary things are cut out. On the GRE, you want to write as much as you can. That doesn't mean that you're filling the screen with blather or repeating yourself a hundred times, but you do want to expand on your ideas as much as possible and explore as many of their ramifications as you can. Be thorough. However, in your quest for length, know that depth is better than breadth. It's much better to have a few well-chosen examples that you explore in depth than many examples that you discuss only superficially. The bottom line is that high-scoring essays are usually long, and low-scoring essays are usually short. Make it as long as time permits. Aiming for about 500 words is a good guideline.

- **Organization.** Remember, the readers are going to go through your essay very quickly, and they're grading holistically. You need to make a good overall impression. No brilliant example, no amazing turn of phrase will save your essay if it is disorganized. One of the primary things the readers are looking for is a well-structured, well-organized piece of writing. In a sense the structure is much more important than the content. No one *really* cares what you say—they're not reading your essay to decide whether they agree with you. They care how you say it—whether you write a well-planned, logical response to the prompt. The easiest way to organize your essay is to use the old boring four- or five-paragraph essay format that you first learned in sixth grade: introduction, two or three body paragraphs, and a conclusion. Hard to believe something so basic could work on the GRE? Believe it. We're not writing real essays here, we're learning how to tackle a standardized test.

- **Introduction and Conclusion.** This is really part of organization, but it's important enough to discuss separately. Your essay must have an introduction and a conclusion. You can't simply launch into an example in the first sentence of your essay—the reader will be jolted. You have to ease the reader into the essay by spreading out a road map of where the essay is going. A good introduction can do a lot for you, because a reader who comes away with a good impression from the introduction is more likely to keep that good impression throughout the rest of your essay. Think of it as building goodwill. A conclusion is also crucial, because you don't want your essay to just en—. Wow. See how jarring that was? Now you probably wouldn't end in mid-word, but the point is that you have to bring your reader home with some kind of summation. The essay needs closure. A strong introduction gives the reader a good first impression; a strong conclusion leaves the reader with a good last impression.

- **Clear Point of View.** Unlike the other points mentioned so far, this one is not structural but rather content-based. It should always be clear to someone reading your essay exactly where you stand. Whether you're presenting your opinion in the Issue essay or critiquing the argument in the Argument essay, your own position should always be clear. When a clear point of view isn't present, your essay is weak and abstract, and the reader doesn't know why you wrote it—you clearly had nothing to say. When this situation arises, most of the time it's because you haven't actually figured out what you think. You're hoping to uncover it by writing about it, but that rarely works. Instead you end up with an essay that reads as though you were trying to discover your point of view along the way—which is exactly what you are doing. In order to write a high-scoring essay, you need to know what it is you want to say. And that means that you have to think before you write. Writing is just thinking on paper, but the thinking has to come first. We'll discuss this in more detail shortly.

- **Proper Grammar and Effective Language.** To some degree, of course, your essay score will be affected by how well you write. If your sentences are all the same length and same structure, your writing will be monotonous. If you make numerous or prominent grammatical errors, it will seem careless and unsophisticated. Using language well is part of good essay writing. We can't really teach you in this book to be a better writer (that's an entire book in itself), but we'll try to give you some helpful guidance along the way. In general, try to write as well as you can, but don't think that you need complicated syntax or fancy rhetorical flourishes to be successful on the Analytical Writing section. Use language that you're comfortable with and you should be fine. This is the GRE. You don't need the essay-writing skills of E. B. White to score well.

THE FOUR RULES

There are four basic rules we're going to follow while writing an essay. Poorly written essays tend to be essays that don't have a clear purpose. Although the Issue and Argument essays each have their own peculiarities we'll have to take into account, remembering the following four rules will keep your essay, whichever one it is, focused.

1. Spend time thinking.
2. Make a plan and stick to it.
3. Include only one thought per paragraph.
4. Clearly link each paragraph to your thesis.

Spend Time Thinking

Time is ticking. We know. It's scary. There's even a little clock, right there in the corner of the screen, counting down tick by tick. Take a deep breath. Even though time is limited, don't rush into writing before you're ready. If you do, you'll find that you quickly run out of things to say, and you'll have a screen full of random, unconnected sentences in front of you. It's better to spend some time up front thinking about what you'll say.

So relax a bit. Read the prompt. You've got scratch paper, so use it. What's your initial thought after you read the prompt? Write it down. Write down all your thoughts, even the stupid ones. The idea is just to get your thoughts down without any inhibitions. (No one will take away points from your essay because you wrote something stupid down on your scratch paper.) Play devil's advocate. Think about the other side of the issue or argument. What examples can you use?

You will probably spend around 5 minutes without typing a single word. If so, good. Trust us, it will pay off later.

Make a Plan and Stick to It

Now you've got some ideas. Perfect. Lay them out into the rough outlines of an essay. What's your introduction? If it's the Issue essay, you'll need to state your opinion, also known as your thesis, clearly. If it's the Argument, it will probably be some variation of "This argument is potentially flawed, and we will need more information to determine whether or not to use it."

How will you support your thesis? What examples will you use, or what flaws will you point out? As soon as you know, you know exactly what your paragraphs will be. Write down that outline on your scratch paper.

That is your roadmap for the essay. Do not deviate from it. It's a good plan. Many people have the impulse to change their entire essay at the last second. Don't. Stick with your plan. Whenever you get lost in your essay, look back to your scratch paper to see what you should be writing about.

Applied Strategies

Include Only One Thought Per Paragraph

The people who grade your essay are not going to take printouts of your essay to a luxurious reading room, sit upon large padded velvet chairs, pour themselves glasses of brandy, light their pipes, and settle in to examine your thoughts. They will read your essay from a computer monitor as quickly as possible while sitting in an office chair with poor back support. They're not going to give you the benefit of the doubt.

Therefore, you need to make each point incredibly easy for them to find. Each paragraph will contain one, and only one, point, and support for that point. Nothing else.

You already know, from your plan, what each paragraph will be about. If you start wandering from that plan, and from the point of the paragraph, you're going to lose the reader. The teddy bear was invented in two places independently of each other: 1902 in the United States, and in 1903 in Germany. If you're confused, you're not alone. Switching from one point to another in the middle of the paragraph makes for jarring, incomprehensible writing.

Clearly Link Each Paragraph to Your Thesis

Once you have your thesis, every single thing you write in your essay should exist for one purpose, and one purpose only: to prove your thesis. If you are not actively supporting your thesis, then you're not answering the question.

It may not be as obvious to the graders how your paragraphs link to your thesis as it is to you. So once again, make life easy for those poor, harried GRE essay graders. Let them know exactly how that paragraph connects to the thesis, and how it answers the question they asked.

In other words, don't assume that if you show them Points A and C, that they will know that point B connects the two. Explicitly write that Point A leads to Point B, and Point B leads to Point C, and Point C leads back to your thesis.

THE ISSUE ESSAY

The first essay that we're going to look at is the Issue essay. We've already discussed the basic tasks for an essay. Now we're going to look at how you do it.

The Prompt

The first thing the GRE will give you is a prompt, a short sentence displayed inside a box. They want to know your opinion about that prompt. The prompt will be what they call a "topic of general interest," which means that ETS thinks almost everyone will have an opinion about it.

Here's a sample Issue Prompt:

> *The best indicator of a glorious nation is the emphasis it places on educating its populace.*

One thing you may have noticed about this prompt is that it not only presents an issue, but it takes a side. The GRE will never simply say "Education: Discuss." Instead they'll take a definite position. It is up to you to agree or disagree with that position, and explain exactly *why* you agree or disagree.

ETS doesn't actually care about your opinion on the Issue Essay. What they are actually looking for is that you *have* a clear opinion, and that you back that opinion up. It's not better to agree than it is to disagree, or vice versa. They don't care. They simply want to see how you support your position.

Directly following the prompt will be an assignment. Although these take a couple different forms, they are always some variation of the following statement:

> *Write a response in which you agree or disagree with the above statement and explain your reasoning for the position you take.*

Most of the prompts will be similar to the one above: a claim about some sort of topic of importance to society as a whole (laws, education, ideals, technology, etc.) which you can agree or disagree with. There are sometimes slight variations such as these:

- Given a claim and a reason for that claim, discuss how much you agree or disagree about the claim and the reason given.
- Given two opposing views, discuss the view that you agree with more and explain your reasons. Address both the side you agree with and the opposing side.

Even these, however, are hardly different from the typical prompt and assignment. ETS still wants you to clearly state your opinion and the reasons you hold it. (For a full list of Issue topics that the GRE will use, go to www.ets.org/gre).

Examples

Once you've read the prompt and the assignment, write down "Yes" and "No" on your scratch paper. Now it's time to brainstorm. Think of examples to support each side of the prompt. Don't worry about which side of the prompt you actually agree with for now. Just focus on the support you could use to argue either side.

For our prompt above, for Yes we could list any glorious nation that emphasized education, or any decidedly non-glorious civilizations that did not emphasize education. Note that we can argue the claim by saying "Doing what we say is good, so do what we say," and we can also argue it by saying "Not doing what we say is bad, so do what we say." The examples could be from history, current events, literature, film, or your personal experiences. Write down anything you can think of to support your position under Yes on your scratch paper.

For No, we could list any glorious nation that did not emphasize educating its citizens, or we could list some non-glorious civilizations that did emphasize education. List anything you can think of to show that education ain't so needed under No on your scratch paper.

Now look at your lists of examples. Was there one side, Yes or No, that had more examples? Are there any particular examples you came up with that you think you could write about particularly well? If so, you've found out what you think about the claim. If you've got better examples under Yes, then you are 100% for education, because it is the most important thing to make a society great. If you've got better examples under No, then you are now wholeheartedly devoted to nations focusing on something other than education, because it's not as necessary as those eggheads think it is.

After you've chosen a side, put a star next to your strongest 2 or 3 examples.

To review: Come up with your examples before you come up with an opinion. Go with whichever opinion has the better examples. Again, the GRE doesn't care about your opinion; it cares about your support. So focus on support first.

Thesis

Now that you know your position, it's time to tell the world. A basic thesis can be something along the lines of

> *Education is the best indicator of a glorious nation.*

Or

> *Education is not the best indicator of a glorious nation.*

These are fine theses. They state directly what we think with a minimum of fuss. Although they don't use the words "Yes" or "No," it's still clear what we think. You can always use this sort of clear, simple thesis. However, let's see if we can do a bit better. Rather than simply restate the claim, we can look at our examples a bit and ask ourselves "How do those examples support my point?" Use that to write your thesis. For instance,

> Without education, a great nation will not last beyond the current generation.

Or

> Education is no substitute for food, jobs, or military might, all of which are the true indicators of a major nation.

Remember that every paragraph you write must link back to your thesis, so feel free to rewrite it a couple times. No matter what, however, make sure it is obvious how your thesis answers the question asked. The most eloquent, profound thesis doesn't do you any good if it doesn't have anything to do with the prompt or the assignment.

Outline

Remember those examples you put stars next to? Each one of those will be a paragraph. Figure out which example will go first, and which next. Keep in mind that you will need to transition from one paragraph to the next, so if you know that mentioning one example will allow you to segue naturally to the next, put them in an order to allow you to use that transition.

Now you've got your outline:

- Thesis (with introduction paragraph)
- Example (tied back to thesis)
- Example (tied back to thesis)
- Conclusion

You won't always stick simply to the above outline, but if you're ever stuck, it's a nice simple format to follow. You may use only 1 example, or 3 examples, but no matter how you lay out your essay, figure out a plan beforehand and stick to it.

You can also (and sometimes will be required to) use one of the examples from the *other* side of the argument, and show why it doesn't actually invalidate your side of the argument. "Sure, some may point to the Athenian city-state as evidence that education is important, but their education was in fact limited almost entirely to a select few. It was Athen's navy that had far more to do…"

Write

Here is where all that planning pays off. Using your outline, start writing your essay. Anytime you're stuck, look back to your outline and ask yourself "What do I need to say right now to support my thesis?"

Although you may decide to sparge your essay with a miscellany of abstruse words in order to give your essay a veneer of erudition, don't. Using advanced vocabulary is fine, but never let it hinder the reader. If you're not sure if you're using a word correctly, just using a vocabulary word to use it, or if you think that using a word may obscure your point rather than clarify it, then use a simpler word or phrase instead.

Whenever you're stuck, say things as directly as possible. If you have time, you can always go back later and modify your sentences if necessary, but it's better to end up with simple, direct sentences at the end than it is to have a couple great sentences that end abruptly because you ran out of time.

Time is incredibly important in this essay. Keep watching the clock. You should spend 5–7 minutes on each paragraph. When you have 10 minutes left, move on to the conclusion as soon as possible.

Sample Essay

> In order to accomplish anything great, one must seek unpopularity.

Write a response in which you agree or disagree with the above statement and explain your reasoning for the position you take. In developing your position, consider situations in which the statement may or may not hold true and explain how these situations shape your decision.

Many people who have achieved important objectives have done so at the cost of being unpopular. It is sometimes argued that unpopularity is necessary in order to accomplish anything great and that nothing important is achieved by those who worry about being liked. While this may be true in some situations, many great things have been achieved by people who needed to court popularity in order to do them. In other cases, great things have been achieved by people for whom popularity or unpopularity were irrelevant. The key factor is the particular nature of the objective.

When the goal is to accomplish a change in society, unpopularity is probably inevitable. Most people resist large changes, and therefore the people who are pushing for the changes are bound to be unpopular with the section of the population that wants to keep things the way they are. For example, when civil rights leaders such as Malcolm X and Martin Luther King, Jr. were pushing for equal civil rights for black Americans, they were despised by much of the country. The goals they were advancing were controversial and confrontational and this made them deeply unpopular with millions of Americans. Despite this, the cause of civil rights was undoubtedly a great and noble one.

In other situations, however, great things can be accomplished and sometimes can only be accomplished by people with popular support. For example, when Britain was in danger of being defeated by Germany in 1940, Franklin Roosevelt was able to use his popularity and political skill to gather support for programs such as the Lend-Lease Act, which gave badly needed supplies to the British military. Without Roosevelt's skill in rallying the American people, the necessary support might not have been there to defeat the Axis powers and win the war. Victory in World War II is an example of a great thing that could only have been accomplished by a popular leader.

Finally, in some circumstances popularity is irrelevant to the achievement of an important task. Some examples of this would be in the realm of scientific and medical research. When Jonas Salk developed the polio vaccine, a dangerous disease was eradicated, which is a great thing. Salk's accomplishment, however, did not depend on whether he was popular. Similarly, when Einstein wrote his 1905 paper on the photoelectric effect, his achievement in recognizing that the speed of light is constant for all observers did not depend on whether other scientists liked him. A scientific advance is not judged by the popularity of the scientist who discovers it. It just doesn't really matter either way.

In the end, to know whether unpopularity will be a necessary component of achieving something great, you need to know the type of achievement under discussion. Achievements that require large-scale social change will probably make those who fight for them unpopular, but other types of achievements will only be possible when their supporters are popular. And with still other types of achievements, such as scientific ones, it doesn't matter if their proponents are well liked or not. It's all a question of circumstance.

Now let's discuss a few things about this essay. First, this is not a flawless essay. It's not supposed to be perfect. However, this would get a high score on the GRE. Here are some of its features.

Introduction

The introduction accomplishes a few things, all of which you want to do in your essays. First, it establishes what the issue under discussion is. It does this by paraphrasing the prompt in the second sentence. Paraphrasing is usually better than quoting it verbatim, because it's less boring to the reader, and even seems less lazy. (If the prompt is very short, you may have a hard time paraphrasing it; if this is so, don't worry about it.) There are other ways to make it clear to the reader what issue is under discussion, but paraphrasing is the simplest.

Second, the introduction clearly establishes the point of view of the essay. After reading this introduction, you know quite clearly that the writer believes the prompt is sometimes true, but not always. And it leads you to believe that the following paragraphs will back up those assertions by providing examples of the different types of situations.

Body Paragraphs

The body paragraphs follow the implicit promise of the introduction to back up the writer's position. The first paragraph not only explains *why* the prompt is sometimes true, but presents concrete examples in Malcolm X and Martin Luther King, Jr., to support the point. You always want to make sure that your body paragraphs have concrete details. Abstractions are not persuasive. Specifics and particulars are needed to back up your thesis.

The third paragraph logically follows by discussing an example of the opposite situation, exactly as the introduction has led you to expect. It gives a concrete example backed up by historical details.

The fourth paragraph continues the logical structure and organization of the essay by giving concrete examples of the last situation described in the introduction. Thus, all the body paragraphs give details and examples that support the basic point of view of the essay.

Conclusion

The most important thing about the conclusion is that it's there. You'll notice that it doesn't really say anything that wasn't already said in the introduction. The purpose of the conclusion is to tie a bow on the essay and give it the feeling of closure. It's a matter of ending the essay on the right note, with the right tone.

Time Guidelines

You have 30 minutes to write the Issue essay. How should you spend your time? Here are some guidelines.

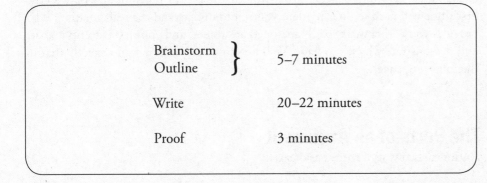

Brainstorm Outline }	5–7 minutes
Write	20–22 minutes
Proof	3 minutes

These are only rough estimates, but they should give you a sense of how to apportion your time. You should develop your own essay-pacing plan by writing some practice essays and adjusting your timing if necessary.

THE ARGUMENT ESSAY

Now it's time to take a look at the Argument essay. You'll find that even though the Argument essay is the more unfamiliar of the two essay types, once you learn how arguments are constructed, it's actually not that difficult to write one. If you read and practice the material in this section, you'll be able to bang out a high-scoring essay on any Argument topic ETS throws at you. Let's begin.

What Is an Argument?

On the GRE, an argument isn't about you and your roommate yelling at each other over whose turn it is to buy toilet paper. An argument is a short paragraph that attempts to convince you of something by providing evidence. Your job on the GRE is to analyze that argument and discuss how well-reasoned it is—whether it's logical and persuasive.

The *Real* Task of the Argument Essay

The directions on the GRE describe your task as "analyzing" the argument. There's a simpler way to understand what you're really supposed to do, however. Your job is to *criticize* the argument. "Analyzing" sounds like an even-handed evaluation of the argument. That's not what you're doing here. On the Issue essay, there's no right answer; you can take any position you like. On the Argument essay, however, there *is* a right answer. How well-reasoned will you find the argument? The answer will always be, "Not very well. In fact, rather poorly. This argument is terrible."

If the argument were a well-reasoned piece of writing, there wouldn't be much to say about it. "Great argument! Airtight logic! The reasoning is ironclad! The conclusion must certainly be true!" That wouldn't make for much of an essay. So the first thing you need to do is reorient yourself to understand the real situation: ETS provides you with a weak, badly reasoned argument, and your job is to rip it apart and demonstrate why it's so bad. We'll be showing you how to do exactly that in the following pages.

The Parts of an Argument

Arguments consist of three basic parts:

- Conclusion
- Premises
- Assumptions

Let's look at each of these components in detail.

Conclusion

The conclusion is the most basic part of an argument. There's no point in writing an argument unless there's some conclusion you're trying to reach. The conclusion is simply the main point of the argument, the primary thing that the author is trying to convince you of.

Let's look at a simple argument.

> *Bobby needs to watch the Red Sox game. His TV is broken. Therefore, he should buy a new TV.*

What is the conclusion of the above argument? Pretty clearly, the ultimate point the author is trying to make is that Bobby should buy a new television. In addition to the general thrust of the argument, the tip-off we have here is the word "therefore." Certain words tend to indicate that the conclusion is about to follow. Among them are *therefore, thus, so, clearly, hence, consequently*, and *in conclusion*.

The first thing you should always do is identify the conclusion of the argument.

Premises

Think of premises as the reasons that the author gives to make you believe the conclusion. An argument can't simply assert something without backing it up. That wouldn't be an argument at all. The author of an argument needs to provide evidence to support the conclusion. Those pieces of evidence are the premises. Let's take another look at our sample argument.

> *Bobby needs to watch the Red Sox game. His TV is broken. Therefore, he should buy a new TV.*

We know that the conclusion is that Bobby should buy a new television. What are the premises of this argument? What evidence did the author provide to support the conclusion? This time it's pretty clear that the premises are the other two sentences in the argument: Bobby needs to watch the Red Sox game; his TV is broken.

After identifying the conclusion, you should always identify the premises of an argument.

The "Why?" Test

There's a simple way to determine if you've correctly identified the conclusion and premises of an argument. It's called the "Why?" test, and this is how it works. After you have identified what you believe to be the conclusion of the argument, ask yourself, "Why should I believe this is true?" The premises should answer that question. For example, ask, "Why should I believe that Bobby should buy a new TV?" The answer here is clearly, "Because he needs to watch the Red Sox, and his TV is busted." That means we've correctly identified the conclusion and premises. What if we'd misidentified them?

Let's say we had thought that the conclusion was the first sentence. When we ask, "Why should I believe that Bobby needs to watch the Red Sox?" there's nothing to point to. Nothing in the argument provides any support for that statement. The argument just says so. We just have to accept it as given.

So the "Why?" test helps us to make sure we've correctly broken down the argument into its basic pieces.

Assumptions

So far, we've seen how to find conclusions and premises. Assumptions are the third part of arguments. Assumptions are similar to premises in that they also provide reasons to support the conclusion. But they have a key difference. While the premises are explicitly stated in the argument, the assumptions are by definition *unstated*.

Assumptions are things that must be true in order for the conclusion to make sense, but that the author left out of the argument. Instead of establishing the truth of those facts, the author simply *assumed* that they were true. Let's go back one more time to our sample argument.

> *Bobby needs to watch the Red Sox game. His TV is broken. Therefore, he should buy a new TV.*

What must the author be assuming in order for the argument to make sense? What else must be true for the conclusion to follow properly from the premises?

Well, for one, we have to assume that Bobby can't get his TV fixed, or can't get it fixed soon enough to watch the game. If he could get it fixed, then he wouldn't have to buy a new one.

Second, we have to assume that there's no other way Bobby can watch the Red Sox game. For example, he can't go over to his friend Johnny's house and watch the game there. Or he can't go to Fenway Park and see the game live. If he could do either of these things, he wouldn't have to buy a new TV.

So, let's summarize the breakdown of this argument:

Conclusion: Bobby should buy a new TV.
Premises: He needs to watch the Red Sox Game. His TV is broken.
Assumptions: He can't get his TV fixed. He can't watch the game some
                    other way.

Why Assumptions Are So Important

It's important to understand that assumptions are necessary for an argument to work. If the assumptions aren't true, the argument falls apart. In the argument above, if Bobby can fix his TV, or watch the game another way, then he doesn't have to buy a new TV. The conclusion is effectively destroyed. This is the key because, as we said, your task on the Argument essay is to weaken the argument. You do that by identifying the assumptions of the argument and attacking them.

Here are a few more tips to help you spot assumptions:

- **Focus on the gap in the argument.** There is always a gap between the premises of an argument and the conclusion, some unjustified leap of logic that needs to be filled by the assumptions. If you look for the gap in the reasoning, and think about what information will bridge that gap, it will be easier to find the assumptions.
- **Look for new stuff in the conclusion.** If the conclusion talks about things that weren't mentioned at all in the premises, then the author must have simply assumed there was a connection.
- **Think about weaknesses in the argument.** What are the possible flaws? An argument is always weakest at its unstated parts. Pretend you're a lawyer in a courtroom and your job is to raise doubt in the minds of the members of the jury about the truth of the argument's conclusion. What could you say? What counterexamples and alternative possibilities could you suggest?

Quick Quiz #1

Try to break down the following arguments. Write down the conclusion and premises, using the "Why?" test to check yourself. Then write down any assumptions you spot. The answers are on page 172.

1. *All the classrooms in the Dover school district have computers. The children in Dover have higher standardized test scores than the children in Wilmington, where there are no computers in the classrooms. Clearly, Wilmington should put computers in its classrooms to raise students' scores.*

    Conclusion: _____

    _____

    Premises: _____

    _____

    Assumptions: _____

    _____

2. *Tony's Macaroni is the best-selling brand of macaroni and cheese at FreshStar supermarket. Therefore, more people in town must prefer its taste to that of any other brand.*

    Conclusion: _____

    _____

    Premises: _____

    _____

    Assumptions: _____

    _____

3. *This new food additive has been shown to cause cancer in laboratory rats. Consequently, any product that uses it will be dangerous for humans.*

Conclusion: _____

_____

Premises: _____

_____

Assumptions: _____

_____

All of the examples we've looked at so far are much shorter and simpler than the arguments you'll get as prompts for the Argument essay, but you break them down in the exact same way. The arguments you'll actually be writing about have a lot more than two assumptions. There will be more things wrong with them than you'll have time to write about. This is good because it means you don't have to find every assumption in order to write a high-scoring essay. You have to find only a few.

The Prompt

Now we're ready to tackle a sample prompt for the Argument essay.

> *The following is a memo from the circulation manager of National News-letter, Inc.*
>
> *"To make the home delivery service of our national newsletter more profitable, we should focus on Holden County rather than Plymouth County. First, the residents of Plymouth County are more geographically spread out, which would require us to spend more money per customer delivering the newsletter to them than to the residents of Holden County. Furthermore, a study by a nearby university indicates that Plymouth County residents prefer local news to national news, since they spend 50 percent more time watching local television news broadcasts than national broadcasts. Lastly, because Holden County has a higher average income per resident than Plymouth County, we can expect to make more money delivering newsletters in Holden County than in Plymouth County."*

The assignment itself can take a variety of forms, but is always some variation of one of the four questions:

- What evidence is needed to evaluate the argument?
- What are the assumptions of the argument?
- What questions would we have to ask to determine the argument's feasibility?
- What other plausible explanations could there be other than the proposed explanation?

Each question type will require a slightly different approach to how we use the argument's assumptions. (For a full list of all the Argument Essay topics the GRE will use, see www.ets.org/gre. If you find you still have trouble breaking down arguments, it's a great place to find some real GRE arguments to tackle.) We'll talk about each specific question type in detail a bit later, but for the first part of your essay, it doesn't matter what question they ask. First, we'll have to look at the parts of the argument.

Find the Assumptions

The conclusion is that National Newsletter, Inc.'s home delivery service will be more profitable if they concentrate on Holden County rather than Plymouth County. The premises are as follows: 1) Plymouth residents are spread out so it will cost more to deliver the newsletter to them; 2) a study suggests that Plymouth residents care more about local news because they watch local news programs more than national programs; and 3) Holden residents have more money on average than Plymouth residents.

So far this is not too difficult because the structure of the argument is fairly straightforward. But now comes the important part: spotting assumptions. So let's think about what else must be true for this argument to work, and what implicit facts are being left out. Where is the gap in the reasoning? How might we challenge this argument? What possibilities could we suggest that would cast doubt on the conclusion?

First, we might notice that they're assuming that the higher per-customer cost of delivering to Plymouth County (due to geographical spread) won't be compensated for by higher sales there, or by a slightly higher subscription rate, or by some other factor.

Second, we can point out that the argument assumes that this university study is valid and accurate.

Third, they're assuming that although the residents of Plymouth County may watch more local TV news than national news (according to the study), the residents of Holden County *don't*. (Remember, the argument is making a comparison between two counties, so the claim about Plymouth County's TV news preferences is helpful to the arguments only if Holden County's preferences are different.)

Fourth, the argument assumes that because Plymouth County residents aren't interested in national TV news programs (compared with local programs), they won't be interested in a national newsletter. In other words, it assumes that their television preferences are the same as their newsletter preferences.

Fifth, we can point to the assumption that higher income leads to higher home-delivery subscription sales.

We could probably find a few more if we kept looking, but five assumptions are more than enough to write the Argument essay.

It's also important during this step to think about some concrete counterexamples you can use in your essay to attack the assumptions. Being specific and using concrete details is just as important in the Argument essay as in the Issue essay. It's not enough to just say, "The argument assumes [insert assumption], but maybe that's not true." You have to demonstrate why it might not be true, why it's a bad assumption.

Let's come up with some specific criticisms of the assumptions we identified for this argument.

> **Assumption 1:**   Higher cost of delivery to spread-out people means less profit.
>
> **Why it's a bad assumption:** Because higher costs can be counterbalanced by higher revenue. If they sell more subscriptions, they could make more money. Or maybe they can charge a higher rate because of the extra delivery distance.

Assumption 2: The university study is valid.

Why it's a bad assumption: We have no idea how it was conducted. We don't know that the sample it used was representative of the Plymouth County population. Maybe it surveyed only people who watch television, rather than people who read to get their news.

Assumption 3: The preference for local TV news by Plymouth County residents does not apply to residents of Holden County.

Why it's a bad assumption: Because maybe residents of Holden County also watch 50 percent more local TV news than national TV news. In fact, perhaps they watch 150 percent more local news than national news. Perhaps they don't watch any national news at all.

Assumption 4: The preference of Plymouth County residents for local television news over national television news indicates that they won't want to read a national newsletter.

Why it's a bad assumption: Because people's preferences for written material may be very different from their television preferences. Perhaps people really like seeing local events covered on television, but prefer to read about national events in newspapers and newsletters.

Assumption 5: Higher average income means more sales and more profits.

Why it's a bad assumption: Because we don't know what the difference in income actually is. It could be $5 a year, which would be insignificant. Furthermore, we have no evidence that the newsletter is expensive and therefore more likely to be bought by wealthier people.

Remember, we're not going to write about all of these assumptions. We have to pick only a few of them.

Outline

Choose two or three of the assumptions you listed. Note that you may spot only two or three assumptions in an argument; that's fine. You won't always come up with five assumptions. Out of the assumptions you could find, however, choose whichever ones you want to write about. You may also find that some of your assumptions are very similar to each other; it may be better to treat them as variations on the same assumption, and use that mega-assumption and one other assumption.

Each assumption will be a separate paragraph. Look to see if you can think of any transitions between assumptions to help you order your paragraphs, but if not then just pick whichever assumption you want to write about first. Your outline will probably look like this:

- Introduction
- Assumption #1
- Assumption #2
- Conclusion

If you have time, you may have a third assumption paragraph. After writing a couple Argument Essays, you'll know whether or not you reliably have time to write 2 or 3 body paragraphs. Writing about 3 assumptions is not necessarily better than writing about two, so don't feel as if you must have 3 separate assumptions to get the highest score. It's far more important to have each assumption you found clearly explained than it is to simply list assumptions. Whatever your specific outline, however, stick to it.

Write

The introduction for every Argument question, no matter which type it is, is always basically the same. The introduction will be a variation of "The argument comes to this conclusion, but that may not necessarily be true. We need more information to know for sure."

The body paragraphs, however can change quite a bit depending on what type of question was asked.

- **State the Assumptions.** As you write your body paragraphs, don't simply state the assumptions and leave it at that. After you state each assumption, describe why that assumption may not be valid. Emphasize as much as possible the difference between the argument's premise and conclusion. If possible, use specific counterexamples to show the problems with each assumption.
- **Necessary Evidence.** The evidence we will need to evaluate the argument will be information to tell us whether or not each assumption is valid. For instance, this argument claims that the higher cost of delivery to spread-out people will result in less profit. To know for sure whether or not that's true we're going to need to provide evidence of exactly how much money is lost due to extra mileage in Plymouth County, and how much revenue we can expect to accrue from those residents. Until we know that the extra revenue won't make up for the added mileage costs, we don't know if it's a good or bad idea to expand into Plymouth County.
- **Ask Some Questions.** The questions we ask will be focused on the argument's assumptions. With each question, we need to make it clear why we need to ask that question, and the results the answers could have on the argument's recommendation. For the current argument, we may need to ask if the preference of Plymouth County

residents for local news applies to the residents of Holden County. If the residents of Holden County similarly prefer local news to national news, then we may need to consider an alternate location for our newsletter, or ignore the study in our recommendation since both locations are similarly biased. If the residents of Holden County do not prefer local news, unlike the residents of Plymouth County, then we would need to know if they would still be interested in the national newsletter. If they watch so much national news, would they need our national newsletter, or do they receive all the national news they require from television broadcasts?

- **Other Explanations.** Here we will use our assumptions to see what other conclusions we could get from the initial premises. The initial argument will give a definitive conclusion or explanation, and we need to show that the conclusion is not necessarily correct. Consider the following argument:

  Students from Astoria High School consistently score better on standardized tests than do students from Midtown High School. The school day at Astoria High School is 30 minutes longer than the school day at Midtown High School. Astoria High School's higher test scores can therefore be attributed to its longer school day.

  There are several assumptions in this argument. Two major ones are 1) Astoria High School and Midtown High School are comparable schools and 2) that extra 30 minutes is connected to the test scores. Either assumption gives us a possible alternative explanation. If the two schools are not comparable, for instance if Astoria High School is well-funded whereas Midtown High School is not, or Astoria High School has small classes and Midtown High School has large classes, then the difference in test scores could be due to either of those reasons. (In an actual essay, we'd explain how each difference could result in higher scores in one school and lower schools in the other.)

As with the Issue essay, timing is important. When you have 10 minutes left, start to transition to your conclusion. You don't want to have a great essay marred by the fact that you didn't get to finish it.

Sample Essay

Write a response in which you discuss the stated or unstated assumptions of the argument. Be sure to explain how the argument depends on these assumptions and what the implications are if the assumptions are unsupported.

The argument concludes that in order to increase the profitability of the home delivery service for its national newsletter, National Newsletter, Inc., should concentrate on Holden County rather than Plymouth County. This conclusion is based on the premises that Plymouth County is more geographically spread out than Holden County, that people in Plymouth County watch more local TV news than national TV news, and that Holden County residents have a higher average income than residents of Plymouth County. The reasoning in the argument is logically flawed, however, because it relies on numerous assumptions that appear to be wholly unsupported.

First, the argument assumes that because the residents of Plymouth County are spread out geographically, making delivery more costly, there is less potential for profit. However, higher costs could be compensated for with higher revenues. For example, if more home delivery subscriptions were sold in Plymouth County than Holden County, the revenue from higher sales would lead to more profit. People in Plymouth County may even be more likely to order home delivery precisely because they live in far-out places. Furthermore, Plymouth County residents might be willing to pay a higher subscription rate because of the distance, compensating for the extra cost of delivery. The argument fails to address any of these potential situations.

Second, the argument ignores the possibility that residents of Holden County watch the same amount of local television news as do the residents of Plymouth County. The argument mentions a university study that says Plymouth County residents watch 50 percent more local TV news than national TV news. However, no information is provided about television viewing in Holden County at all. For all we know, everyone in Holden County also watches 50 percent more local TV news than national TV news. In fact, Holden County residents might not watch any national TV news at all. If any of this is true, it would severely weaken the argument.

Finally, the argument fails to take into account that the higher average income of Holden County does not necessarily mean more sales and more profit. We don't even know how much higher the average income is, for one thing. It could be higher by an insignificant amount. Moreover, there's no reason to believe that higher income will lead to more newsletter subscriptions. A newsletter isn't a luxury item like a yacht that can only be afforded by the wealthy.

In conclusion, the argument that focusing on Holden County rather than Plymouth County will make home delivery of the newsletter more profitable is rather weak. If the author demonstrated that higher delivery costs couldn't be balanced with higher revenues, that Holden County residents watch more national news than residents of Plymouth County, and that higher incomes lead to higher subscription sales, the argument would be greatly strengthened. Without this additional support, however, there is no reason to accept the conclusion of the argument.

As was true of the sample Issue essay earlier, this is not a perfect essay. It's not a particularly creative essay, but it gets the job done and would rate a high score on the GRE. Let's look a little closer.

Introduction

The introduction accomplishes a few things. It demonstrates understanding of the argument (and of arguments in general), and it establishes the point of view of the essay very clearly. This introduction follows a very easy template that you can use for your essays.

The argument concludes [paraphrase conclusion]. This conclusion is based on the premises [paraphrase premises]. The reasoning in the argument is logically flawed, however, because it relies on assumptions that appear to be wholly unsupported.

The first two sentences of the introduction demonstrate that you understand the argument and that you understand how arguments work. You're using the jargon of arguments such as "conclusion" and "premises" and later "assumptions." You're not giving your own opinion at all. Instead, you're showing the reader that you understand the task of the Argument essay. The final sentence of the introduction establishes your point of view, which will always be the same: This argument is terrible because of its unsupported assumptions.

Body Paragraphs

The body paragraphs logically follow the introduction and proceed to systematically address major assumptions of the argument and show them to be dubious. Each body paragraph does two things. First, it identifies an assumption, and then, it criticizes that assumption with specific, concrete details and counterexamples.

There are many ways to introduce assumptions. Here are a few good ones.

> The argument assumes [assumption]. However...

> The argument fails to consider that [assumption may be false]. For example...

> The argument ignores the possibility that [assumption may be false]. For example...

> The argument does not take into account that [assumption may be false]. For example...

Notice that the body paragraphs make heavy use of structure words to indicate the overall organization of the essay and the organization of the paragraphs themselves—words like, *first, second, finally, last, furthermore, in addition, moreover, for example.*

Also notice that the body paragraphs use specific details and counterexamples to attack the assumptions. If the assumption is false, then something else must be true, and you should always suggest what that alternative could be. Otherwise your argument will be too abstract and too vague.

Conclusion

As in the Issue essay, the conclusion is really just restating the basic perspective of the introduction. Here it recaps the three assumptions from the point of view of how the argument could be improved. After all, if you're ripping the argument to shreds, it's only polite to suggest ways that the author could begin to fix it. Ultimately, though, your goal is to wrap up the essay with a final restatement of your position and end the whole thing on a conclusive note.

Time Guidelines

You have 30 minutes to write the Argument essay. Here are some guidelines on how to use your time.

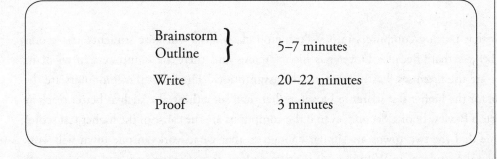

Brainstorm	}	5–7 minutes
Outline		
Write		20–22 minutes
Proof		3 minutes

Again, these are only suggestions. You have to find something that works for you. With practice, you'll become better and faster at producing these essays, so you'll feel less pressed for time.

FINAL THOUGHTS

Now you have the knowledge you need in order to raise your score on the Analytical Writing section. The only thing missing is the experience. Practice writing these essays and you'll find that they become easier and easier. Writing GRE essays is a craft, not an art, and anyone can learn how to do it. Work hard, and when your real test comes you'll finish the first 60 minutes with confidence. Those essays aren't going to hold you back.

ANSWERS AND EXPLANATIONS

Quick Quiz #1

1.   The conclusion is that putting computers into Wilmington classrooms will raise students' test scores. Why should we believe that? Because Dover has higher scores and there are computers in all of its classrooms. Those are the premises. Lastly, what are the assumptions? First, that the computers are the actual explanation for the higher test scores in Dover, rather than something else such as better teachers or access to Princeton Review books. Second, even if the computers are the cause of the higher test scores, you have to assume that the two towns are similar enough so that what works in one town will work in the other. Maybe the students in Wilmington don't know how to use computers and so computers won't help them.

2.   The conclusion is that Tony's Macaroni is the best-tasting brand of mac and cheese in town. The evidence for this conclusion (in other words, the premises) is that it's the best-selling brand at FreshStar supermarket. What are the big assumptions here? One is that the sales at FreshStar are representative of the sales at all other supermarkets in town. Maybe Tony's Macaroni sells very poorly at other stores. (If you were thinking that FreshStar is the only supermarket in town, you were just assuming that. The argument never says it.) The second big assumption is that best sales = best taste. In other words, the argument assumes that Tony's Macaroni sells well because it tastes better than other brands. But that's not necessarily true. Maybe it's just cheaper.

3.   The conclusion is that any product using the food additive will be dangerous for humans. The premise is that it caused cancer in lab rats. The assumptions? Well, for one, they're assuming that humans are like lab rats (kind of like how ETS views you when you're working on the multiple-choice experimental section). More precisely, they're assuming that something that is dangerous to lab rats will also be dangerous to humans—that humans and lab rats are similar in this way. The second assumption is that any product using the additive will use similar quantities to those that were given to the lab rats. After all, if the rats were fed 20 grams of the additive per day, and a typical product for human consumption would use only .05 grams, maybe we shouldn't be as concerned (especially given the difference in body weight between rats and humans).

SAMPLE ESSAYS

The following essays are intended to give you additional exposure to the points that were made in this chapter. They are not models of perfection and are not supposed to be. Despite their flaws, however, they do the important things well enough to receive high scores on the GRE. Remember, reading these essays is not a substitute for practicing writing essays yourself. Ultimately, you're the one who has to sit at the computer and type out two essays—this book can't do it for you. But these essays will help you get a better feel for what the graders are looking for.

Issue Essays

Issue Essay #1

> *A good decision is one that takes into account its future consequences more than its present benefits.*

Write a response in which you agree or disagree with the above statement and explain your reasoning for the position you take. In developing your position, consider situations in which the statement may or may not hold true and explain how these situations shape your decision.

When trying to decide a course of action, it is important to consider both its short-term and long-term consequences. Looking at only one of these factors may lead to sound decisions sometimes, but in other cases will bring on disaster. Some argue that the future ramifications of a decision are more important than whatever present advantages it may have, but that will not always be true. Sometimes, the immediate benefits of a choice are important so that steps should be taken to achieve them even at the cost of future problems. Two examples from history demonstrate that neither present benefits nor future consequences are enough to justify a decision by themselves.

First, consider the compromise that British Prime Minister Neville Chamberlain struck with Nazi Germany. The Munich Compromise was supposed to accomplish "peace in our time," but Hitler soon seized more territory and invaded Poland. Seeking to avoid war is a good thing, and Chamberlain's actions kept Britain out of the war longer than it otherwise would have been. However, all it really did was postpone the day when appeasement would no longer be possible and confrontation would become necessary. In the meantime, Hitler became stronger and solidified his hold over more and more of Europe. Britain would likely have lost far fewer men in the war had it been more willing to sacrifice the short-term benefits of appeasing Hitler for the longer-term necessity of defeating him. In this case, the future costs far outweighed the present advantages.

In contrast, however, sometimes the immediate benefits of a decision are so great that they outweigh future problems. For example, when the U.S. Constitution was being drafted, a controversy arose over how representatives would be apportioned. The Southern states wanted black slaves to be counted for population purposes, because this would give them more representatives in Congress. The Northern states did not want to do this and argued that only free men should be counted. Eventually, the 3/5 compromise was adopted, which determined that a slave would count as three fifths of a free man. Condoning and recognizing slavery in the Constitution led to tremendous problems, culminating 75 years later in the Civil War. However, without that compromise the Constitution would never have been ratified and the states would never have been able to form a unified country. In this situation, the importance of establishing a new country and government was high enough that making such a compromise was necessary. Despite the terrible future consequences that almost destroyed the country, at least there was a country to be preserved.

In conclusion, as the above examples demonstrate, neither the long-term consequences nor the short-term benefits of a decision can determine definitively whether that decision was proper. Rather, it is the relative importance of the benefits and consequences themselves that determine the best course of action. In some situations, the immediate advantages will be great enough to justify future problems. In others, shortsighted decisions will lead to terrible costs down the road. Good decisions must be based on circumstances, not principles alone.

Analysis

The introduction of this essay makes clear that the author believes that the prompt is sometimes true, and sometimes not. The point of view is clear. Furthermore, it gives some general description of why that might be. There are two solid body paragraphs that back up the author's thesis, contrasting the importance of focusing on long-term consequences vs. short-term benefits. The body paragraphs also use concrete, specific examples rather than vague assertions or hypothetical situations. The body paragraphs are well developed, giving the essay depth and length. Finally, the conclusion restates the point of view and ends with a good sentence to give the essay a proper note of closure. This is an example of a well-organized essay that uses only two examples, but uses them well to support its point.

Issue Essay #2

> The arts (music, dance, visual arts) are much less important to students' futures than academic subjects such as math, history, English, and science. The arts should be deemphasized in schools.

Write a response in which you agree or disagree with the above statement and explain your reasoning for the position you take. In developing your position, consider situations in which the statement may or may not hold true and explain how these situations shape your decision.

The question of how to use limited time and resources in schools is a contentious one. Schools are where kids learn the basic skills and knowledge they will need in life, such as reading and math. Schools traditionally are also where kids are exposed to other important aspects of a well-rounded education, such as sports and the arts. Many people believe that academic subjects like history and science are much more important than music, dance, or the visual arts, and therefore that the arts should not receive much emphasis in schools. However, the arts are an important aspect of what gives life beauty and meaning. Depriving kids of exposure to the arts would leave them less able to understand and enjoy one of the primary things that can give their lives satisfaction and purpose.

For example, music education gives a tremendous number of benefits to students. Nearly all students listen to music, but far fewer know much about how it actually works. Studying music gives one a new appreciation for composers and songwriters that enhances the experience of listening to music. Furthermore, studying music gives students the chance to make music themselves, by singing or learning to play an instrument. The ability to play music even gives some students career opportunities, but more often it gives students the opportunity to find a lifelong passion and hobby. The joys of having music in one's life are hard to calculate.

Another reason why the arts should be taught in school is that students will develop skills that are not emphasized in academic subjects. For instance, students that practice drawing and painting develop hand-eye coordination and the ability to translate things from the imagination to the reality of paper. Students that practice dance learn about their own bodies and how to express themselves with body language and gestures. These are all useful skills that are neglected in regular classroom subjects.

Finally, studying the arts taps into students' inborn sense of creativity and stimulates their work in other academic subjects. Someone who studies painting or photography is likely to be able to write in a more visually descriptive way. Someone who has learned about the history of sculpture and tried to make pottery will have a greater appreciation for the history of ancient civilizations and their cultural artifacts. Studying the arts can in fact enhance the study of academic subjects.

In conclusion, it would be a terrible mistake to de-emphasize the arts in schools. While no one can deny that it is important for students to learn math and English and history, ways should be found to teach these subjects better, rather than simply giving them more time at the expense of the arts. Students who get no exposure to the arts in school are likely never to be exposed to them later. Without the arts, their lives will not be as full and fulfilling as they would otherwise have been, and that would be a terrible loss.

Analysis

This essay also shows an author arguing one side of a prompt, but unlike the previous essay, this one disagrees with the prompt. The introduction begins by outlining the problem, pointing out one perspective on the problem, and then clearly rejecting that perspective to argue that the arts are important. We know what the issue is and we know where this author stands. The three body paragraphs use clear transition words (*for example, another reason, finally*) to make the structure and organization obvious. They show three specific ways that the arts are beneficial to students, thus providing solid support to back up the thesis of the essay. The conclusion paragraph reiterates the main point and sums up the author's argument, ending on the right kind of conclusory note.

Issue Essay #3

> *Today's world offers many ways to learn; reading books is no longer necessary to become a well-educated person.*

Write a response in which you agree or disagree with the above statement and explain your reasoning for the position you take. In developing your position, consider situations in which the statement may or may not hold true and explain how these situations shape your decision.

For centuries, books were the primary means of passing on knowledge. There was no television, no radio, no Internet, no study-at-home videotapes. Now that all these things exist, books no longer have a monopoly on information. This leads some to the conclusion that reading books isn't necessary for becoming educated anymore. There is some truth to this. Today, people learn things in other ways and from other sources. However, much of the world's knowledge is still only available in books, and therefore reading them will continue to be an important part of people's education. How important will depend to some degree on what exactly we mean by education.

For example, if we consider an educated person to be one who knows the basic facts of history, then there are many sources for this information outside of books. Much information about world history can be found online and can help a person learn about the basic facts and dates and people that we believe educated people should know. History is also available on CD-ROM encyclopedias. Beyond the computer, there are many historical documentary films that can educate people about the realities of the past. Even some Hollywood movies convey accurate historical information that can properly be called educational.

However, many kinds of information that we feel educated people should know are not available anywhere but in books. Literature is an obvious example. Most people would not consider an education complete if it did not include exposure to some of the world's great literature. Shakespeare and Milton and Dickens and Austen have much to teach us through their stories and characters. And right now, experiencing literature still means reading books. Despite such things as books on tape and e-books, reading books is still the only realistic way for people to become knowledgeable about literature.

Finally, if we believe that being a well-educated person means having some special knowledge about a particular field, then reading books will also be essential. Becoming a lawyer requires reading case books on contracts and evidence in law school. Becoming a doctor requires reading textbooks on anatomy and neurology. Being a scientist requires reading scientific journals to learn about new scientific discoveries. For almost any "major" in college, the information that one would need to study is only available in books, whether you want to study sociology, religion, anthropology, philosophy, or something else.

In conclusion, while there are many sources outside of books for some types of information, many other types of information are still largely restricted to books. Radio, movies, television, the Internet, and other sources of knowledge are certainly places where you can educate yourself, but their scope is limited. Whether the reading of books is truly "necessary" to be a well-educated person will depend on how exactly you define "well-educated," but most people will probably define it in a way that will make the reading of books essential still.

Analysis

This essay is finding truth in both sides of the issue, similar to the way the first essay did, although the introduction shows it to be leaning somewhat toward the claim that reading books will still be necessary. The first body paragraph describes one situation that could support the idea that education can be obtained outside of books, but the second and third suggest two other definitions of education that indicate that books are still necessary. So this essay entertains the thesis of the prompt, but ultimately moves in the direction of rejecting it. Remember, there is no right answer, no correct perspective to take. As long as you support your opinion, your essay will be fine. The conclusion here recaps the points made in the introduction and body paragraphs, which is the main thing it needs to do.

Argument Essays

Argument Essay #1

> *The following is from a state report on safety procedures in various towns.*
>
> *The Peabody health department requires that all mine workers be screened at least once every four months for health problems that may arise from working underground. However, this requirement may be unnecessary and of no benefit to workers. In the town of Orange, the health department has no such requirement, and surveys show that workers are screened on average only once every three years. Not only is the reported number of workers with job-related illnesses lower in Orange, but the number of deaths known to be the result of exposure to harmful agents on the job is half as large. Clearly, increased frequency of health screenings neither prevents illness nor saves lives.*

Write a response in which you discuss the stated or unstated assumptions of the argument. Be sure to explain how the argument depends on these assumptions and what the implications are if the assumptions are unsupported.

The argument concludes that more frequent screenings for job-related health problems don't reduce illness or save lives. The conclusion is based on the premises that although Peabody screens workers every four months and workers in Orange are screened on average every three years, the reported number of sick workers is lower in Orange and the number of deaths is half as much. The argument is not logically persuasive, however, because it relies on numerous shaky assumptions for which no evidence has been given.

First, the argument does not address the possibility that the populations of Peabody and Orange may be very different. The argument claims that half as many people die in Orange from exposure to harmful agents as do in Peabody. But comparisons of absolute numbers are only valid if the populations are similar. For example, say the population of Peabody was 1,000 and 10 people died, while the population of Orange was 100 and 5 people died. Even though twice as many people died in Peabody as in Orange, Peabody's rate was only 1 percent while Orange's rate was 5 percent. The argument fails to address this issue.

Moreover, the argument assumes that the condition of mine workers is identical in Peabody and Orange except for the difference in frequency of screening. However, there are many other potential explanations for the reported differences. Perhaps the mine workers in Orange have better protective equipment, which means they get sick less often. Or perhaps they work in less toxic mines. There could even be differences in screening procedures that account for the differences. No information has been presented to show that other plausible explanations have been ruled out.

Lastly, the argument fails to consider that workers in Orange may be screened more often than the averages suggest. Averages can be deceptive because they are subject to distortion by extreme values. For example, most workers in Orange could be screened every few months, but if there were a minority who refused to be screened at all, and hadn't been screened for, say, 20 years, then the average of once every three years would not truly be representative.

In sum, the argument that frequent screening does not prevent illness or save lives is logically unsound. If the author showed that the populations of Peabody and Orange are similar, that there are no other significant differences between the towns other than the frequency of screening, and that the average frequency of screening in Orange is actually representative, the argument would be much stronger. In the absence of this additional evidence, however, we should be wary about accepting the truth of the argument's conclusion.

Analysis

This essay begins by identifying the conclusion and premises of the argument and taking the position that the argument is flawed because of its shaky assumptions. Remember, this is always our position. The argument is always weak because of its assumptions. Each body paragraph follows the pattern of identifying an assumption made by the argument, and then criticizing that assumption with concrete objections. The argument essay is almost a mechanical exercise once you learn how to find the assumptions, so these essays will sound very much alike. The conclusion restates the main point and recaps the assumptions.

Argument Essay #2

> *A recent study reported that people who own dogs live healthier and longer lives than people who are not dog owners. In particular, people who own dogs have much lower rates of strokes than the general population. Therefore, the city of Weston should create a program that selects dogs from the Weston animal shelter and gives them to stroke patients when they return home to convalesce. Not only will this speed their recovery, but it will save the city money by reducing the number of return visits to the hospital. Furthermore, the stroke patients will tell their friends, which means that more people will become dog owners, reducing the number of people who have strokes in the future.*

Write a response in which you discuss the stated or unstated assumptions of the argument. Be sure to explain how the argument depends on these assumptions and what the implications are if the assumptions are unsupported.

The argument concludes that the city of Weston will save money and reduce the number of people who suffer strokes by creating a program that selects dogs from the local animal shelter and giving them to recently discharged stroke patients as pets. This conclusion is based on the premises that dog owners have lower rates of strokes than the general population does, according to a recent study. The logic of the argument is not convincing, however, because it assumes the truth of many things that have not in fact been demonstrated.

To start with, the argument assumes that dog ownership is in fact the cause of the lower incidence of stroke among dog owners, rather than a mere correlated fact. But noting that people who have dogs also have low rates of stroke does not demonstrate that the former is the cause of the latter. It's quite possible that both of these facts are explained by something the argument does not mention. For example, perhaps energetic people who like to lead active lives are less likely to have strokes because of the exercise they get, and are also more likely to own dogs that they run with and take to the park to play frisbee. If that is the case, then it is the active lifestyle that is the real cause of better health, and giving a dog to an inactive person will do nothing to prevent a stroke.

In addition, the argument assumes that giving dogs to people after they have had strokes will have healing benefits. But the evidence provided by the study does not support that idea. The study says that people who own dogs have lower rates of strokes than most people. It suggests that owning a dog may be a good measure to prevent strokes. But once a person has actually had a stroke, there is no evidence that a dog will help them get better. Brushing your teeth may help prevent cavities, but once you have one, brushing won't do anything to fix it.

Finally, the argument fails to address the possibility that the program will not save money after all. The program itself will cost money to implement and no figures have been presented that show that there will be a net savings to the town of Weston once the program has been put in place. It might turn out to be quite expensive to find the right dog for each stroke patient. The patients might have to be driven to the shelter to see the dogs first. The dogs would have to be transported to their homes. People would have to be hired to make all of this happen. Furthermore, we have no idea how many return visits will be prevented by this program. It could be very few, or even none at all. Without some evidence that allows us to at least estimate these numbers, it's difficult to have any confidence in this claim.

In conclusion, the argument that giving dogs to stroke patients will save money and reduce the number of strokes in Weston is dubious. If the author demonstrated that dog ownership was the actual cause of the lower rate of strokes in dog owners, showed that owning a dog could heal a stroke as well as prevent one, and provided some evidence to back up the claim of saving money, the argument would be substantially stronger. As it currently stands, however, there is little reason to follow its recommendation.

Analysis

The introduction presents the components of the argument and establishes our permanent point of view: The argument is terrible. The first body paragraph identifies a very common assumption, namely that a correlation of two things implies a causal relationship. The second body paragraph criticizes a common unjustified leap of logic and uses a comparison with brushing teeth to make the criticism easier to understand. The third body paragraph addresses a third claim that the argument makes, and gives concrete reasons why that claim might not be true. Finally, the conclusion wraps it all up. The argument has been thoroughly demolished.

Argument Essay #3

> Excelsior Corporation provides subsidized daycare to its employees and is usually ranked among the top 10 companies for employee satisfaction. Excelsior's competitor, Sigma corporation, is hoping to boost its productivity and take some market share from Excelsior. Sigma intends to provide free daycare for its employees as the cornerstone of this strategy. Clearly, Sigma will soon command a bigger piece of market share than Excelsior.

Write a response in which you discuss the stated or unstated assumptions of the argument. Be sure to explain how the argument depends on these assumptions and what the implications are if the assumptions are unsupported.

The argument concludes that Sigma Corporation will soon have a greater share of the market than Excelsior Corporation. The evidence provided for this conclusion is that Excelsior gives subsidized daycare to its employees and is highly ranked in employee satisfaction, and Sigma plans to give its employees free daycare. The argument's logic is faulty, however, since it relies on several unsupported assumptions to bridge the gap between its premises and conclusion.

First of all, the argument does not address the possibility that the high employee satisfaction rating enjoyed by Excelsior is due to factors unrelated to its subsidized daycare. No direct causal relationship has been established between subsidized daycare and employee satisfaction. The author simply mentions the former and assumes a connection to the latter. But the high employee satisfaction rating could be caused by excellent salaries, health benefits, a good working environment, respectful treatment by company management, or a host of other factors. There is no reason to assume that subsidized daycare is the main explanation for employee satisfaction.

Furthermore, the argument fails to take into account that the market share currently possessed by Excelsior may have nothing to do with its high employee satisfaction ranking. We know nothing about Excelsior's business—what it does or how it does it. Excelsior's market share could be caused by patented designs, or excellent branding, or attractive pricing, or exceptional management. Nothing indicates that the satisfaction of the employees is directly responsible for the company's market share, and that Sigma could take some of that market share or boost its productivity by raising the satisfaction level of its employees.

Finally, the argument assumes that giving free daycare to Sigma's employees will increase their level of satisfaction and raise productivity. However, we don't know anything about the current levels of satisfaction of Sigma employees. The employees could be so demoralized by horrible working conditions, low salaries, and other negatives that free daycare won't be nearly enough to satisfy them. Or, alternatively, Sigma's employees might already be extremely satisfied, so much so that adding free daycare won't change things much. Perhaps Sigma is already ranked among the top five companies in employee satisfaction. All of these possibilities remain unexamined by the author.

To sum up, the argument that Sigma will steal market share from Excelsior by giving free daycare to its employees is quite weak. If the author demonstrated that Excelsior's level of employee satisfaction is due to its subsidized daycare, that Excelsior's current market share is caused by the satisfaction of its employees, and that free daycare will raise the level of satisfaction for Sigma employees, the argument would be on much firmer ground. Without additional support, however, there isn't much reason to believe the conclusion.

Analysis

Are you bored yet? Yet again, we have an essay that follows a very clear template. But more important, we have an essay that accomplishes the task, and would receive a high score on the GRE. This is an example of an argument that has a few tricky assumptions because they seem quite natural. For example, you might not have thought at first to criticize the idea that Excelsior's high employee satisfaction is the reason for its current market share, because that idea seems so natural. In other words, you yourself may have made that assumption. It's often difficult to identify the assumptions we ourselves are making. However, this essay did take that into account, and a solid paragraph of criticism resulted. Two other key assumptions were also identified and criticized, and the conclusion ties a bow on the essay, giving it the right tone of completion. Length is good. Transitions and organization are good. Do something similar on your GRE, and you'll score well on the Analytical Writing section.

Chapter 7
Vocabulary

WORDS, WORDS, WORDS

As we mentioned in the Strategies chapter, one of the most important things you need to do to improve your score on the GRE Verbal section is to improve your vocabulary. There is simply no getting around it. It's also very important that you learn the techniques and apply them on the test, but relying on technique alone is like relying on exercise alone to keep you healthy. Exercise is great, but to be as healthy as possible you also have to focus on nutrition and eating the right things. Likewise, think of words as your GRE verbal nutrition. You need a healthy diet of vocabulary as well as good technique to get your maximum score on the Verbal section.

The best way to learn words is to read good books and magazines and newspapers throughout your life. However, since you presumably can't put off the GRE for a few more years while you beef up your reading, we need to find other ways.

Key Terms

The Key Terms List is a tally of about 300 words that appear with great frequency on the GRE. It was compiled by analyzing every written GRE available, as well as dozens of computer-based GREs. This is the first task in your vocabulary preparation: Learn these key terms cold. We have split the list into four groups, and each group of words is followed by quizzes, drills, and some sample questions that make use of those words. Make sure to spend some time learning each group before you tackle the practice material. Use the drills and questions to see how well you've mastered that particular group. When you have the first group down, move on to the second, and so on.

The Key Terms List also appears in our book *Cracking the GRE*, but the drills in this book are slightly different. You can use these drills as extra practice if you already own *Cracking*.

Beyond the Key Terms

The Key Terms List is the beginning, not the end, of your vocabulary workout. Once you've mastered all the words in this list, you should move on to the additional vocabulary lists we've provided. Remember, every new word you learn makes it more likely you'll score higher on the GRE Verbal section. Furthermore, learning vocabulary is the only part of your GRE preparation that is actually useful to you in grad school and in life.

How to Learn New Words

Before we give you the lists, we're going to talk a bit about how to learn words. There are many different ways because everyone is a little different, and what works well for someone else might not work well for you. In the end, you'll have to find the method that helps you the most. However, there are several things that most people find useful. Here are some suggestions.

- **Write them down.** In order to learn words, you have to make them your own. One of the first ways you do that is by writing them and their definitions down, rather than just reading them on a list. Whether you write them in a notebook or on flash cards or on the palm of your hand is your call, but write them down somewhere.

- **Make flash cards.** In addition to the benefits of writing down vocabulary mentioned above, making flash cards helps in several other ways. Most important is that flash cards are very portable. Many people study vocabulary in the same way they study for everything else: Sit down and stare. Those words are rarely going to end up in your long-term memory that way. Instead, focus on spending a little bit of time with each vocabulary word throughout the day. If you look over your words for a couple minutes before your commute, and then again for a couple minutes after your commute, your brain will have been working on those words in the meantime. By working on them again, you're telling your brain "Hey, these words are important! They keep coming up, so you better remember them." We have a set of fantastic flash cards called *Essential GRE Vocabulary* that we recently released. You can purchase them online or at your local bookstore.

- **Connect flash cards and ideas.** Say you're learning words like *panacea* and *nostrum*. A panacea is a cure-all, something that cures everything. A nostrum is a quack medicine that was probably advertised as a panacea, but isn't one. Rather than just keeping those words as abstract concepts, connect them to objects in your life. Tape those flash cards up next to your medicine cabinet. Next time you walk by, your brain will start to connect those words to medicine. If the word *nostrum* made you think of a particular sham medicine ("Order SuperMagnetPills now and receive a MagicBandage for free!"), then draw or cut out a picture of that medicine and paste it to your flash card. If a word makes you think of a particular person, put a picture of that person or write his or her name on that flash card. Give your brain multiple ways of remembering a word. Our Princeton Review flash cards are written this way, to help you memorize the meanings using helpful techniques and tricks.

- **Use a dictionary.** You probably have a dictionary, but you might not have a paperback dictionary that you can carry with you easily. Get one. Or better yet, bookmark an online dictionary if you have a smartphone and you'll have a dictionary with you all the time!

You're much more likely to look up a word and check its definition if you have easy access to a dictionary. A dictionary will also give you secondary meanings of words that you might not have known, as well as information about their history and etymology that may make it easier to remember them.

- **Say them out loud.** This is related to writing them down, because saying them aloud is another way that you make words your own. It also brings another sense into play (hearing) and makes it more likely that you'll remember the meaning of the word. (Just don't say words aloud during your test. The other test takers in the room may hurt you.)

- **Create mnemonic devices.** A mnemonic device is a memory trick that helps you remember something by tying it to a rhyme, story, sentence, song, acronym, or anything that you already know or can remember more easily. A simple example of a mnemonic device that many students are taught is the sentence "Every Good Boy Does Fine," used to remember the notes represented by lines on the treble clef in music. Making a mnemonic is one of the best ways to nail down those words that keep eluding you no matter how many times you seem to read their definitions.

- **Visualize.** Another great way to remember words is to visualize them—to associate them with some image. One of the more creative visualizations we've heard in our classes involved the word *sycophant*, which is someone who attempts to win advancement by flattering influential people—basically, a brownnoser. This student imagined a psychotic elephant putting its trunk into a giant puddle of mud—brownnosing—and then, every time she saw the word *sycophant*, she thought of her "psycho-elephant." We doubt she'll ever forget the meaning of that word.

- **Look at word roots.** You can also help yourself remember words by learning a little bit about their etymology. Many English words have prefixes and suffixes that come from Latin and Greek. So perhaps you remember the word *anachronism* (something out of its proper time, like an automobile showing up in a movie about the eighteenth century) by remembering that *chron* is a root that means time. For example, think of the words *chronology, synchronize, chronic,* and others.

- **Make sentences with them.** One of the hard things about learning words from lists is that the words have no context. Writing down a sentence for each word not only ensures that you understand the definition, but also gives you context for the meaning of the word, which makes it easier to remember. When you make a sentence like, "My grandfather was from a small, bucolic town in Kansas," it's easier to remember that bucolic means "rustic, pastoral, rural."

- **Use them.** Try to incorporate as many new words as you can into your writing and your conversation. Not only will you impress people with your superior command of language (unless they want to smack you for showing off), but you'll also truly be internalizing these words and making them part of your permanent vocabulary. Ultimately, it's through constant reinforcement that you expand your vocabulary.

- **Make it a priority.** This is just one final reminder that in order to increase your vocabulary you have to work at it. If you don't put effort into learning words, don't expect to get results. You'll just be wasting your time. Remember, there is no way to get a high score on the GRE Verbal section without a strong vocabulary, and there is no way to get a huge improvement in your score without expanding your vocabulary.

So, bring on the words!

KEY TERMS GROUP 1

aberrant	adjective	deviating from the norm (noun form: *aberration*)
abscond	verb	to depart clandestinely; to steal off and hide
alacrity	noun	eager and enthusiastic willingness
anomaly	noun	deviation from the normal order, form, or rule; abnormality (adj. form: *anomalous*)
approbation	noun	an expression of approval or praise
arduous	adjective	strenuous; taxing; requiring significant effort
assuage	verb	to ease or lessen; to appease or pacify
audacious	adjective	daring and fearless; recklessly bold (noun form: *audacity*)
austere	adjective	without adornment; bare; severely simple; ascetic (noun form: *austerity*)
axiomatic	adjective	taken as a given; possessing self-evident truth (noun form: *axiom*)
canonical	adjective	following or in agreement with accepted, traditional standards (noun form: *canon*)
capricious	adjective	inclined to change one's mind impulsively; erratic; unpredictable
censure	verb	to criticize severely; to officially rebuke
chicanery	noun	trickery or subterfuge
connoisseur	noun	an informed and astute judge in matters of taste; expert
convoluted	adjective	complex or complicated

More Great Books
Check out *Essential
GRE Vocabulary*—a box
of flashcards from your
besties at The Princeton
Review.

disabuse	verb	to undeceive; to set right
discordant	adjective	conflicting; dissonant or harsh in sound
disparate	adjective	fundamentally distinct or dissimilar
effrontery	noun	extreme boldness; presumptuousness
eloquent	adjective	well-spoken; expressive; articulate (noun form: *eloquence*)
enervate	verb	to weaken; to reduce in vitality
ennui	noun	dissatisfaction and restlessness resulting from boredom or apathy
equivocate	verb	to use ambiguous language with a deceptive intent (adj. form: *equivocal*)
erudite	adjective	very learned; scholarly (noun form: *erudition*)
exculpate	verb	exonerate; to clear of blame
exigent	adjective	urgent; pressing; requiring immediate action or attention
extemporaneous	adjective	improvised; done without preparation
filibuster	noun	intentional obstruction, esp. using prolonged speechmaking to delay legislative action
fulminate	verb	to loudly attack or denounce
ingenuous	adjective	artless; frank and candid; lacking in sophistication
inured	adjective	accustomed to accepting something undesirable
irascible	adjective	easily angered; prone to temperamental outbursts
laud	verb	to praise highly (adj. form: *laudatory*)
lucid	adjective	clear; easily understood
magnanimity	noun	the quality of being generously noble in mind and heart, esp. in forgiving (adj. form: *magnanimous*)
martial	adjective	associated with war and the armed forces
mundane	adjective	of the world; typical of or concerned with the ordinary
nascent	adjective	coming into being; in early developmental stages
nebulous	adjective	vague; cloudy; lacking clearly defined form
neologism	noun	a new word, expression, or usage; the creation or use of new words or senses
noxious	adjective	harmful; injurious
obtuse	adjective	lacking sharpness of intellect; not clear or precise in thought or expression
obviate	verb	to anticipate and make unnecessary
onerous	adjective	troubling; burdensome
paean	noun	a song or hymn of praise and thanksgiving
parody	noun	a humorous imitation intended for ridicule or comic effect, esp. in literature and art

perennial	adjective	recurrent through the year or many years; happening repeatedly
perfidy	noun	intentional breach of faith; treachery (adj. form: *perfidious*)
perfunctory	adjective	cursory; done without care or interest
perspicacious	adjective	acutely perceptive; having keen discernment (noun form: *perspicacity*)
prattle	verb	to babble meaninglessly; to talk in an empty and idle manner
precipitate	adjective	acting with excessive haste or impulse
precipitate	verb	to cause or happen before anticipated or required
predilection	noun	a disposition in favor of something; preference
prescience	noun	foreknowledge of events; knowing of events prior to their occurring (adj. form: *prescient*)
prevaricate	verb	to deliberately avoid the truth; to mislead
qualms	noun	misgivings; reservations; causes for hesitancy
recant	verb	to retract, esp. a previously held belief
refute	verb	to disprove; to successfully argue against
relegate	verb	to forcibly assign, esp. to a lower place or position
reticent	adjective	quiet; reserved; reluctant to express thoughts and feelings
solicitous	adjective	concerned and attentive; eager
sordid	adjective	characterized by filth, grime, or squalor; foul
sporadic	adjective	occurring only occasionally, or in scattered instances
squander	verb	to waste by spending or using irresponsibly
static	adjective	not moving, active, or in motion; at rest
stupefy	verb	to stun, baffle, or amaze
stymie	verb	to block; thwart
synthesis	noun	the combination of parts to make a whole (verb form: *synthesize*)
torque	noun	a force that causes rotation
tortuous	adjective	winding; twisting; excessively complicated
truculent	adjective	fierce and cruel; eager to fight
veracity	noun	truthfulness; honesty
virulent	adjective	extremely harmful or poisonous; bitterly hostile or antagonistic
voracious	adjective	having an insatiable appetite for an activity or pursuit; ravenous
waver	verb	to move to and fro; to sway; to be unsettled in opinion

Quick Quiz #1

Define the following words.

Assuage: _____

_____

Axiomatic: _____

_____

Ennui: _____

_____

Paean: _____

_____

Perspicacious: _____

_____

Voracious: _____

_____

Capricious: _____

_____

Precipitate: _____

_____

Virulent: _____

_____

Prevaricate: _____

_____

Equivocate: _____

_____

Obviate: _____

_____

Tortuous: _____

_____

Laud: _____

_____

Mundane: _____

_____

Quick Quiz #2

Match the following words to their definitions. The answers are on page 239.

A. Aberrant   _____ Urgent; pressing

B. Disabuse   _____ To babble meaninglessly

C. Prescience   _____ Truthfulness; honesty

D. Solicitous   _____ Harmful; injurious

E. Veracity   _____ To undeceive; to set right

F. Audacious   _____ Deviating from the norm

G. Noxious   _____ Misgivings; reservations

H. Qualms   _____ Coming into being

I. Nascent   _____ To stun, baffle, or amaze

J. Enervate   _____ Daring and fearless; recklessly bold

K. Exigent   _____ Foreknowledge of events

L. Prattle   _____ To loudly attack or denounce

M. Fulminate   _____ To weaken; to reduce in vitality

N. Stupefy   _____ Concerned and attentive

Quick Quiz #3

Try the following questions. The answers are on page 239.

Friendly Reminder
For the first three questions here, remember that you should select TWO words that can apply.

1. While health care reform was being debated in the legislature, the opposition repeatedly _____ to filibuster the bill.

   ☐ refused
   ☐ endeavored
   ☐ consented
   ☐ strived
   ☐ declined
   ☐ hesitated

2. Given the lack of popular protest against the strident and polarized character of modern political discourse, observers must ask whether the American people have become _____ to it or are simply apathetic.

   ☐ drawn
   ☐ antipathetic
   ☐ inured
   ☐ habituated
   ☐ averse
   ☐ committed

3. The nation's recent ill-starred series of foreign entanglements, each undertaken on a more tenuous basis than the last, cautioned the president, a voracious acolyte of history's lessons, against the danger of taking _____ action.

   ☐ precipitate
   ☐ prudent
   ☐ deliberate
   ☐ compulsory
   ☐ martial
   ☐ rash

4. The stainless steel fabrication process requires the machinist to be extremely _____; even a measurement off by less than the width of a hair can make the entire project unusable.

   | pristine |
   | tenacious |
   | nice |
   | feckless |
   | perfunctory |

5. Given that *Saturday Night Live* has been on the air since the 1970s, it is unsurprising that it has become somewhat (i) _____. For example, since Dan Aykroyd and Chevy Chase's celebrated impersonations of Presidents Nixon and Ford, respectively, it has become (ii) _____ for the program frequently to feature (iii) _____ of the current president.

Blank (i)	Blank (ii)	Blank (iii)
progressive	anomalous	biographies
temporal	perfunctory	analyses
ossified	superfluous	parodies

6. Altruism is thought by some to be a purely human trait, developed during our evolution as a tribal species. However, studies of other animals (i) _____ this notion. Chimps will adopt orphaned infants, and many species of birds will warn others, at the risk of exposing themselves, when a predator approaches the flock. These displays of animal altruism (ii) _____ that animals other than humans also evolved to exhibit this trait.

Blank (i)	Blank (ii)
belie	assuage
confirm	intimate
promote	rescind

7. Books on statistics frequently use the (i) _____ paradox between attitudes about flying and driving as evidence of the public's (ii) _____ understanding of probability. Even though fliers have a much lower risk of injury or death than drivers, people consistently attest to having fewer (iii) _____ about driving than flying.

Blank (i)	Blank (ii)	Blank (iii)
variegated	nebulous	disputes
ostensible	nefarious	antitheses
sibilant	obligatory	qualms

8. During the series between the Hawks and the Bears, the Bears' coach wrongly accused Archer, the Hawks' star player, of using (i) _____ performance enhancing drugs. At the inquiry, despite Archer's eloquent (ii) _____ of his innocence, the tribunal chose to censure him as punishment. A few months later however, Archer was (iii) _____ when another player from the Bears confessed his coach's perfidy.

Blank (i)	Blank (ii)	Blank (iii)
deleterious	attestation	consternated
illicit	repudiation	habituated
irregular	abridgement	exculpated

9. Poverty can be a function not only of absolute wealth, but also of comparison in a community; in an area with _____ income levels, those at the very bottom will suffer cost-of-living increases brought on by those in the middle and top income brackets.

disparate
reticent
arduous
onerous
wavering

10. Though Adam was incredulous upon hearing Madam Sofia's psychic reading, after a few weeks had passed, he was (i) _____ by how remarkably (ii) _____ she had turned out to be.

Blank (i)	Blank (ii)
dubious	prescient
stupefied	exhaustive
blasé	mundane

KEY TERMS GROUP 2

abate	verb	to lessen in intensity or degree
accolade	noun	an expression of praise
adulation	noun	excessive praise; intense adoration
aesthetic	adjective	dealing with, appreciative of, or responsive to art or the beautiful
ameliorate	verb	to make better or more tolerable
ascetic	noun	one who practices rigid self-denial, esp. as an act of religious devotion
avarice	noun	greed, esp. for wealth (adj. form: *avaricious*)
axiom	noun	a universally recognized principle (adj. form; *axiomatic*)
bucolic	adjective	rustic and pastoral; characteristic of rural areas and their inhabitants
burgeon	verb	to grow rapidly or flourish
cacophony	noun	harsh, jarring, discordant sound; dissonance (adj. form: *cacophonous*)
canon	noun	an established set of principles or code of laws, often religious in nature (adj. form: *canonical*)
castigation	noun	severe criticism or punishment (verb form: *castigate*)
catalyst	noun	a substance that accelerates the rate of a chemical reaction without itself changing; a person or thing that causes change
caustic	adjective	burning or stinging; causing corrosion
chary	adjective	wary; cautious; sparing
cogent	adjective	appealing forcibly to the mind or reason; convincing
complaisance	noun	the willingness to comply with the wishes of others (adj. form: *complaisant*)
contentious	adjective	argumentative; quarrelsome; causing controversy or disagreement
contrite	adjective	regretful; penitent; seeking forgiveness (noun form: *contrition*)
culpable	adjective	deserving blame (noun form: *culpability*)
cupidity	noun	eager or excessive desire to possess something; greed; avarice
dearth	noun	smallness of quantity or number; scarcity; a lack
demur	verb	to question or oppose
didactic	adjective	intended to teach or instruct
discretion	noun	cautious reserve in speech; ability to make responsible decisions (adj. form: *discreet*)

disinterested	adjective	free of bias or self-interest; impartial
dogmatic	adjective	expressing a rigid opinion based on unproved or unprovable principles (noun form: *dogma*)
ebullience	adjective	the quality of lively or enthusiastic expression of thoughts and feelings (adj. form: *ebullient*)
eclectic	adjective	composed of elements drawn from various sources
elegy	noun	a mournful poem, esp. one lamenting the dead (adj. form: *elegiac*)
emollient	adjective/ noun	soothing, esp. to the skin; making less harsh; mollifying; an agent that softens or smoothes the skin
empirical	adjective	based on observation or experiment
enigmatic	adjective	mysterious; obscure; difficult to understand (noun form: *enigma*)
ephemeral	adjective	brief; fleeting
esoteric	adjective	intended for or understood by a small, specific group
eulogy	noun	a speech honoring the dead (verb form: *eulogize*)
exonerate	verb	to remove blame
facetious	adjective	playful; humorous
fallacy	noun	an invalid or incorrect notion; a mistaken belief (adj. form: *fallacious*)
furtive	adjective	marked by stealth; covert; surreptitious
gregarious	adjective	sociable; outgoing; enjoying the company of other people
harangue	verb/noun	to deliver a pompous speech or tirade; a long, pompous speech
heretical	adjective	violating accepted dogma or convention (noun form: *heresy*)
hyperbole	noun	an exaggerated statement, often used as a figure of speech (adj. form: *hyperbolic*)
impecunious	adjective	lacking funds; without money
incipient	adjective	beginning to come into being or to become apparent
inert	adjective	unmoving; lethargic; sluggish
innocuous	adjective	harmless; causing no damage
intransigent	adjective	refusing to compromise (noun form: *intransigence*)
inveigle	verb	to obtain by deception or flattery
morose	adjective	sad; sullen; melancholy
odious	adjective	evoking intense aversion or dislike
opaque	adjective	impenetrable by light; not reflecting light
oscillation	noun	the act or state of swinging back and forth with a steady, uninterrupted rhythm (verb form: *oscillate*)

penurious	adjective	penny-pinching; excessively thrifty; ungenerous
pernicious	adjective	extremely harmful; potentially causing death
peruse	verb	to examine with great care (noun form: *perusal*)
pious	adjective	extremely reverent or devout; showing strong religious devotion (noun form: *piety*)
precursor	noun	one that precedes and indicates or announces another
preen	verb	to dress up; to primp; to groom oneself with elaborate care
prodigious	adjective	abundant in size, force, or extent; extraordinary
prolific	adjective	producing large volumes or amounts; productive
putrefy	verb	to rot; to decay and give off a foul odor (adj. form: *putrid*)
quaff	verb	to drink deeply
quiescence	noun	stillness; motionlessness; quality of being at rest (adj. form: *quiescent*)
redoubtable	adjective	awe-inspiring; worthy of honor
sanction	noun/verb	authoritative permission or approval; a penalty intended to enforce compliance; to give permission or authority to
satire	noun	a literary work that ridicules or criticizes a human vice through humor or derision (adj. form: *satirical*)
squalid	adjective	sordid; wretched and dirty as from neglect (noun form: *squalor*)
stoic	adjective	indifferent to or unaffected by pleasure or pain; steadfast (noun form: *stoicism*)
supplant	verb	to take the place of; supersede
torpid	adjective	lethargic; sluggish; dormant (noun form: *torpor*)
ubiquitous	adjective	existing everywhere at the same time; constantly encountered; widespread
urbane	adjective	sophisticated; refined; elegant (noun form: *urbanity*)
vilify	verb	to defame; to characterize harshly
viscous	adjective	thick; sticky (noun form: *viscosity*)

Quick Quiz #4

Define the following words.

Pernicious: _____

_____

Eulogy: _____

_____

Aesthetic: _____

_____

Castigation: _____

_____

Prodigious: _____

_____

Penurious: _____

_____

Satire: _____

_____

Ebullience: _____

_____

Incipient: _____

_____

Penurious: _____

_____

Quaff: _____

_____

Emollient: _____

_____

Harangue: _____

_____

Inveigle: _____

_____

Facetious: _____

_____

Caustic: _____

_____

Cogent: _____

_____

Quick Quiz #5

Match the following words to their definitions. The answers are on page 239.

A.	Pious	_____ Drawn from different sources or styles
B.	Intransigent	_____ Evoking intense aversion or dislike
C.	Torpid	_____ To examine with great care
D.	Eclectic	_____ To defame; to characterize harshly
E.	Heretical	_____ Unwilling to compromise
F.	Peruse	_____ Impenetrable by light
G.	Culpable	_____ Lethargic; sluggish
H.	Ascetic	_____ Extremely reverent or devout
I.	Enigmatic	_____ Argumentative; quarrelsome
J.	Supplant	_____ Mysterious; obscure
K.	Opaque	_____ Deserving blame
L.	Odious	_____ One who practices rigid self-denial
M.	Vilify	_____ Violating accepted dogma or convention
N.	Contentious	_____ To take the place of

Try the following questions. The answers are on page 239.

Try the following questions. The answers are on page 239.

Another Friendly Reminder

You know what we're going to say, don't you? Remember to select TWO answer choices for questions 1, 2, and 3 here.

1. The two colleagues made a concerted effort to steer clear of the ongoing argument between their respective supervisors, preferring instead to continue their _____ until the hearing.

   ☐ neutrality
   ☐ stoicism
   ☐ cynicism
   ☐ skepticism
   ☐ disinterest
   ☐ disagreement

2. Roger's personality was described by all of his literary critics as _____, but this description was widely regarded as hyperbole by those who knew him well and ultimately came to appreciate his even-handed and flexible approach to his analyses.

   ☐ pernicious
   ☐ facetious
   ☐ doctrinaire
   ☐ dogmatic
   ☐ sarcastic
   ☐ didactic

3. The naked _____ endemic in our corporate culture was well documented in the criminal trial of the CEO, who confessed to embezzling employee retirement funds in order to purchase his third Italian villa.

   ☐ opprobrium
   ☐ magnanimity
   ☐ avarice
   ☐ altruism
   ☐ cupidity
   ☐ conservatism

4. The retiree's testimonial dinner was a great mixture of (i) _____ that highlighted his many accomplishments as well as some good-natured (ii) _____ that caused everyone to break into laughter.

Blank (i)	Blank (ii)
insults	gravity
accolades	malevolence
inquiries	satire

5. Considering the (i) _____ upbringing he sings about in his ferociously bitter lyrics, it was a total surprise to his fans that Randy's autobiography had such a(n) (ii) _____ tone when describing his childhood.

Blank (i)	Blank (ii)
wretched	unhappy
substantial	innocuous
successful	troubled

6. For some, the power of omens and signs is easy to dismiss as (i) _____ belief, based on (ii) _____ evidence, that the future can be foretold by specific, unrelated events. For others, though, those same omens and signs are clear and reliable markers of (iii) _____ events.

Blank (i)	Blank (ii)	Blank (iii)
a dogmatic	empirical	incipient
an irrational	substantiated	hypothetical
a heretical	circumstantial	erroneous

7. The hostilities between the party's candidates began to (i) _____ once the primary election was over and they no longer had any reason to (ii) _____ each other in their intense fight for the nomination.

Blank (i)	Blank (ii)
reconvene	champion for
escalate	abrogate
abate	vilify

8. At every single public event, the country legend appeared in his (i) _____ boots and cowboy hat. However, those who knew him personally could attest to the fact that his fashion sense was a bit more (ii) _____, with items in his closet ranging from a (iii) _____ old sports jersey to brand-new, hand-tailored suits.

Blank (i)	Blank (ii)	Blank (iii)
customary	garish	bedraggled
profound	staid	pristine
stereotypical	eclectic	imposing

9. After failing to advance to the final round of the state spelling bee for the third year in a row, Heather's mood could only be described as _____.

morose
chary
contrite
impecunious
detestable

10. The success of the espionage mission depended on the ability of the mole to feign (i) _____ in order to ingratiate herself within the company ranks. Otherwise, all the mission plans would be compromised and the spies would have to (ii) _____ the mission.

Blank (i)	Blank (ii)
nescience	actualize
irascibility	truncate
complaisance	execute

KEY TERMS GROUP 3

acumen	noun	keen, accurate judgment or insight
adulterate	verb	to reduce purity by combining with inferior ingredients
amalgamate	verb	to combine several elements into a whole (noun form: *amalgamation*)
archaic	adjective	outdated; associated with an earlier, perhaps more primitive, time
aver	verb	to state as a fact; to declare or assert
bolster	verb	to provide support or reinforcement
bombastic	adjective	pompous; grandiloquent (noun form: *bombast*)
diatribe	noun	a harsh denunciation
dissemble	verb	to disguise or conceal; to mislead
eccentric	adjective	departing from norms or conventions
endemic	adjective	characteristic of or often found in a particular locality, region, or people
evanescent	adjective	tending to disappear like vapor; vanishing
exacerbate	verb	to make worse or more severe
fervent	adjective	greatly emotional or zealous (noun form: *fervor*)
fortuitous	adjective	happening by accident or chance
germane	adjective	relevant to the subject at hand; appropriate in subject matter
grandiloquence	noun	pompous speech or expression (adj. form: *grandiloquent*)
hackneyed	adjective	rendered trite or commonplace by frequent usage
halcyon	adjective	calm and peaceful
hedonism	noun	devotion to pleasurable pursuits, esp. to the pleasures of the senses (a *hedonist* is someone who pursues pleasure)
hegemony	noun	the consistent dominance of one state or ideology over others
iconoclast	noun	one who attacks or undermines traditional conventions or institutions
idolatrous	adjective	given to intense or excessive devotion to something (noun form: *idolatry*)
impassive	adjective	revealing no emotion
imperturbable	adjective	marked by extreme calm, impassivity, and steadiness
implacable	adjective	not capable of being appeased or significantly changed
impunity	noun	immunity from punishment or penalty

inchoate	adjective	in an initial stage; not fully formed
infelicitous	adjective	unfortunate; inappropriate
insipid	adjective	without taste or flavor; lacking in spirit; bland
loquacious	adjective	extremely talkative (noun form: *loquacity*)
luminous	adjective	characterized by brightness and the emission of light
malevolent	adjective	having or showing often vicious ill will, spite, or hatred (noun form: *malevolence*)
malleable	adjective	capable of being shaped or formed; tractable; pliable
mendacity	noun	the condition of being untruthful; dishonesty (adj. form: *mendacious*)
meticulous	adjective	characterized by extreme care and precision; attentive to detail
misanthrope	noun	one who hates all other humans (adj. form: *misanthropic*)
mitigate	verb	to make or become less severe or intense; to moderate
obdurate	adjective	unyielding; hardhearted; intractable
obsequious	adjective	exhibiting a fawning attentiveness
occlude	verb	to obstruct or block
opprobrium	noun	disgrace; contempt; scorn
pedagogy	noun	the profession or principles of teaching, or instructing
pedantic	adjective	the parading of learning; excessive attention to minutiae and formal rules
penury	noun	poverty; destitution
pervasive	adjective	having the tendency to permeate or spread throughout
pine	verb	to yearn intensely; to languish; to lose vigor
pirate	verb	to illegally use or reproduce
pith	noun	the essential or central part
pithy	adjective	precise and brief
placate	verb	to appease; to calm by making concessions
platitude	noun	a superficial remark, esp. one offered as meaningful
plummet	verb	to plunge or drop straight down
polemical	adjective	controversial; argumentative
prodigal	adjective	recklessly wasteful; extravagant; profuse; lavish
profuse	adjective	given or coming forth abundantly; extravagant
proliferate	verb	to grow or increase swiftly and abundantly
queries	noun	questions; inquiries; doubts in the mind; reservations
querulous	adjective	prone to complaining or grumbling; peevish
rancorous	adjective	characterized by bitter, long-lasting resentment (noun form: *rancor*)

recalcitrant	adjective	obstinately defiant of authority; difficult to manage
repudiate	verb	to refuse to have anything to do with; disown
rescind	verb	to invalidate; to repeal; to retract
reverent	adjective	marked by, feeling, or expressing a feeling of profound awe and respect (noun form: *reverance*)
rhetoric	noun	the art or study of effective use of language for communication and persuasion
salubrious	adjective	promoting health or well-being
solvent	adjective	able to meet financial obligations; able to dissolve another substance
specious	adjective	seeming true, but actually being fallacious; misleadingly attractive; plausible but false
spurious	adjective	lacking authenticity or validity; false; counterfeit
subpoena	noun	a court order requiring appearance and/or testimony
succinct	adjective	brief; concise
superfluous	adjective	exceeding what is sufficient or necessary
surfeit	noun/verb	an overabundant supply; excess; to feed or supply to excess
tenacity	noun	the quality of adherence or persistence to something valued; persistent determination (adj. form: *tenacious*)
tenuous	adjective	having little substance or strength; flimsy; weak
tirade	noun	a long and extremely critical speech; a harsh denunciation
transient	adjective	fleeting; passing quickly; brief
zealous	adjective	fervent; ardent; impassioned; devoted to a cause (a *zealot* is a zealous person)

Quick Quiz #7

Define the following words.

Tirade: _____

_____

Solvent: _____

_____

Idolatrous: _____

_____

Opprobrium: _____

_____

Obsequious: _____

_____

Luminous: _____

_____

Tenuous: _____

_____

Reverent: _____

_____

Iconoclast: _____

_____

Fervent: _____

_____

Amalgamate: _____

_____

Repudiate: _____

_____

Specious: _____

_____

Pervasive: _____

_____

Surfeit: _____

_____

Hedonism: _____

_____

Quick Quiz #8

Match the following words to their definitions. The answers are on page 240.

A. Zealous

B. Malleable

C. Grandiloquence

D. Proliferate

E. Evanescent

F. Impassive

G. Misanthrope

H. Tenacity

I. Spurious

J. Pith

K. Querulous

L. Specious

M. Polemical

N. Succinct

_____ The essential or central part

_____ Tending to disappear like vapor

_____ Brief; concise

_____ Controversial; argumentative

_____ Lacking authenticity; false; counterfeit

_____ Capable of being shaped or formed

_____ Fervent; ardent; devoted to a cause

_____ Persistent determination

_____ One who hates other human beings

_____ Revealing no emotion

_____ Pompous speech or expression

_____ To grow or increase swiftly

_____ Prone to complaining; whiny

_____ Seemingly true, but actually false

Quick Quiz #9

Try the following questions. The answers are on page 240.

Last Reminder
By now, you know what to do on questions 1, 2, 3.

1. After months of speculation drove it upward, the pharmaceutical company's stock price _____ upon news that its experimental drug did not receive governmental approval.

   ☐ stymied
   ☐ assuaged
   ☐ plummeted
   ☐ rebounded
   ☐ retreated
   ☐ ascended

2. The researcher's colleagues marveled at how he could review income tax law in such a _____ manner at work, yet complete his own tax return in such a careless way at home.

   ☐ meticulous
   ☐ plodding
   ☐ unhurried
   ☐ lackadaisical
   ☐ painstaking
   ☐ efficient

3. Faced with a(n) _____ of subpar therapy choices, the doctor consulted a colleague, who, once she had reviewed all patient records and available research on the subject, helped the doctor wade through the multitude of options and actually suggested a course of action the doctor had not considered.

   ☐ dearth
   ☐ potpourri
   ☐ exiguousness
   ☐ confusion
   ☐ surfeit
   ☐ overabundance

4. The Pashupatinath temple in Nepal contains the most frequently used cremation site in the Kathmandu Valley. Among its attractions are a two-tiered pagoda where the (i) _____ are able to worship. Images of Ganesh, with his huge trunk and regal bearing, (ii) _____ the walls. The temple is not accessible to non-Hindus, but an excellent (iii) _____ can be seen from the opposite riverbank.

Blank (i)	Blank (ii)	Blank (iii)
fortuitous	adorn	vista
reverent	placate	paragon
luminous	bolster	zenith

5. Many car rental companies will not rent vehicles to customers under the age of 25, claiming that these drivers have higher than average rates of accidents, rendering the risk of loss too great. This argument, however, is (i) _____; senior citizens also have higher than average rates of accidents, and yet their rental privileges are not (ii) _____.

Blank (i)	Blank (ii)
eccentric	adulterated
pedantic	restricted
spurious	dissembled

6. It is ironic that Mary Shelley's focus on Victor's passivity renders the reader incapable of sympathizing with the protagonist, much as Dostoyevsky's depiction of the darkest places in the human psyche once caused his empathy for his characters to be _____.

rescinded
commiserated
occluded
disregarded
lambasted

7. Although Marian thought that the oft-repeated tale was (i) _____, Barbara never tired of telling the story, believing that the lessons it contained were timeless and (ii) _____.

Blank (i)	Blank (ii)
hackneyed	archaic
inchoate	immutable
substantial	evanescent

8. While some in the field of psychology believe that intelligence is a purely genetic trait, and that any new research will demonstrate this fact, the current research on the nature versus nurture debate is by no means (i) _____. Studies on race, environment, and other factors have shown that heredity and the environment one grows up in affect intelligence. One's intelligence can be (ii) _____ by a strongly enriching environment, or neglected by an extremely impoverished one. Studies on genetics are also not decisive; there is not one single "intelligence gene," but more likely there is a (iii) _____ of different genetic markers.

Blank (i)	Blank (ii)	Blank (iii)
incipient	exscinded	maladaptive liturgy
incontrovertible	cultivated	refulgent sojourn
indeterminate	descanted	complicated amalgam

9. Ellen and Suzanne had not planned to have lunch together on Friday, and thus running into each other at the sushi restaurant was simply _____ occurrence.

an infelicitous
a fortuitous
a profuse
a transient
a suggestive

10. Many critics of Vice President Al Gore point to the (i) _____ claim that he "invented the Internet" in an attempt to discredit him. While, at face value, it seems doubtful that a politician could be responsible for a technological breakthrough, an argument can be made that Gore, as an early champion of the power of technology to drive political change, helped create the vision of a world with high-speed computing and communications. In 1991, he crafted the *High Performance and Computing Act* which led to the development of the National Information Infrastructure, which was (ii) _____ the later telecommunications web which came to be called the Internet.

Blank (i)	Blank (ii)
dubious	an alternative to
indefatigable	a precursor to
guileless	a surrogate for

KEY TERMS GROUP 4

acerbic	adjective	having a sour or bitter taste or character; sharp; biting
aggrandize	verb	to increase in intensity, power, influence, or prestige
alchemy	noun	a medieval science aimed at the transmutation of metals, esp. base metals into gold (an *alchemist* is one who practices alchemy)
amenable	adjective	agreeable; responsive to suggestion
anachronism	noun	something or someone out of place in terms of historical or chronological context
astringent	adjective/noun	having a tightening effect on living tissue; harsh; severe; an astringent agent or substance
bombast	noun	self-important or pompous writing or speech (adj. form: *bombastic*)
contiguous	adjective	sharing a border; touching; adjacent
convention	noun	a generally agreed-upon practice or attitude
credulous	adjective	tending to believe too readily; gullible (noun form: *credulity*)
cynicism	noun	an attitude or quality of belief that all people are motivated by selfishness (adj. form: *cynical*)
decorum	noun	polite or appropriate conduct or behavior (adj. form: *decorous*)
derision	noun	scorn; ridicule; contemptuous treatment (adj. form: *derisive*; verb form: *deride*)
desiccate	verb	to dry out or dehydrate; to make dry or dull
dilettante	noun	one with an amateurish or superficial interest in the arts or a branch of knowledge
disparage	verb	to slight or belittle
divulge	verb	to disclose something secret
fawn	verb	to flatter or praise excessively
flout	verb	to show contempt for, as in a rule or convention
garrulous	adjective	pointlessly talkative, talking too much
glib	adjective	marked by ease or informality; nonchalant; lacking in depth; superficial
hubris	noun	overbearing presumption or pride; arrogance
imminent	adjective	about to happen; impending
immutable	adjective	not capable of change

impetuous	adjective	hastily or rashly energetic; impulsive and vehement
indifferent	adjective	having no interest or concern; showing no bias or prejudice
inimical	adjective	damaging; harmful; injurious
intractable	adjective	not easily managed or directed; stubborn; obstinate
intrepid	adjective	steadfast and courageous
laconic	adjective	using few words; terse
maverick	noun	an independent individual who does not go along with a group or party
mercurial	adjective	characterized by rapid and unpredictable change in mood
mollify	verb	to calm or soothe; to reduce in emotional intensity
neophyte	noun	a recent convert; a beginner; novice
obfuscate	verb	to deliberately obscure; to make confusing
obstinate	adjective	stubborn; hardheaded; uncompromising
ostentatious	adjective	characterized by or given to pretentious display; showy
pervade	verb	to permeate throughout (adj. form: *pervasive*)
phlegmatic	adjective	calm; sluggish; unemotional
plethora	noun	an overabundance; a surplus
pragmatic	adjective	practical rather than idealistic
presumptuous	adjective	overstepping due bounds (as of propriety or courtesy); taking liberties
pristine	adjective	pure; uncorrupted; clean
probity	noun	adherence to highest principles; complete and confirmed integrity; uprightness
proclivity	noun	a natural predisposition or inclination
profligate	adjective	excessively wasteful; recklessly extravagant (noun form: *profligacy*)
propensity	noun	a natural inclination or tendency, penchant
prosaic	adjective	dull; lacking in spirit or imagination
pungent	adjective	characterized by a strong, sharp smell or taste
quixotic	adjective	foolishly impractical; marked by lofty romantic ideals
quotidian	adjective	occurring or recurring daily; commonplace
rarefy	verb	to make or become thin, less dense; to refine

recondite	adjective	hidden; concealed; difficult to understand; obscure
refulgent	adjective	radiant; shiny; brilliant
renege	verb	to fail to honor a commitment; to go back on a promise
sedulous	adjective	diligent; persistent; hardworking
shard	noun	a piece of broken pottery or glass
soporific	adjective	causing drowsiness; tending to induce sleep
sparse	adjective	thin; not dense; arranged at widely spaced intervals
spendthrift	noun	one who spends money wastefully
subtle	adjective	not obvious; elusive; difficult to discern
tacit	adjective	implied; not explicitly stated
terse	adjective	brief and concise in wording
tout	verb	to publicly praise or promote
trenchant	adjective	sharply perceptive; keen; penetrating
unfeigned	adjective	genuine; not false or hypocritical
untenable	adjective	indefensible; not viable; uninhabitable
vacillate	verb	to waver indecisively between one course of action or opinion and another; waver
variegated	adjective	multicolored; characterized by a variety of patches of different color
vexation	noun	annoyance; irritation (noun form: *vex*)
vigilant	adjective	alertly watchful (noun form: *vigilance*)
vituperate	verb	to use harsh condemnatory language; to abuse or censure severely or abusively; berate
volatile	adjective	readily changing to a vapor; changeable; fickle; explosive (noun form: *volatility*)

Quick Quiz #10

Define the following words.

Soporific: _____

_____

Rarefy: _____

_____

Ostentatious: _____

_____

Variegated: _____

_____

Unfeigned: _____

_____

Terse: _____

_____

Glib: _____

_____

Disparage: _____

_____

Cynicism: _____

_____

Contiguous: _____

_____

Neophyte: _____

_____

Mercurial: _____

_____

Flout: _____

_____

Volatile: _____

_____

Phlegmatic: _____

_____

Mollify: _____

_____

Vexation : _____

_____

Quick Quiz #11

Match the following words to their definitions. The answers are on page 240.

A. Obstinate   _____ To go back on a promise

B. Sedulous   _____ Using few words; terse

C. Pungent   _____ One who spends money wastefully

D. Fawn   _____ To dry out or dehydrate

E. Vigilant   _____ An overabundance; a surplus

F. Shard   _____ Stubborn; uncompromising

G. Trenchant   _____ Alertly watchful

H. Desiccate   _____ Characterized by a strong, sharp smell

I. Spendthrift   _____ To flatter or praise excessively

J. Laconic   _____ To permeate throughout

K. Plethora   _____ Excessively wasteful

L. Renege   _____ A piece of broken pottery or glass

M. Profligate   _____ Diligent; hardworking; persistent

N. Pervade   _____ Sharply perceptive; keen; penetrating

Quick Quiz #12

Try the following questions. The answers are on page 240.

1. Because the agreement between the two dueling factions was _____, rather than formal, it was more easily broken.

   ☐ tacit
   ☐ contentious
   ☐ terse
   ☐ volatile
   ☐ implied
   ☐ trivial

2. When my niece came to visit New York City for a weekend, she was in awe of the _____ sights and sounds that I, as a lifelong New Yorker, rarely even notice.

   ☐ quotidian
   ☐ eccentric
   ☐ pragmatic
   ☐ untenable
   ☐ garrulous

3. While the poet believed that his recent choice of _____ themes indicated a maturation of his work, the critics lambasted the lack of whimsical subject matter that they had become accustomed to in his verses.

   ☐ lyrical
   ☐ laconic
   ☐ quotidian
   ☐ pragmatic
   ☐ quixotic
   ☐ metaphorical

4. Haile Selassie, the Emperor of Ethiopia for most of the twentieth century, blamed the rise of evil on the _____ of people who, because they had never seen the country firsthand, showed no concern for the plight of the downtrodden.

approbation
cognizance
indifference
corruption
vileness

5. It is only because the towns along the river's shore are (i) _____ populated, and therefore generate little pollution, that the river's waters can remain so (ii) _____.

Blank (i)	Blank (ii)
contiguously	pristine
substantially	adulterated
sparsely	hastily

6. A successful moderator must have a soothing personality; (i) _____ any offended parties is an important part of his responsibilities, and (ii) _____ manners will only succeed in exacerbating his clients' indignation.

Blank (i)	Blank (ii)
mollifying	amenable
touting	credulous
coveting	crass

7. The (i) _____ adoration the collectors felt for the current gallery display was evident in the number of paintings purchased, despite the (ii) _____ cost of each piece.

Blank (i)	Blank (ii)
phony	exorbitant
phlegmatic	spendthrift
unfeigned	tawdry

8. The debate between nature and nurture in determining personality traits is a long–standing one. A (i) _____ in the psychology profession may readily defend one particular side of the argument, but the more (ii) _____ professional will acknowledge that there are too many undecided factors, the existence of which precludes taking a firm stance on this (iii) _____ issue.

Blank (i)	Blank (ii)	Blank (iii)
maverick	fledgling	enduring
scholar	cynical	subtle
neophyte	seasoned	transitory

9. Taking a few art classes had convinced Elaine that she was an expert in sculpture, but the museum curators viewed her instead as a mere _____.

bystander
fraud
dilettante
anachronism
maverick

10. The (i) _____ nature of the protagonist is clearly developed in the first few chapters of the book and contributes to the vacillating emotions the author hopes to evince in his readers. The decisions the principal character makes in later chapters, though, are more fitting of a (ii) _____ personality.

Blank (i)	Blank (ii)
exaggerated	bombastic
mercurial	steadfast
glib	acerbic

EXTRA VOCABULARY

The 300 or so words on the Key Terms List are the most important part of your vocabulary building, but they shouldn't be the end. After you've mastered those, learn as many more words as you can. For you hardcore vocabulary students, here are another 200 good GRE words that you should study. Once you've learned them, test yourself with the exercises at the end. Remember, every new word you learn makes it more likely you'll score well on the GRE Verbal section. So keep it up!

abash	verb	to make ashamed; to embarrass
abject	adjective	hopeless; extremely sad and servile; defeated
abnegate	verb	to deny oneself things; to reject; to renounce
abrogate	verb	to abolish or repeal formally; to set aside; to nullify
abstemious	adjective	sparing or moderate, especially in eating and drinking
abstruse	adjective	hard to understand or grasp
abysmal	adjective	extremely hopeless or wretched; bottomless
accede	verb	to give in; to yield; to agree
accrete	verb	to increase by growth or addition
adduce	verb	to bring forward as an example or as proof; to cite
adroit	adjective	skillful; dexterous; clever; socially at ease
advent	noun	arrival; coming; beginning
affable	adjective	easy to talk to; friendly
affectation	noun	unnatural or artificial behavior, usually intended to impress
aggregate	noun	sum total; a collection of separate things mixed together
aghast	adjective	terrified; shocked
allege	verb	to assert without proof
allusion	noun	an indirect reference to something else; a hint
ambience	noun	atmosphere; mood; feeling
ambivalent	adjective	undecided; having opposing feelings simultaneously
amiable	adjective	friendly; agreeable
amorphous	adjective	shapeless; bloblike
anathema	noun	something or someone loathed or detested; a formal ecclesiastical curse and excommunication
ancillary	adjective	subordinate; providing assistance
animosity	noun	resentment; hostility; ill will
antecedent	noun	something that went before; a preceding cause or event

antipathy	noun	firm dislike; a strong feeling of aversion
antithesis	noun	the direct opposite
apex	noun	highest point
aphorism	noun	a brief, witty saying; a proverb
apocryphal	adjective	of dubious authenticity; fictitious
apostasy	noun	abandonment or rejection of faith or loyalty
apposite	adjective	distinctly suitable; pertinent
appropriate	verb	to take without permission; to set aside for a particular use
arbiter	noun	one who decides; a judge
arcane	adjective	mysterious; known only to a select few
archetype	noun	an original model or pattern
arrant	adjective	utter; unmitigated; very bad
astute	adjective	shrewd; keen in judgment
attrition	noun	a gradual wearing away, weakening, or loss; a natural decrease in numbers or size
augment	verb	to make bigger; to add to; to increase
auspicious	adjective	favorable; promising
avow	verb	to claim; to declare boldly; to admit
banal	adjective	unoriginal; ordinary
belabor	verb	to go over repeatedly or to an absurd extent
beleaguer	verb	to surround; to besiege; to harass
belie	verb	to give a false impression of; to contradict
benign	adjective	gentle; not harmful; kind; mild
bereave	verb	to deprive or leave desolate, especially through death
blithe	adjective	carefree; cheerful
broach	verb	to open up a subject for discussion, often a delicate subject
brook	verb	to bear or tolerate; to put up with something
callow	adjective	immature
cardinal	adjective	most important; chief
catholic	adjective	universal; embracing everything
cavil	verb	to quibble; to raise trivial objections
chagrin	noun	humiliation; embarrassed disappointment
choleric	adjective	hot-tempered; quick to anger
circumspect	adjective	cautious
coalesce	verb	to come together as one; to fuse; to unite
coda	noun	a passage concluding a musical composition

cognizant	adjective	fully informed; knowledgeable; aware
collusion	noun	conspiracy; secret cooperation
commensurate	adjective	equal; proportionate
conciliatory	adjective	making peace; attempting to resolve a dispute through goodwill
consecrate	verb	to make or declare sacred
consonant	adjective	harmonious; in agreement
consummate	adjective	perfect; complete; supremely skillful
contumely	noun	rudeness; insolence; arrogance
convivial	adjective	fond of partying; festive
copious	adjective	abundant; plentiful
corroborate	verb	to confirm; to back up with evidence
coterie	noun	a select group of close associates
countenance	noun	face; facial expression
covet	verb	to wish for enviously
cull	verb	to pick out from among many; to select; to collect
cursory	adjective	hasty; superficial
daunt	verb	to make fearful; to intimidate
debacle	noun	a sudden disastrous collapse, downfall, or defeat; a rout
debauchery	noun	corruption by sensuality; intemperance; wild living
decorous	adjective	in good taste; orderly; proper
deleterious	adjective	harmful
deluge	noun	a flood
deprecate	verb	to express disapproval of
dilapidated	adjective	broken-down; fallen into ruin
discomfit	verb	to confuse; to disconcert; to thwart the plans of; to defeat in battle
discourse	noun	to converse; to formally discuss a subject
doggerel	noun	comic, loose verse
egregious	adjective	extremely bad; flagrant
elucidate	verb	to explain; to make understandable
empirical	adjective	relying on experience or observation; not merely theoretical
endemic	adjective	native; belonging to a specific region or people
enormity	noun	extreme evil or wickedness
epicure	noun	a person with refined taste in wine and food
epitome	noun	the perfect example of something; a paradigm
equanimity	noun	composure; calm

eschew	verb	to avoid; to shun
espouse	verb	to support; to advocate
evince	verb	to show or demonstrate clearly; manifest
exhort	verb	to urge strongly
exposition	noun	a setting forth of meaning or intent; a discourse intended to explain
extol	verb	to praise highly
facile	adjective	fluent; skillful in a superficial way; easy
fatuous	adjective	foolish; silly; idiotic
fetter	verb	to restrain; to hamper
flag	verb	to weaken; to slow down
flippant	adjective	frivolously shallow and disrespectful
foment	verb	to stir up; to instigate
forbear	verb	to refrain from; to abstain
founder	verb	to fail; to collapse; to sink
fulsome	adjective	offensively flattering or insincere; repulsive
gainsay	verb	to deny; to speak or act against
gambit	noun	a scheme to gain an advantage; a ploy
genial	adjective	cheerful and pleasant; friendly; helpful
germane	adjective	applicable; pertinent; relevant
gratis	adjective	free of charge
gratuitous	adjective	given freely (said of something bad); unjustified; unprovoked; uncalled for
guile	noun	cunning; duplicity; artfulness
harbinger	noun	a forerunner; a signal of
hermetic	adjective	impervious to external influence; airtight
idyllic	adjective	charming in a rustic way; naturally peaceful
ignominy	noun	deep disgrace
impecunious	adjective	without money; penniless
impromptu	adjective	without preparation; on the spur of the moment
impugn	verb	to attack as false or questionable
incandescent	adjective	brilliant; giving off heat or light
incipient	adjective	beginning; emerging
incorrigible	adjective	incapable of being reformed
indolent	adjective	lazy
indulgent	adjective	lenient; yielding to desire
ineluctable	adjective	inescapable; unavoidable
inept	adjective	clumsy; incompetent

inert	adjective	inactive; sluggish; not reacting chemically
inexorable	adjective	relentless; inevitable; unavoidable
inherent	adjective	part of the essential nature of something; intrinsic
inundate	verb	to flood; to overwhelm
inveterate	adjective	habitual; deeply rooted
itinerant	adjective	moving from place to place
judicious	adjective	exercising sound judgment
lament	verb	to mourn
largess	noun	liberality in giving gifts; money or gifts bestowed; generosity of attitude
lascivious	adjective	lustful; obscene; lewd
latent	adjective	present but not visible or apparent; potential
levee	noun	an embankment designed to prevent the flooding of a river
levity	noun	lightness; frivolity; unseriousness
licentious	adjective	lascivious; lewd; promiscuous; amoral
magnate	noun	a rich, powerful, or very successful businessperson
manifest	adjective	visible; evident
maudlin	adjective	tearfully sentimental; silly or weepy
maxim	noun	a fundamental principle; an old saying
mendicant	noun	a beggar
motility	noun	spontaneous movement
noisome	adjective	offensive or disgusting; stinking; noxious
nominal	adjective	in name only; insignificant
novel	adjective	new; original
oblique	adjective	indirect; at an angle
palliate	verb	to make less severe or intense; to make an offense seem less serious
panacea	noun	something that cures everything
paradigm	noun	a model or example
paradox	noun	a true statement or phenomenon that seems to contradict itself
parsimonious	adjective	stingy; miserly
partisan	adjective	having a bias in support of a party, group, or cause
partisan	noun	one who supports a particular party, group, or cause
patina	noun	surface discoloration caused by age and oxidation
paucity	noun	scarcity
pedestrian	adjective	unoriginal; banal
perturb	verb	to disturb greatly

piquant	adjective	pleasantly pungent or tart
placid	adjective	pleasantly calm; peaceful
plaintive	adjective	expressing sadness or sorrow
plumb	verb	to measure the depth of something
portent	noun	an omen; a sign of something coming in the future
precipitous	adjective	steep
predilection	noun	a natural preference for something
presage	verb	to portend; to foreshadow; to forecast or predict
privation	noun	lack of comforts or necessities; poverty
provincial	adjective	limited in outlook to one's own small corner of the world; narrow
prurient	adjective	having lustful thoughts or desires; causing lust
putative	adjective	commonly accepted; supposed; reputed
quay	noun	a landing on the edge of the water; wharf; pier
queue	noun	a line of waiting people or things
queue	verb	to get in line
quintessential	adjective	being the most perfect example of
rampart	noun	a fortification; a bulwark of defense
redolent	adjective	fragrant; aromatic; suggestive or reminiscent
remonstrate	verb	to argue against; to protest; to raise objections
remuneration	noun	payment; recompense
renaissance	noun	a rebirth or revival
replete	adjective	completely filled; abounding
reproach	verb	to scold, usually in disappointment; to blame; to disgrace
reprobate	noun	a wicked, sinful, depraved person
reprove	verb	to criticize mildly
respite	noun	a period of rest or relief
ribald	adjective	characterized by vulgar, lewd humor
sagacious	adjective	wise
sagacity	noun	wisdom
sage	noun	a wise person
salutary	adjective	healthful; remedial; wholesome
sanguine	adjective	cheerful; optimistic; hopeful
surreptitious	adjective	sneaky; secret
sycophant	noun	one who sucks up to others; a servile, self-seeking flatterer
taciturn	adjective	untalkative by nature

temerity	noun	recklessness; audacity; foolhardy disregard of danger
turpitude	noun	shameful wickedness or depravity
unalloyed	adjective	undiluted; pure
usury	noun	lending money at an extremely high rate of interest
venal	adjective	capable of being bribed; corrupt
verdant	adjective	covered with green plants; leafy; inexperienced
vestige	noun	a remaining bit of something; a last trace
vitiate	verb	to make faulty or defective; to impair; to corrupt morally
wizened	adjective	shriveled; withered; shrunken

Quick Quiz #13

Define the following words.

Quintessential: _____

_____

Surreptitious: _____

_____

Apex: _____

_____

Affable: _____

_____

Belie: _____

_____

Inexorable: _____

_____

Debacle: _____

_____

Founder: _____

_____

Gainsay: _____

_____

Largess: _____

_____

Mendicant: _____

_____

Queue: _____

_____

Sycophant: _____

_____

Apostasy: _____

_____

Impugn: _____

_____

Quick Quiz #14

Match the following words to their definitions. The answers are on page 241.

A. Panacea   _____ Pleasingly pungent or tart

B. Cavil   _____ Rudeness; insolence; arrogance

C. Itinerant   _____ To explain; to make understandable

D. Aghast   _____ To make ashamed; to embarrass

E. Guile   _____ Moving from place to place

F. Piquant   _____ Extreme evil or wickedness

G. Banal   _____ Terrified; shocked

H. Enormity   _____ Cunning; duplicity

I. Abash   _____ Unoriginal; ordinary

J. Contumely   _____ Something that cures everything

K. Fetter   _____ To quibble; to raise trivial objections

L. Apposite   _____ To argue against; to protest

M. Elucidate   _____ Distinctly suitable; pertinent

N. Remonstrate   _____ To restrain; to hamper

Quick Quiz #15

Try the following questions. The answers are on page 241.

1. Though high, the _____ the artisan received for the sale of his wares was commensurate with his skill level and years of experience.

   ☐ remuneration
   ☐ commendation
   ☐ remonstration
   ☐ compensation
   ☐ deprecation
   ☐ renown

2. The _____ of a wise test taker is one who studies every day, becomes familiar with good test-taking strategies, and gets plenty of sleep the night before the test.

   ☐ nadir
   ☐ debacle
   ☐ archetype
   ☐ epitome
   ☐ harbinger
   ☐ antecedent

3. Despite grandiose hopes that the fall of the Berlin Wall would lead to rapid economic equality and integration of the Eastern and Western German blocs, one still finds that the preponderance of _____ German citizens lives in the east, while the luxury-automobile-driving citizens are more likely to live in the west.

   ☐ arrant
   ☐ indigent
   ☐ hermetic
   ☐ fatuous
   ☐ deleterious
   ☐ impecunious

4. The new task force that was created by the city to deal with the (i) _____ houses that were abandoned long ago due to foreclosure was a (ii) _____ task force only. Though the devoted members had (iii) _____ their commitment to improving the neighborhoods, they had neither a budget nor the influence to affect any true change.

Blank (i)	Blank (ii)	Blank (iii)
flippant	cognizant	avowed
dilapidated	nominal	broached
provincial	impromptu	reproved

5. The director gave the playwright's latest work only (i) _____ reading before dismissing it as superficial. Had he read it more carefully, he would have found the underlying themes quite (ii) _____.

Blank (i)	Blank (ii)
a cursory	glib
a novel	indulgent
an illusory	profound

6. The theory that women are more verbally skilled than men (i) _____ anthropological history. This theory also gives credence to why men might have better spatial analysis skills. In traditional hunter-gatherer groups, the men used spatial skills to figure out puzzling tasks, such as how to catch their food. They needed to remain (ii) _____ during their hunts to avoid scaring off the prey. On the other hand, women spent their days doing (iii) _____ tasks, such as picking berries, while talking to other women and socializing their young.

Blank (i)	Blank (ii)	Blank (iii)
has no basis in	taciturn	simpler
is supported by	strident	culinary
is disputed by	melodic	complicated

7. No one has suggested that the professor is not (i) _____; nonetheless, some have suggested that the affection shown to him by the faculty is more a result of his (ii) _____ nature than his academic skill.

Blank (i)	Blank (ii)
sagacious	prurient
witless	convivial
parsimonious	incipient

8. Benjamin Franklin was born the son of a candlemaker, and his first marriage proposal was rejected due to his lack of financial standing or prospects. Nonetheless, Franklin became, through industry and (i) _____ that made him sometimes appear (ii) _____, quite (iii) _____ during his accomplished lifetime.

Blank (i)	Blank (ii)	Blank (iii)
inimicality	pedantic	squalid
improvidence	penurious	intransigent
frugality	prodigal	affluent

9. Alice was shocked at her brother's _____ when he stood up in class and interrupted the teacher to disagree with her.

equanimity
debauchery
temerity
animosity
countenance

10. According to her later testimony, it was because of his indecorous conduct that the senator chose not to _____ his appointment.

countenance
belabor
remonstrate
ramify
impugn

ADVANCED VOCABULARY

You want more? Wow, you really are a glutton for vocabulary. Congratulations, that's great! Here is a list of about 100 very challenging vocabulary words for your perusal. Enjoy!

abjure	verb	to repudiate; to take back; to refrain from
adumbrate	verb	to foreshadow vaguely; to suggest or outline sketchily; to obscure or overshadow
anodyne	adjective/ noun	soothing; something that assuages or comforts; something that allays pain
apogee	noun	the most distant point in the orbit of the moon or of an artificial satellite
apotheosis	noun	an exalted or glorified example; elevation to divine standard
artful	adjective	crafty; wily; sly
artless	adjective	completely without guile; natural; without artificiality
assay	verb	to examine by trial or experiment; to evaluate or assess
asseverate	verb	to aver; to allege; to assert
augur	verb	to serve as an omen or sign; to predict or foretell
baleful	adjective	sinister; pernicious; ominous
beatify	verb	to bless, make happy, or ascribe a virtue to; to regard as saintly
bilious	adjective	ill-tempered; cranky
calumny	noun	slander; a maliciously false statement
captious	adjective	disposed to point out trivial faults; calculated to confuse or entrap in argument
carapace	noun	a protective shell
celerity	noun	swiftness of action or motion; speed
coeval	adjective	of the same period; coexisting
contretemps	noun	an embarrassing occurrence; a mishap
contumacious	adjective	stubbornly rebellious or disobedient
corrigible	adjective	capable of being set right; correctable; reparable
denouement	noun	an outcome or solution; the unraveling of a plot
descry	verb	to discriminate or discern
desuetude	noun	disuse
desultory	adjective	moving or jumping from one thing to another; disconnected; occurring haphazardly
diaphanous	adjective	of such fine texture as to be transparent or translucent; delicate; insubstantial
diffident	adjective	reserved; shy; unassuming; lacking in self-confidence

diurnal	adjective	occurring every day; occurring during the daytime
dulcet	adjective	melodious; harmonious; mellifluous
egress	noun	exit
encomium	noun	a formal expression of praise; a tribute
essay	verb	to test or try; attempt; experiment
estimable	adjective	worthy; formidable
excoriate	verb	to censure scathingly; to upbraid
execrate	verb	to denounce; to loathe
exegesis	noun	critical examination; explication
expiate	verb	to make amends for; to atone
fecund	adjective	fertile; productive
fell	verb/ adjective	to cause to fall by striking; cruel; lethal; dire; sinister
fractious	adjective	quarrelsome; rebellious; unruly; irritable
hirsute	adjective	hairy; shaggy
hoary	adjective	gray or white with age; ancient; stale
husband	verb	to use sparingly or economically; to conserve
imbroglio	noun	difficult or embarrassing situation
importune	verb	to urge with annoying persistence; to trouble
indefatigable	adjective	not easily exhaustible; tireless; dogged
insouciant	adjective	nonchalant; lighthearted; carefree
invidious	adjective	causing envy or resentment; offensively harmful
jejune	adjective	vapid; uninteresting; childish; immature; puerile
lachrymose	adjective	causing tears; tearful
lassitude	noun	exhaustion; weakness
ligneous	adjective	woodlike
limn	verb	to draw; to outline in detail; to delineate; to describe
list	verb	to tilt or lean to one side
loquacious	adjective	very talkative; garrulous
lubricious	adjective	lewd; wanton; greasy; slippery
lugubrious	adjective	exaggeratedly mournful
meet	adjective	fitting, proper
mellifluous	adjective	sweetly flowing
meretricious	adjective	plausible but false or insincere; gaudy; showy; tawdry; flashy
minatory	adjective	menacing; threatening
nadir	noun	low point
nice	adjective	exacting; fastidious; extremely precise
nonplus	verb	to baffle; to bewilder; to perplex
nugatory	adjective	of little or no importance; trifling; inconsequential

obstreperous	adjective	noisily and stubbornly defiant; aggressively boisterous
ossify	verb	to convert into bone; to become rigid
otiose	adjective	lazy; of no use; futile
panegyric	noun	formal or elaborate praise
parry	verb	to deflect or ward off; to evade or avoid
pellucid	adjective	transparent; easy to understand; limpid
peripatetic	adjective	wandering; traveling continually; itinerant
perorate	verb	to speak formally
plangent	adjective	pounding; thundering; resounding
pluck	noun	courage; spunk; fortitude
prize	verb	to pry; to press or force with a lever
prolix	adjective	long-winded; verbose
propinquity	noun	nearness; proximity
propitiate	verb	to appease; to conciliate
propitious	adjective	marked by favorable signs or conditions
puerile	adjective	childish; immature
puissant	adjective	powerful
pulchritude	noun	physical beauty
pusillanimous	adjective	cowardly; craven
salacious	adjective	lustful; lascivious; bawdy
saturnine	adjective	melancholy or sullen; of a gloomy disposition
sententious	adjective	given to pompous moralizing; preachy; self-righteous
sidereal	adjective	astral; relating to stars or constellations
sinecure	noun	a position requiring little or no work and usually providing an income
stentorian	adjective	extremely loud and powerful
stygian	adjective	gloomy; dark
succor	noun	assistance; relief in time of distress
succor	verb	to give assistance in time of need
sundry	adjective	various; miscellaneous; separate
supine	adjective	lying face upward; offering no resistance
tendentious	adjective	argumentative; biased
turbid	adjective	murky; opaque; unclear
tyro	noun	novice; rank amateur
unctuous	adjective	oily, both literally and figuratively; characterized by earnest insincerity
vagary	noun	whim; unpredictable action; wild notion
voluble	adjective	fluent; verbal; having easy use of spoken language
wag	noun	a wit; a joker

Gimme A Break!
Whew! How are you holding up? Give yourself a break and go for a walk or step away from the book for a moment.

ANSWER KEY

Key Terms Group 1

Quick Quiz #2
K
L
E
G
B
A
H
I
N
F
C
M
J
D

Quick Quiz #3
1. B and D
2. C and D
3. A and F
4. C
5. ossified, perfunctory, parodies
6. belie, intimate
7. ostensible, nebulous, qualms
8. illicit, attestation, exculpated
9. A
10. stupefied, prescient

Key Terms Group 2

Quick Quiz #5
D
L
F
M
B
K
C
A
N
I
G
H
E
J

Quick Quiz #6
1. A and E
2. C and D
3. C and E
4. accolades, satire
5. wretched, innocuous
6. irrational, circumstantial, incipient
7. abate, vilify
8. customary, eclectic, bedraggled
9. A
10. complaisance, truncate

Key Terms Group 3

Quick Quiz #8

J
E
N
M
I
B
A
H
G
F
C
D
K
L

Quick Quiz #9

1. C and E
2. A and E
3. E and F
4. reverent, adorn, vista
5. spurious, restricted
6. D
7. hackneyed, immutable
8. incontrovertible, cultivated, complicated amalgamation
9. B
10. dubious, a precursor to

Key Terms Group 4

Quick Quiz #11

L
J
I
H
K
A
E
C
D
N
M
F
B
G

Quick Quiz #12

1. A and E
2. A and B
3. C and D
4. indifference
5. sparsely, pristine
6. mollifying, crass
7. unfeigned, exorbitant
8. neophyte, seasoned, enduring
9. C
10. mercurial, steadfast

Extra Vocabulary

Quick Quiz #14

F
J
M
I
C
H
D
E
G
A
B
N
L
K

Quick Quiz #15

1. A and D
2. C and D
3. B and F
4. dilapidated, nominal, avowed
5. a cursory, profound
6. is supported by, taciturn, simpler
7. sagacious, convivial
8. frugality, penurious, affluent
9. C
10. A

Chapter 8
Mixed Drills

Drill #1

Try the following questions. The answers are on page 256.

1. One major _____ that some scientists have about the practice of cloning is their fear of the potentially negative outcomes associated with a homogenous population.

gambit
rampart
conviction
qualm
certitude

2. While the life of _____ may appeal to some, others hold interests they believe are more intellectually based than cultivating a discriminating taste in food.

an epicure
a sage
a hedonist
a connoisseur
an ascetic

3. The intentions of the restaurant critic were (i) _____; he accepted the assignment to review the new bistro not as (ii) _____ journalist, but as a private citizen seeking revenge against the owner, who had wronged him in a business deal years before.

Blank (i)	Blank (ii)
squalid	a surreptitious
discreet	a discerning
malevolent	an indifferent

4. It is part of human nature to resist change and (i) _____ new ideas. This fact is evidenced in many teachers' (ii) _____ adherence to archaic methodologies, which makes educational reform difficult to enact. Until some (iii) _____ teachers and administrators begin to welcome new classroom techniques, the attempts of the current administration at modifying the system will be ineffective.

Blank (i)	Blank (ii)	Blank (iii)
eschew	inept	sagacious
aver	partisan	superfluous
covet	dogged	obstinate

5. Near the end of his life, author Leo Tolstoy was increasingly influenced by aspiring communist revolutionaries. Tolstoy came to believe that excessive personal wealth was (i) _____ to the well-being of his Russian countrymen, and was persuaded to bequeath his copyrights and much of his fortune to the Russian state; his wife, Sophia, who believed in her right to be an aristocrat, regarded this as (ii) _____ decision.

Blank (i)	Blank (ii)
convivial	a heretical
inimical	an opulent
stupefying	a refulgent

6. Doctors have remained (i) _____ in the face of the incredible news that a Swedish research team has discovered a gene that causes cancer. Their reluctance to show excitement is due to their awareness that transforming the mere identification of this gene into usable medicine is (ii) _____ task and will not (iii) _____ the need for uncomfortable and lengthy treatments any time in the near future.

Blank (i)	Blank (ii)	Blank (iii)
felicitous	a prized	obviate
morose	an arduous	aggrandize
impassive	an austere	effect

A tenured art history professor at a major university recently asserted that **the head of the Art History department is incompetent**, pointing to the decline in enrollment in art history courses despite an increase in enrollment overall at the university. While one may argue that professors who lash out at department heads are rarely likely to achieve anything constructive, **in this case the complaint is entirely unwarranted**. It is true that a decrease in enrollment within a department often indicates incompetence on the part of the department head, but not so here. Rather, the decline in enrollment in art history courses is entirely due to the university's admissions committee's decision to admit far more students who plan to enroll exclusively in pre-medicine courses.

Line (5) ... *(10)* ... *(15)*

7. In the argument, the two boldfaced portions play which of the following roles?

   ◯ The first provides evidence intended to support a claim that the argument overall opposes; the second provides information to undermine the strength of that evidence.

   ◯ The first provides evidence intended to support a claim that the argument overall opposes; the second states the conclusion of the argument overall.

   ◯ The first provides evidence intended to support a claim that the argument overall opposes; the second provides evidence to undermine the claim being opposed.

   ◯ The first states a claim that the argument overall opposes; the second provides evidence to undermine the claim being opposed.

   ◯ The first states a claim that the argument overall opposes; the second states the conclusion of the argument overall.

The London Board of Trade limited the quantity of pound sterling banknotes permitted in circulation in the American colonies, citing fear of devaluation induced by overprinting. The Board also denied the necessity of paper money, considering the ever-increasing colonial exports purchased by foreign nations that rendered payments in gold and silver. However, in 1749, Governor Glen of South Carolina contended that access to more paper currency was essential because there was actually a deficit of gold and silver. This shortfall led to difficulties in exchanging goods for these precious metals, forcing many merchants to earn their success only through continued reliance on the barter system. Such a system limited the colonists' ability to obtain certain goods for which they had no apparently comparable trade, severely hampering widespread economic growth in the colonies.

Line (5) ... *(10)* ... *(15)*

8. Select the sentence that suggests the final phrase, *severely hampering widespread economic growth in the colonies,* may be an exaggeration.

9. Which of the following statements, if true, would most strengthen Governor Glen's argument in favor of paper currency?

   ◯ It was difficult for the colonists to maintain high levels of foreign exports during the winter months.

   ◯ Although colonists were not always able to find trade partners in their local communities, there were strong domestic trade links among the various colonies.

   ◯ Since the value of a pound sterling banknote was linked directly to that of silver, the two methods of payment were equally acceptable to a merchant.

   ◯ Foreign countries often wanted to barter with colonial exporters, but the value of some foreign goods was difficult to determine.

   ◯ Because some colonies had already developed their own form of legal tender and no longer used the British pound sterling, the Board of Trade should not have been worried about devaluation.

El Niño-Southern Oscillation is a climate pattern that occurs across the tropical Pacific Ocean approximately every five years. The phenomenon
Line includes a change in ocean temperature—the "El
(5) Niño" component—and a change in air surface pressure—the "Southern Oscillation" component. When prolonged, above-average ocean warming coincides with higher air surface pressure, the phenomenon is popularly called El Niño; when
(10) prolonged, above-average ocean cooling coincides with lower air surface pressure, the phenomenon is popularly called La Niña. El Niño or La Niña events typically last between five and nine months.

El Niño begins with increased surface pressure
(15) over the Indian Ocean and reduced air pressure over the central and eastern Pacific Ocean, a combination which causes trade winds traveling from Peru to the Eastern Pacific to subside. Under normal conditions, these trade winds blow warm water near the
(20) surface away from Peru along the Equatorial Current, leading to an upwelling of cold, nutrient-rich water. During an El Niño, however, this effect is reduced. Because the Pacific Ocean has a potent impact on climate throughout the world, El Niño disturbs
(25) weather patterns more powerfully than does any other known force. Typical effects include severe droughts in Indonesia, Australia, and the Philippines, and substantially increased rainfall in parts of South America.

(30) The effects of El Niño can be economically devastating in South America. Because of the increased rainfall, flooding in Peru and Ecuador is common. Moreover, El Niño significantly diminishes the amount of cold water that usually rises from the
(35) deep, depriving local fish populations of the important nutrients brought up with the cold water. In the absence of these nutrients, fish swim deeper, head south, or die off, causing great harm to the fishing industry. Indeed, during the 1972 El Niño, the world's
(40) largest fishery collapsed. In addition, these same fish feed local bird populations; during an El Niño event, birds, the droppings of which are used in the fertilizer industry, leave to find new food sources.

Although no one knows how long El Niño has
(45) existed, evidence suggests that there may have been El Niño phenomena for thousands of years. Coral records suggest a warming of sea surface temperatures as early as 3,000 B.C.E. Five hundred years ago, fishermen in Peru saw their anchovy catch
(50) diminish substantially when water temperatures warmed. The most destructive El Niño event occurred in 1982–1983, when droughts and associated wildfires killed nearly 2,000 people; this incident sparked intense occupation among scientists
(55) worldwide with the causes of El Niño.

10. In the last sentence of the passage, the word *occupation* most nearly means

○ function
○ employment
○ concern
○ affair
○ professionalism

11. The passage suggests which of the following about phenomena associated with El Niño?

☐ The surface water of the Pacific Ocean near South America is warmer because of reduced trade winds.
☐ Severe droughts are seen in some parts of the world, while increased flooding is seen in other parts of the world.
☐ Because many fish relocate or die, fewer fish are caught by many people in the South American fishing industry.

12. On the basis of the passage, it can be inferred that

○ In the absence of an El Niño event, drought conditions are rarely present in Indonesia, Australia, or the Philippines.
○ No observable phenomenon influences global weather patterns to a magnitude greater than does an El Niño event.
○ Because of the changes in surface pressure and reduction in trade winds associated with El Niño events, many South American birds are forced to relocate.
○ The El Niño event of 1982–1983 caused more deaths than did any other climate-related event that year.
○ The effects of the 1972 El Niño event were felt most profoundly in Peru and Ecuador.

13. Although we had planned the vacation trip to the sunny spa for weeks, no one could have predicted the _____ onset of rainy weather that spoiled most of our outdoor activities.

   ☐ welcome
   ☐ precipitous
   ☐ unforeseen
   ☐ fortunate
   ☐ fruitless
   ☐ lethargic

14. The _____ outcries from the disgruntled union workers were apparently to no avail; the supervisor decided to reject the enhanced benefits package without any further discussion.

   ☐ pristine
   ☐ fervent
   ☐ quizzical
   ☐ redolent
   ☐ allusive
   ☐ impassioned

15. David's report card stated he is sometimes regarded as _____ student by his teachers when his narrow-minded interpretations and adamant attitudes dominate his classroom discussions.

   ☐ an intransigent
   ☐ an assiduous
   ☐ an intractable
   ☐ a gregarious
   ☐ a pensive
   ☐ a diligent

16. With the inception of numerous exorbitant tolls throughout the state's major highways, the popularity of long-distance automobile travel _____ while the rate of train travel experienced a concomitant upswing.

   ☐ waned
   ☐ equivocated
   ☐ intensified
   ☐ importuned
   ☐ abated
   ☐ surged

Late Victorian writers obsessed about the relationship between art and the artist—as Basil Hallward lamented in *The Picture of Dorian Gray*,
Line "We live in an age when men treat art as if it were
(5) meant to be a form of autobiography." Yet Oscar Wilde, the author of that very novel, himself made fortunes from the rampant speculation about the connections between his work and life. The irony inherent in this contradiction seems obvious: only by
(10) recognizing and manipulating the public's tendency to impute biographical meaning to the aesthetic can the artist maneuver the perception of his art to his own advantage. But if the "art of art" is really all about "the art of the ruse," then what value does
(15) any of it have, anyway?

For the following question, consider each of the choices separately and select all that apply:

17. An example of treating "art as if it were meant to be a form of autobiography" would be

☐ reading a novel about a young girl as an allegory for modern political circumstances.

☐ viewing the bare shoulders in a painting of a well-known society figure as an indication of her seductive nature.

☐ observing that the director of a film had a childhood injury similar to that of one of the characters in the film.

18. Click on the sentence in which the author refers to a creation of an artist to support an assertion about a conundrum that was commonly faced by artists in the time period discussed in the passage.

Recently, scientists studying how the brain interprets expressive gestures that communicate emotional states undertook a study comparing
Line neural activity relating to hand gestures expressing
(5) emotions such as "I don't care" to neural activity relating to instrumental gestures intended to change behavior through spoken commands such as "sit down." Volunteers undergoing fMRI testing were shown brief videos of both expressive gestures
(10) and instrumental gestures and were asked to interpret the import of the gestures. As anticipated, expressive gestures activated different neural networks than did instrumental gestures. Expressive gestures activated neurons in the paracingulate
(15) cortex and the amygdala, both of which are known to be activated during social interaction. Instrumental gestures, by contrast, activated neurons in a region of the brain associated with language.

19. In context, the word *import (Line 11)* most nearly means

◯ enticement
◯ influx
◯ transmission
◯ magnitude
◯ connotation

Recently, scientists studying how the brain
interprets expressive gestures that communicate
emotional states undertook a study comparing neural
Line activity relating to hand gestures expressing emotions
(5) such as "I don't care" to neural activity relating to
instrumental gestures intended to change behavior
through spoken commands such as "sit down."
Volunteers undergoing fMRI testing were shown brief
videos of both expressive gestures and instrumental
(10) gestures and were asked to interpret the import of
the gestures. Expressive gestures activated different
neural networks than did instrumental gestures.
Expressive gestures activated neurons in the
paracingulate cortex and the amygdala, both of which
(15) are known to be activated during social interaction.
Instrumental gestures, by contrast, activated neurons
in a region of the brain associated with language.

20. The function of the highlighted portion of the
     passage is to

   ◯ describe the role that neural networks play
        in perception
   ◯ refute a hypothesis anticipated at the outset
        of the study
   ◯ highlight the definitive nature of certain
        aspects of neurology
   ◯ summarize the conclusion to be drawn from
        a study
   ◯ explain the appropriateness of a particular
        methodology

Drill #2

Try the following questions. The answers are on page 260.

1. Although the Modern Library Board selected Joyce's *Ulysses* as its number one novel of all time, Friendswood Library disagrees and instead chose Fitzgerald's *The Great Gatsby* as its _____ of literature.

antithesis
escutcheon
apotheosis
litigation
demotion

2. Polonius, one of Shakespeare's most _____ characters, speaks some of the bard's classic epigrammatic lines such as, "To thine own self be true," and, "Neither a borrower nor lender be."

obsequious
auriferous
sententious
dysphonic
mellifluous

3. Maggie decided that decorating her denim jacket with rhinestones was an easy way to (i) _____ her look, changing it from a run-of-the-mill outfit to (ii) _____ creation.

Blank (i)	Blank (ii)
regard	an inimitable
isolate	a laughable
personalize	an austere

4. The researcher expected to find only (i) _____ medical tips in the medieval texts and was surprised to find information about things such as lemon balm, cayenne pepper, and onions, items that modern medical experts recommend for their (ii) _____ benefits.

Blank (i)	Blank (ii)
commodious	tenebrious
antediluvian	lugubrious
extant	salubrious

5. (i) _____ debating whether bread should be buttered on the top or the bottom was impossible for the Yooks and the Zooks, who each felt strongly that their own perspective was the correct way and refused to consider any alternative. Instead of recognizing the absurdity of the conflict, they allowed things to (ii) _____, with each side developing bigger and better weapons that ultimately led them to the threat of (iii) _____ destruction.

Blank (i)	Blank (ii)	Blank (iii)
Tempestuously	confabulate	predisposed
Dogmatically	stagnate	mutual
Rationally	escalate	incongruous

6. Lower taxes would have many (i) _____ effects on the nation as a whole. In addition to encouraging businesspeople to be more optimistic and (ii) _____ in their investments, tax cuts would encourage the mass hiring of employees, which is not (iii) _____ given the current payroll tax rate.

Blank (i)	Blank (ii)	Blank (iii)
execrable	bullish	feasible
salutary	bearish	malleable
indeterminate	birdlike	atypical

In *The Great Gatsby,* F. Scott Fitzgerald created a protagonist who was a staunch believer in the agrarian myth espoused by Thomas Jefferson and Benjamin Franklin, yet was simultaneously
(5) entrenched in the corruption and materialism of American society during the 1920s. This dual nature of the title character has commonly been viewed as a thinly disguised reflection of Fitzgerald himself, who, as reviewer Allen claimed, maintained
(10) a "catholic sensibility" his whole life despite well-known episodes of public drunkenness and debauchery. Fitter agreed, perceiving in Fitzgerald a "deep-seated conservative quietism" not dissimilar to Jay Gatsby's adherence to the principles of
(15) honorable living dictated by Benjamin Franklin in *Poor Richard's Almanack.* The parallels were so apparent to Mencken that he regarded the book as little more than a "glorified anecdote." Other critics have rejected this narrow, egocentric interpretation
(20) and given far more credence to the novel as shrewd social commentary. Trask, for example, considered the eyes of Dr. T.J. Eckleburg, featured prominently on a billboard in the novel, not those of an all-seeing god evaluating Gatsby's personal shortcomings, but
(25) those of Thomas Jefferson mourning the collective American abandonment of his belief in hard work and integrity as the paths to fortune. Even Trask, though, conceded that the hedonistic Fitzgerald spoke clearly through the character of Nick Carraway in an ironic
(30) plea for the preservation of a more austere way of life.

7. Select the sentence that best defines one of the two contradictory facets of Jay Gatsby's character.

8. According to the passage, which of the following statements about *The Great Gatsby* cannot be shown to be accurate in the estimation of at least one critic?

○ The novel was merely a description of an episode from Fitzgerald's life.

○ The symbolism in the novel sometimes reflected Fitzgerald's lack of self-worth.

○ The novel provided insight into American culture of the 1920s.

○ Fitzgerald used the novel as a vehicle to voice his opinions about changes in America.

○ The novel's main character provided a truthful depiction of the author.

9. Which of the following situations is most analogous to Fitter's belief about the character of Jay Gatsby?

○ A job candidate in an interview mimics the actions of the interviewer in an unconscious effort to establish rapport and familiarity.

○ A photographer chooses to repeatedly use a model who has many of the same mannerisms and facial expressions as the photographer.

○ A character in a movie written by a health-conscious playwright has a gym membership and buys only organic foods.

○ A college student relates strongly to a character in a novel and begins to take an interest in that character's hobbies.

○ An actor improvises many of his character's lines in order to add depth to the role.

Newton's theory of universal gravitation states that every massive particle in the universe attracts every other massive particle with a force proportional to *Line* the mass of the particles and their proximity to one (5) another. Consequently, cosmologists would expect that calculations based on this theory would yield an accurate measure of the mass in the universe; in fact, though, the total amount of observable matter in the universe does not contain enough mass to (10) account for the organization of the universe into clusters of galaxies. To explain this discrepancy, cosmologists have developed the theory of "dark matter:" they postulate that the missing mass consists of elementary particles too small to be (15) detected by electromagnetic radiation, and that these particles provide the mass necessary to hold the universe together. According to available evidence, these particles can only account for a maximum of 20 percent of the missing mass in the universe, yet (20) their existence brings us one important step closer to solving the mystery of the missing matter.

10. According to the passage, which of the following factors is believed to help account for the missing mass in the universe?

○ Massive particles with a force proportional to the mass of the particles attract additional mass to the universe.

○ Tiny particles that are not currently observable by humans compose some of the missing mass.

○ "Dark matter" adheres to mass and causes it to expand.

○ Galaxies organize themselves into clusters to compensate for the lack of other mass in the universe.

○ The proximity of certain particles to each other forces an attraction that creates mass.

For the following question, consider each of the choices separately and select all that apply:

11. The passage suggests that a massive particle would be most likely to attract another particle

☐ with a force related to the mass of each particle.

☐ at a distance related to the mass of each particle.

☐ by using an elementary particle as an intermediary.

High tax rates, not the new regulations on carbon emissions, are responsible for the poor industrial production in Country A since its new government was elected. Neighboring Country B imposes the same regulations on carbon emissions, but while industrial production in Country A has been declining, it has been improving in Country B.

12. Which one of the following statements, if true, would most weaken the argument?

  ○ While Country B has a regional airport, Country A has an international airport.
  ○ Country A's newly elected government raised taxes with the goal of guaranteeing a more just distribution of wealth.
  ○ The type of coal always burned in Country A is different from the type of coal always burned in Country B.
  ○ Both Country A and Country B have been in a recession.
  ○ Agricultural production is also falling in Country A.

13. An aspiring pop star should be _____, playing concert after concert and sending out hundreds of demo tapes, even though in the end, fame may depend solely on having the right connections.

  ☐ idolatrous
  ☐ dogged
  ☐ tenuous
  ☐ notorious
  ☐ tenacious
  ☐ advantageous

14. In many Western cultures, the four-leaf clover is easily identified as _____ symbol; in Buddhist cultures, it is the wheel that is widely recognized as a good omen.

  ☐ an auspicious
  ☐ a facetious
  ☐ a pious
  ☐ a pervasive
  ☐ a propitious
  ☐ a prophetic

15. Because he had initially feared public displays of outrage from constituents who felt their taxes were already too high, the governor was shocked to hear so many people _____ his decision to sign the new bill that would generate much-needed revenue for the state.

  ☐ effectuate
  ☐ reproach
  ☐ annul
  ☐ laud
  ☐ extol
  ☐ flout

16. After a brief, but vexing, attempt at living in the countryside without the amenities that are readily accessible to the modern urbanite, the young lawyer, who previously had found a certain _____ charm in the lifestyle of the Pennsylvania Dutch, quickly changed his mind.

  ☐ bucolic
  ☐ erudite
  ☐ pedestrian
  ☐ idyllic
  ☐ banal
  ☐ lugubrious

The ubiquity of jeans across social classes in modern America might be surprising given that throughout history jeans have transmitted very
Line specific cultural messages. Their crude, durable
(5) fabric initially made them symbolic of poor, working-class men, but when women hung up their skirts in order to take their turns at the heavy machinery while their husbands fought fascism in Europe, jeans were transformed into a hallmark of patriotism and
(10) early feminism. In the 1950s, after exposure in films as the garments of choice of brooding icons such as Marlon Brando and James Dean, jeans also served as an emblem of rebellious youth. Ultimately, their rise to dominance over the American wardrobe in
(15) the 1970s did nothing to lessen the ability of jeans to align the wearer with a certain social group, thanks to the scope of brands and styles that became available.

17. The passage implies all of the following about people who have worn jeans throughout history EXCEPT

⊙ their social affiliations are not exclusive to one particular social class
⊙ they found jeans more suitable for some working environments
⊙ the early adopters wore jeans in order to identify with certain social groups
⊙ they progressively gained more control over the symbolism of the jeans they wore
⊙ they were members not only of a variety of economic classes, but age groups as well

The ubiquity of jeans across social classes in modern America might be surprising given that throughout history they have transmitted very
Line specific cultural messages. Their crude, durable
(5) fabric initially made them symbolic of poor, working-class men, but when women hung up their skirts in order to take their turns at the heavy machinery while their husbands fought fascism in Europe, jeans were transformed into a hallmark of patriotism and
(10) early feminism. In the 1950s, after exposure in films as the garments of choice of brooding icons such as Marlon Brando and James Dean, jeans also served as an emblem of rebellious youth. Ultimately, their rise to dominance over the American wardrobe in
(15) the 1970s did nothing to lessen the ability of jeans to align the wearer with a certain social group, thanks to the scope of brands and styles that became available.

18. What is the function of the highlighted portion?

⊙ to provide a specific example of another shift in the symbolism of jeans
⊙ to present a viewpoint that differs from that of the initial premise
⊙ to summarize an argument in favor of the inconsistent historical symbolism of jeans
⊙ to weaken the author's premise by conclusively demonstrating why jeans gained widespread popularity
⊙ to reconcile an apparent contradiction presented in an earlier sentence

Precipitation—in the form of dew in the warmer months and frost in the colder ones—often forms on grass and leaves during the night. But since this *Line* precipitation results from a change between surface *(5)* and atmospheric temperatures, how can similar water droplets also appear on some houseplants? The answer is that some globules are the result of guttation. Occurring only in vascular plants, guttation begins when water moves from saturated soil *(10)* into drier plant roots. Water accumulation in roots creates pressure, which, in daytime, is offset through evaporation. At night, however, these plants use the pipe-like elements of their tissue to draw the excess water upwards and push it out the tips of their leaves.

For the following question, consider each of the choices separately and select all that apply:

19. There is sufficient evidence in the passage to support which of the following inferences about guttation?

    ☐ Guttation is more likely to occur in climates that have only rainy and dry seasons, as opposed to ones with four distinct seasons ranging from winter to summer.
    ☐ Analyzing the quantity of moisture in the soil and the type of plant one were dealing with would be inadequate to determine whether certain droplets were the result of guttation or were simply dew.
    ☐ In arid climates, guttation is not likely to occur under natural conditions.

20. In the passage, *vascular (Line 8)* most nearly means

    ◯ containing channels
    ◯ needing excessive moisture
    ◯ needing little sunlight
    ◯ absorbent
    ◯ suitable for moderate climates

ANSWERS AND EXPLANATIONS

Drill #1

1. **D** The clue that you need to fill in the blank is *fear of potentially negative outcomes*. If the scientists are afraid of an outcome, they must have a *problem* with cloning. *Qualm* is the only synonym here for *problem*. *Conviction* and *certitude* may seem like possible answers, but the outcomes are described as *potential*. *Gambit* (tactic) and *rampart* (barrier wall) do not make sense in context.

2. **A** The *others* referred to in the sentence have interests that are not related to food, so the blank must refer to a person whose interest *is* food. Choice (A) is the correct answer. Choice (D) is tempting because *connoisseur* is a word often used in conjunction with fine food or wine. However, a *connoisseur* is a general term for someone who has expertise in a subject, which may or may not be food. *Epicure* is a term that necessarily involves food. *Sage* means *wise person*, which is not a match. A *hedonist* is someone who pursues pleasure as a priority, and is the opposite of an *ascetic*.

3. **malevolent** and **an indifferent**

    Given that the critic is seeking *revenge against the owner*, his intentions must be bad. A critic should be *discreet* so that he doesn't ruin his cover, but *malevolent* is the word that matches the clues. *Squalid* means *filthy*, and is irrelevant. In the second blank, you need a word that is dissimilar to vengefulness and conveys impartiality and good intentions. Neither *surreptitious*, which means sneaky, nor *discerning*, which means *discriminating*, has the desired meaning. *Indifferent* is a good synonym for *impartial*, and is the best choice.

4. **eschew, dogged**, and **obstinate**

    From the transition word *and* you know that the first blank has to be similar to *resist change*. *Covet* means to desire greatly and *aver* means to assert, so *eschew* is the correct choice. The next two blanks have to work together. If the *adherence* is strong, then the teachers will be stubborn, and if it is weak, then the teachers will be uncertain. The transition word *Until* makes it clear that the teachers are preventing changes. Therefore, you need the first situation given above, which would lead to *dogged* and *obstinate*. *Inept* means *unskilled*, and is not a match. *Partisan* may seem plausible for the second blank, but then the teachers would be *biased*, for which there is no available synonym for the third blank. *Sagacious* means *shrewd* and *superfluous* means *unnecessary*, and thus neither one fits the meaning of the third blank.

5. **inimical** and **a heretical**

    The first blank describes Tolstoy's belief regarding *excessive personal wealth* in relation to his *countrymen*; since he was *influenced by aspiring communist revolutionaries*, and relinquished *his copyrights and much of his fortune* to the state, a word like *harmful* would make sense. Of the choices, only *inimical* means harmful. The second blank describes the decision as seen by Sophia; since *she believed in her right to be an aristocrat*, she probably thought it was a *foolish* or *incorrect* decision. Of the choices, only *heretical*, which means contrary to accepted custom, is sufficiently negative.

6. **impassive**, **arduous**, and **obviate**

Start with the first blank; the clue there is in the second sentence, which says the doctors have a *reluctance to show excitement*. The only choice for the first blank that expresses a suitable lack of emotion is *impassive*. The second blank describes the task of turning the discovery into useful medicine; since the doctors aren't excited, and the end of the passage suggests that significant change is far in the future, you need something like *long and difficult* in the blank. Of the choices, *an arduous* is the best fit. The third blank describes what the new medicine will, hopefully, eventually do to the need for uncomfortable treatments—*eliminate* it. Of the choices, only *obviate* means eliminate. Be careful with *effect*: As a verb, it means to cause, not to have an effect on.

7. **E**   First, identify the main conclusion of the argument, using the Why Test. The second boldfaced portion is the main conclusion, which is supported by the remainder of the passage. Thus, eliminate (A), (C), and (D), which wrongly assert that the second boldfaced portion is information or evidence. Once you have identified the conclusion, you can see that the first boldfaced portion is a claim with which the main conclusion disagrees. Thus, eliminate (B), as the first boldfaced portion is not evidence. Choice (E) is correct.

8. **"The Board also denied the necessity of paper money, considering the ever-increasing colonial exports purchased by foreign nations that rendered payments in gold and silver."** *(Lines 4–7)*

Keep in mind that the question says *may* be an exaggeration, but still look for the sentence that provides the strongest support. The correct sentence says that, according to the Board, the colonies were exporting more goods as time went on, and therefore were obtaining more gold and silver. In the face of an increase in gold and silver, the inability to obtain some goods through barter, though limiting, as the text says, likely did not *severely hamper* growth.

9. **D**   Governor Glen's argument relies on the fact that colonists were often forced to barter, but bartering was an unreliable method of doing business. Choice (D) supports that point of view not only by pointing out that the Board was wrong about the colonists' ability to obtain gold and silver from foreign trading partners, but also by giving another example of how barter is a poor system. Choice (A) is incorrect because although trade is low at one point during the year, it may be high enough during the rest of the year for the colonists to save up plenty of gold and silver to last them through the slow months. Choice (B) weakens the argument by widening the range of partners with whom the colonists can barter, thus lessening the need for paper currency. Choice (C) does not address any of the main points of the governor's argument and neither does (E).

10. **C** Come up with your own word to replace *occupation*, based on the context of the sentence. You might choose a word like *interest* to describe what a destructive El Niño event would likely spark among the world's scientists. Of the choices, only *concern* can mean interest.

11. **A, B, and C**

Each choice is supported. According to the second paragraph, the reduced trade winds during an El Niño fail to bring as much warm water away from South America as is typical. The second paragraph also mentions droughts in places such as Indonesia and flooding in South America. The third paragraph confirms that fish dive deeper, move south, or die off, which negatively affects the fishing industry.

12. **B** In an inference question, the correct answer must be supported by the text of the passage. Choice (B) is supported: The second paragraph states that *El Niño disturbs weather patterns more powerfully than does any other known force*. Choice (B) is a fair paraphrase of this statement. Choice (A) is not supported: While drought conditions may be severe in these locations during El Niño, the passage offers no information about drought conditions in the absence of El Niño. Choice (C) is wrong because the birds relocate due to reduced food supplies, not the changes in pressure and winds. Choice D is not supported: The 1982–1983 El Niño was the worst El Niño, but the passage does not make a comparison with other climate-related events of that year. Choice (E), finally, is also not supported: While the passage describes some of the effects of the 1972 El Niño event in Peru and Ecuador, no information is provided to make a comparison between those countries and other countries.

13. **B and C**

The transition word *although* indicates that the plans for a sunny vacation were overturned unexpectedly in the second half of the sentence, so you need a word that means something like *sudden* or *unexpected* in the blank. Neither *welcome* nor *fortunate* means sudden or unexpected, so eliminate (A) and (D). Neither *fruitless*, which means useless, nor *lethargic*, which means sluggish, makes sense in the blank; eliminate (E) and (F). Both *precipitous* and *unforeseen* can mean sudden and unexpected, so (B) and (C) give you appropriate, equivalent sentences.

14. **B and F**

The *disgruntled* workers registered *outcries*, signifying they had intense feelings about their enhanced benefits package that was later rejected; thus, you want a word for the blank that means *passionate* or *emotional*. Neither *pristine*, which means clean, nor *quizzical*, which means puzzling, makes sense in the sentence, so eliminate (A) and (C). Choices (D) and (E) give roughly synonymous meanings, but nothing in the sentence supports the description of the cries as suggestive. Both *fervent* and *impassioned* can mean passionate, so (B) and (E) give you appropriate, equivalent sentences.

15.   **A and C**

David is characterized as *narrow-minded* and *adamant*; you can recycle either of those clues into the blank, or you can use a simple word like *stubborn*. Choices (B) and (F) give roughly synonymous meanings, but nothing in the sentence supports the idea that David is hardworking. Neither *gregarious*, which means social, nor *pensive*, which means thoughtful, is supported by the sentence, so eliminate (D) and (E). Both *intransigent* and *intractable* mean stubborn, so (A) and (C) give you appropriate, equivalent sentences.

16.   **A and E**

You have two clues about *the popularity of long-distance automobile travel*: *[N]umerous exorbitant tolls* indicate that such travel is now more expensive due to excessively high costs, and the *upswing* on the other side of the transition *while* suggests that the popularity of traveling by car is swinging in the other direction. Hence, you need a word like *decreased* in the blank. Both *intensified* and *surged* are nearly the opposite of what you're looking for, so eliminate (C) and (F). Neither *equivocated*, which means spoke in an ambiguous manner, nor *importuned*, which means begged, is supported by the sentence, so eliminate (B) and (D). Both *waned* and *abated* mean decreased, so (A) and (E) give you appropriate, equivalent sentences.

17.   **B and C**

In (B), the viewer sees the *bare shoulders* as an indication of the woman's character, relating an artistic feature to speculation about the woman's life. In (C), the viewer notices a relationship between the life of the director and the life of a character in his film. Both of these choices contain autobiographical observations. In (A), the reader sees the novel as an *allegory*, a story about something different from the main plot. In this case, the allegory is about politics, not an autobiography.

18.   **"Late Victorian writers obsessed about the relationship between art and the artist—as Basil Hallward lamented in *The Picture of Dorian Gray*, 'We live in an age when men treat art as if it were meant to be a form of autobiography.'"** *(Lines 1–5)*

In this passage, writers are defined as artists, and as a character in Wilde's novel, Basil Hallward is one of Wilde's creations. The quotation from Hallward is about the autobiographical assumptions that the public makes about art. The problem, or *conundrum*, that the Victorian writers faced concerned the public's inclination to infer information about the artist from his art. Basil Hallward's complaint illustrates their frustration with this tendency.

19. **C** Come up with your own word, based on the context of the sentence. You might come up with something like *meaning*. Of the choices, only *connotation* means meaning. Choice (E) is correct.

20. **D** Begin by considering what role the highlighted portion plays. Before the highlighted portion, the author describes the nature of an experiment. After the highlighted portion, the author describes the details of the results of the experiment. The highlighted portion presents the results in summary form. Thus, (D) is correct. Although the passage discusses neurons and perception, (A) is too broad. Choice (B) is wrong as no hypothesis was offered, let alone refuted. While (C) may seem appealing, the author never commented upon the definitive nature of neurology or any science. Choice (E) is wrong because the author did not attempt to defend the methodology used.

Drill #2

1. **C** The text tells you that the first novel was *selected as the number one novel*, which means that novel is at the peak and is the *best of all time*. The missing word should mean something that relates to that idea. Eliminate (A) and (E) because they both go in the opposite direction of *best of all time*. Choice (D) could be slightly attractive simply because it looks a little like the word *literature*, but it means *engaging in lawsuit* and you can eliminate it. Choice (B) deals with coats of arms and shield and ships, and has nothing to do with books; eliminate it. This leaves you with (C), which means *ideal example*.

2. **C** Although several of the answer choices may describe Polonius, you have to use the clues to determine the best answer. The sole clue is that he *speaks epigrammatic lines*, so you're looking for something that means *using maxims* or *pompously moralizing*. Choice (C) means exactly that, so it's your best answer. *Obsequious* means *excessively obedient* and *auriferous* means *containing gold;* neither one has the meaning suggested. Choices (D) and (E) pertain to vocal quality, and are irrelevant.

3. **personalize** and **an inimitable**

    Start with the second blank: The outfit is *changing*, so you know the second blank has to contrast with *run-of-the-mill outfit*. Something like *extraordinary* or *unique* would make sense. Of the choices, only *inimitable* makes sense. Once you have that, it's easy to fill in the first blank: If she's *changing her look* from something *run-of-the-mill* to something *inimitable*, she's *making it her own*. Of the choices, *personalize* is the best fit.

4. **antediluvian** and **salubrious**

    You know that the texts the researcher is working with are *medieval*, so the medical tips are likely to be *old* or *outdated*. Thus, the best word for the first blank would be *antediluvian*, and not *commodious* (comfortable) or *extant* (existing). When the researcher finds the tips, they *surprise* him because they are things that *modern medical experts recommend*. Because of the contrast with *old*, the second blank could mean *current*, or it could mean *healthy* because the medical experts are recommending them. *Salubrious* means *healthful*, and matches one of the possible meanings. Neither *tenebrious* (gloomy) nor *lugubrious* (sad) fits either of the options, so you can eliminate both choices.

5.   **Rationally, escalate, mutual**

From the word *absurdity*, you know the argument was foolish and that each side *felt strongly* about its viewpoint and *refused to consider alternatives*. These clues could make *Tempestuously* attractive for the first blank. However, you have to consider the clue *was impossible for*, which signals that the missing word will contrast with the irrational nature of the argument. Based on the context, *Rationally* is the best choice. For the second blank, the clues tell you that both groups work to *develop bigger and better weapons*, meaning things are getting worse. *Escalate* is the best choice. *Confabulate*, which means *talk over*, and *stagnate*, which means *stop moving*, are irrelevant. Finally, the clues tell you that *each side* is participating, making *mutual* the best choice for the third blank.

6.   **salutary, bullish,** and **feasible**

The author argues that lower taxes would *encourage businesspeople*, so the effects that the lower taxes have must be positive. *Indeterminate* would mean that the effects are *in doubt* and *execrable* would mean they were *negative*. *Salutary* means *positive*, so it's a good fit for the first blank. The second blank must mean that the people's attitude toward investments is *optimistic*. *Bearish* means *cautious*, and *birdlike* means delicate, so those words aren't what you're looking for. *Bullish* means *optimistic*, so it's a good fit for the second blank. The purpose of the tax cuts is to encourage something that is not currently *possible*, so the third blank must mean something like *possible*. *Malleable* means *changeable*, and *atypical* means *unusual*, so those words don't fit here. *Feasible* means *possible*.

7.   **"Trask, for example, considered the eyes of Dr. T.J. Eckleburg, featured prominently on a billboard in the novel, not those of an all-seeing god evaluating Gatsby's personal shortcomings, but those of Thomas Jefferson mourning the collective American abandonment of his belief in hard work and integrity as the paths to fortune."** *(Lines 21–27)*

The two contradictory aspects of Gatsby's personality are given in the first sentence; he believed in the *agrarian myth* and yet was entrenched in *corruption and materialism*. The passage does not elaborate on the corruption or materialism, so you need to find the sentence that explains what is meant by the *agrarian myth*. You also know from the first sentence that Thomas Jefferson was a proponent of this myth. The correct sentence choice is linked clearly to the myth and gives a solid definition with the phrase *of his belief in hard work and integrity as the paths to fortune*. The sentence that begins *Fitter agreed, perceiving in Fitzgerald . . .* may seem like a good answer, but there is not enough information to connect *Poor Richard's Almanack* to the *agrarian myth*. Furthermore, the phrase *principles of honorable living* is quite vague and cannot really be considered a definition. The final sentence may also seem like a plausible answer, but, again, there is no direct link to prove the connection between *an austere way of life* and the *agrarian myth*.

8. **B** The question asks which statement can *not* be shown to be accurate for at least one critic, so you can eliminate any answer for which you can find support in the passage. Choice (A) is supported by Mencken's view of the novel, and (C) is supported by the phrase *shrewd social commentary*, attributed to *other critics*. Choice (D) is supported by the information in the last sentence on Trask, and (E) is supported by the use of the phrase *a thinly disguised reflection of Fitzgerald himself* to describe how Gatsby *has commonly been viewed*. Only (B) is not accurate: Although you know that Trask does not think Dr. T.J. Eckleburg's eyes represent god, it cannot be shown that someone else does. Additionally, Gatsby can recognize his *personal shortcomings* without affecting his *self-worth*.

9. **C** Given the placement of the sentence in the paragraph shortly after the phrase *has commonly been viewed as a thinly disguised reflection of Fitzgerald himself*, you know that Fitter believed Fitzgerald intentionally attributed his own personal characteristics to Gatsby. Choice (C) gives the best analogy. Choice (A) is not analogous because the action was unintentional; (B) is not analogous because the photographer did not force the model to act as she does. Choice (D) is not analogous because the sequence of events is backward: The character existed before the student acquired certain habits. And, finally, (E) is not analogous because the actor may or may not be expressing himself through the role.

10. **B** According to the passage, cosmologists believe that the missing mass is partially accounted for by *elementary particles too small to be detected by electromagnetic radiation*. Choice (B) rephrases this statement, and so it's the best response. Choices (A) and (E) recycle words from the first sentence of the passage, but they have different meanings; moreover, the first sentence is referring to the problem the cosmologists are trying to solve, whereas the question asks for the solution. Choice (C) is wrong because the passage doesn't say anything about dark matter causing the expansion. Choice (D) also doesn't work: The galaxies are the evidence that shows that Newton's theory has a problem, not the solution.

11. **A** Newton's theory states that massive particles attract each other *with a force proportional to the mass of the particles and their proximity to one another*, so the strength with which the particles attract each other is related to their mass and the distance between them. Choice (B) is tempting, but incorrect: It relates *distance* and *mass* to each other, when it needs to relate them both to *force*. Choice (C) is also incorrect, because it uses the idea of *elementary particles* presented later in the passage out of context—the passage doesn't say that these particles are used as *intermediaries* between massive particles. Choice (A) is supported by the passage: It forms a relationship between *force* and *mass*, which is one of the relationships contained in the theory.

12. **C** This argument contains one of GRE's favorite flaw patterns: The author makes a comparison between Country A and Country B and assumes that those two countries are the same in all relevant respects. Any time you see a comparison flaw, the answer will address whether the comparison is a fair one; in this weaken question, the answer must show that the countries are different in a relevant respect. Choice (C) does so: If the types of coal that the two countries use always differ, it is possible that the regulations on emissions have a negative effect on Country A's industrial production but not on Country B's industrial production. While (A) also provides a difference between the two countries, the link connecting the type of airport, the regulations, and industrial production is less strong than that connecting coal, the regulations, and industrial production in (C). Choices (B) and (E) do not establish any difference between the two countries. Choice (D) establishes a similarity between the countries and so does not help explain the differences in industrial production.

13.   **B and E**

The blank should be a word that describes someone who will play lots of concerts and send out many demos of his work. So, the word should be similar to *persistent*. Both *dogged* and *tenacious* are close synonyms for *persistent*. Choices (A), (D), and (F) are detractor answers that you may think are associated with fame, but they do not work with the clue words.

14.   **A and E**

The same-directional semicolon transition and the clue words *good omen* are evidence that you need a positive word in the blank. You can recycle the word *good* to describe the symbol. *Prophetic* and *pious* are loosely related to the ideas of symbols and Buddhism, but are not supported by the clues. *Facetious*, meaning *humorous*, and *pervasive*, meaning *spread throughout*, do not fit the context of this sentence. The correct answers are *auspicious* and *propitious*.

15.   **D and E**

The time transition word *initially*, as well as the clue word *shocked* in the main clause, tells you that the people must not have displayed outrage and were instead happy with the decision. You need a supportive word in the blank, but (B), (C), and (F) are all negative words. Choice (A), *effectuate*, means *to bring about*, which is also incorrect.

16.   **A and D**

Although the connection between the first part of the sentence and the Pennsylvania Dutch may not be immediately obvious, the first part must be describing the way these people live, or there would be no reason for the lawyer to change his mind about their lifestyle. So you need to find words that reflect the idea of *living without amenities* and *non-urban*. Both *bucolic* and *idyllic* are used to describe the perfect country setting. *Banal* and *pedestrian* are synonyms that mean *ordinary* or *unimaginative*, so neither of them work. There is no support for *lugubrious*, which means excessively mournful, or *erudite*, which means very learned. The correct answers are (A) and (D).

17. **C** You are looking for a choice that is not supported by the passage. Choice (A) is supported by the first sentence, which describes the *ubiquity of jeans across social classes*. You also know the women *hung up their skirts . . . machinery*, and that action prompted a shift in the symbolism of jeans. The women must have been wearing the jeans and gave up their skirts specifically for factory work; (B) is supported and can be eliminated. Choice (D) is supported by the final phrase *the scope of brands and styles that became available*, and (E) is supported by the sentence concerning jeans and *rebellious youth*. There is no support for (C) because there is no evidence that *poor, working-class men*, or even women a little later on, were actively trying to make a statement. The sequence is backward; their use of jeans actually created the symbolism.

18. **E** The contradiction referred to in the correct answer is in the first sentence, as indicated by the word *surprising*. Jeans should not be universally popular if they send a narrow message. The highlighted sentence reconciles the contradiction by pointing out that everyone can wear jeans, but the brands and styles still send specific messages. Choice (A) is incorrect because the highlighted sentence is a general comment about the 1970s, not an example. Choice (B) is incorrect because the viewpoint is not different as stated. The highlighted sentence is also not a summary, but rather a continuation of the evolution of the symbolism of jeans, and so (C) is incorrect. Finally, the word *conclusively* eliminates (D). While the variety of jeans could have been a reason for their increased popularity, there is no evidence that it certainly was the only reason.

19. **B and C**

Choice (A) is incorrect because the passage says that guttation occurs only in vascular plants, and there is no discussion of the difference in the number of vascular plants that exist in the two climates mentioned. Choice (B) is supported because the text says that dew *results from a change between surface and atmospheric temperatures.* Therefore, an analysis that does not factor in those measurements would be *inadequate,* as this answer indicates. The described analysis is also *inadequate* because the passage provides no information on which process is more likely to occur, given that the conditions for both exist. Choice (C) is supported because the passage says that *guttation begins when water moves from saturated soil.* In an arid climate, the soil is not likely to be saturated with moisture. The phrase *under natural conditions* in (C) should eliminate exceptions, such as irrigation systems, when considering this choice.

20. **A** In the last sentence, the plants are described as having *pipe-like elements* that enable the process of guttation to take place. *Containing channels* in (A) is a good synonym for this description. Choices (C) and (E) may seem plausible, given the reference to houseplants. However, there is no proof that all houseplants are vascular plants, or vice versa. Furthermore, houseplants do not necessarily receive only *little sunlight,* nor do they necessarily have a *moderate climate* in which to grow. Choice (B) is incorrect because you know only that the plants *take in* the moisture, not that they *need it,* and (D) is incorrect because the plants actually *push out* the moisture, instead of *absorbing* it.